PRESENTATION PITFALLS

10 Traps Business Professionals Fall Into and How to **Avoid Them**

JOHN POLK
JUSTIN HUNSAKER

WILEY

Copyright © 2025 by John Polk and Justin Hunsaker. All rights reserved.

Published by John Wiley & Sons, Inc., Hoboken, New Jersey.
Published simultaneously in Canada.

No part of this publication may be reproduced, stored in a retrieval system, or transmitted in any form or by any means, electronic, mechanical, photocopying, recording, scanning, or otherwise, except as permitted under Section 107 or 108 of the 1976 United States Copyright Act, without either the prior written permission of the Publisher, or authorization through payment of the appropriate per-copy fee to the Copyright Clearance Center, Inc., 222 Rosewood Drive, Danvers, MA 01923, (978) 750-8400, fax (978) 750-4470, or on the web at www.copyright.com. Requests to the Publisher for permission should be addressed to the Permissions Department, John Wiley & Sons, Inc., 111 River Street, Hoboken, NJ 07030, (201) 748-6011, fax (201) 748-6008, or online at http://www.wiley.com/go/permission.

The manufacturer's authorized representative according to the EU General Product Safety Regulation is Wiley-VCH GmbH, Boschstr. 12, 69469 Weinheim, Germany, e-mail: Product_Safety@wiley.com.

Trademarks: Wiley and the Wiley logo are trademarks or registered trademarks of John Wiley & Sons, Inc. and/or its affiliates in the United States and other countries and may not be used without written permission. All other trademarks are the property of their respective owners. John Wiley & Sons, Inc. is not associated with any product or vendor mentioned in this book.

Limit of Liability/Disclaimer of Warranty: While the publisher and the authors have used their best efforts in preparing this work, including a review of the content of the work, neither the publisher nor the authors make any representations or warranties with respect to the accuracy or completeness of the contents of this work and specifically disclaim all warranties, including without limitation any implied warranties of merchantability or fitness for a particular purpose. No warranty may be created or extended by sales representatives, written sales materials or promotional statements for this work. The fact that an organization, website, or product is referred to in this work as a citation and/or potential source of further information does not mean that the publisher and authors endorse the information or services the organization, website, or product may provide or recommendations it may make. This work is sold with the understanding that the publisher is not engaged in rendering professional services. The advice and strategies contained herein may not be suitable for your situation. You should consult with a specialist where appropriate. Further, readers should be aware that websites listed in this work may have changed or disappeared between when this work was written and when it is read. Neither the publisher nor authors shall be liable for any loss of profit or any other commercial damages, including but not limited to special, incidental, consequential, or other damages.

For general information on our other products and services or for technical support, please contact our Customer Care Department within the United States at (800) 762-2974, outside the United States at (317) 572-3993 or fax (317) 572-4002.

Wiley also publishes its books in a variety of electronic formats. Some content that appears in print may not be available in electronic formats. For more information about Wiley products, visit our web site at www.wiley.com.

ISBN: 9781394345991 (Paperback)
ISBN: 9781394393558 (FF ePub)
ISBN: 9781394346011 (ePDF)
ISBN: 9781394386918 (Print Replica)

Library of Congress Cataloging-in-Publication Data:

Cover design: Wiley
Cover image: © OlenapolII/Shutterstock

SKY10122212_071825

Dedication

To Marty
John's four-leaf-clover finder.
This book, this business, this life,
wouldn't be the same without you.

To Kathryn
Justin's favorite Trapp.
Thank you for being my unwavering
partner on this crazy adventure.

To Our Families

Clichéd, but true. You made us who we are. Jack and Meredith, I'm proud of the humans you've become. SharonDebbieLoriSuzi, still hard to believe we all like each other. Mom and Dad, sorry you missed this.

May and Karl, I'm proud of the incredible people you're growing into. Brady and Krystal, I cherish every vacation we share with your families. Mom, Scott, Dad, and Sarah, thank you for everything.

Acknowledgments

Capital One Leaders. We cut our presentation teeth on your strategy and analysis decks. You set the bar for how to engage, influence, and drive action through presentations. Amanda Aghdami, Ron Andrews, Jeff Bennett, David Brown, Don Busick, Katherine Busser, Gus Cheatham, Jason Dandridge, Cetin Duransoy, Hannes Endhardt, Rich Fairbank, John Feldman, Rob Finnegan, Tanmay Gautam, Keri Gohman, Kevin Goldstein, Karthik Govindankutty, Brian Guthrie, Paul Halpern, Caribou Honig, Aravind Immaneni, Kathy Kauffman, Gagan Kanjila, Jeff Killian, Rick Long, Ed Maino, Sharon McGinty, Erin Mical, Derek Mohar, Steve O'Neill, Eric Schweikert, Karl Werwath, Rich Walker, Jeff Wolfe, Tom York, and Jamie Warder.

The Presentation Workshop Professors at Capital One. You volunteered to help spread the good word. You continuously made the workshop better. And you made this a fun side project. Eric Bowers, Mike Bury, Mark Cohen, Chad Dally, Ritin Dhawan, Mike Fraizer, John Humphrey, David Kapella, Vishal Keswani, Darryl Lang, Vishnu Narayanasamy, Rick Nishimoto, Ricardo Ortiz, Dave Parker, Aaron Parks, Stephen Phillips, Missy Poccia, Louise Schutte, Hanna Turner, and Courtney Williams.

Clients. Teaching makes us better coaches. Coaching makes us better teachers. You enabled this process, expanded our offerings, and let us buy health insurance. Hearing your success makes this all worthwhile.

Book Advisors. You freely shared your book-writing experience and feedback. This book wouldn't be as good without you. James Abbott, Susan Berge, Roy Bivens, Susan Cerra, Katherine Cording, Bill Falloon, Maureen Forys, Mimi Heft, Erin Henry, Dwight Jaggard, Danessa Knaupp, Cole Knaflic, David Martin, Gio Rainey, Alison Schwartz, Todd Silverstein, Megan Torrance, and Emily Troiano.

If we forgot to thank you, let us know. We'll make it up to you in the second edition.

Contents at a Glance

	Foreword	xi
	Introduction	**1**
1	**The Frankenstein Trap**	11
2	**The Bury the Lede Trap**	37
3	**The Black Hole Trap**	71
4	**The Just the Facts Trap**	103
5	**The Expert Trap**	133
6	**The Piece of Cake Trap**	161
7	**The Lipstick on a Pig Trap**	185
8	**The Under (or Over) Confidence Trap**	219
9	**The Virtual Fatigue Trap**	241
10	**The First and Last Impression Trap**	263
	Conclusion	**283**
	Notes	293
	Further Reading	301
	Index	305
	About the Authors	319

Contents

Foreword   xi

Introduction   1
Elevate your career with effective presentation skills   2
Take a systematic approach to improving presentation skills   4
Accept that presentations are the work   4
Raise the bar on presentations in your organization   5
Avoid presentation pitfalls   6

1 The Frankenstein Trap   11
Follow the Platinum Rule of Presentations   13
Understand the audience, their backgrounds, and their concerns   15
Clarify the purpose   21
Adjust for the unique challenges of the setting   24
Determine the design based on the audience, purpose,
    and setting assessment   25
Design decks for others to present   28
Reuse slides safely   29
Key Takeaways   34

2 The Bury the Lede Trap   37
Declare the subject and goal in your presentation title   38
Create a mind map to jump-start presentation planning   39
Plan and organize content with a storyboard   43
Avoid giving a history lesson   45
Favor storylines that give the answer up front   46

Include relevant content in a pitch deck or business case ... 51
Emphasize the main point of the slide in the title ... 56
Craft compelling, concise, and complete sentence titles ... 59
Write an executive summary, even if you don't present it ... 64
Guide the audience with agendas, bumpers, and running heads ... 65
Key Takeaways ... 69

3 The Black Hole Trap ... 71

Understand the causes of poor signal-to-noise ratio ... 72
Visualize the data ... 73
Organize with useful tables ... 74
Include relevant images ... 78
Incorporate icons to visualize concepts quickly ... 86
Improve bulleted lists with engaging visual elements ... 88
Put slides on a word diet ... 90
Use an appendix, but avoid "appendicitis" ... 93
Animate complex slides ... 94
Avoid the MBR paradox ... 97
Key Takeaways ... 100

4 The Just the Facts Trap ... 103

Use stories to illustrate key points ... 104
Structure anecdotes ... 106
Make stories memorable ... 106
Don't show the sausage-making ... 109
Don't leave data up for interpretation ... 110
Use preattentive attributes to focus the audience's attention ... 125
But don't misrepresent the facts ... 129
Key Takeaways ... 131

5 The Expert Trap ... 133

Quickly give the background necessary to understand core concepts ... 134
Reverse engineer your expertise ... 135
Create frameworks ... 136
Make frameworks easy to digest ... 148
Build on the audience's existing knowledge with analogies ... 152

Use idioms carefully	154
Define acronyms and limit jargon	157
Review your work with experts and nonexperts	158
Key Takeaways	159

6 The Piece of Cake Trap — 161

Write like you speak	162
Ensure content has parallel structure	164
Learn the grammar and style rules many presenters get wrong	166
Proofread and edit your work	170
Find an editor	176
Avoid the Perfectionist Trap by embracing drafts	179
Key Takeaways	183

7 The Lipstick on a Pig Trap — 185

Make intentional design decisions not driven by arbitrary preference	186
Avoid inherently noisy presentation software capabilities	187
Remove the noise from charts	188
Employ eye-flow principles and white space	190
Establish a consistent design baseline	197
Reserve contrast for engagement, emphasis, and professional feel	207
Incorporate accessible design, a.k.a. good design	213
Invest in slide and content libraries to improve efficiency and effectiveness	214
Key Takeaways	217

8 The Under (or Over) Confidence Trap — 219

Prepare	220
Practice	224
Pump yourself up	227
Display confidence in delivery	230
Demonstrate leadership presence in presentations	234
Read and react to the audience	235
Create space for discussion	237
Beware the overconfidence trap	237
Critically assess your performance	238
Key Takeaways	239

9 The Virtual Fatigue Trap — 241

   Understand virtual fatigue and its impacts — 242
   Improve your home studio — 245
   Structure presentations to minimize fatigue — 252
   Engage, engage, engage — 253
   Adjust your performance — 256
   Dress for virtual success — 256
   Do all this and more for a hybrid presentation — 259
   Key Takeaways — 260

10 The First and Last Impression Trap — 263

   So, like, reduce, um, filler words, you know — 264
   Don't insult the audience — 268
   Introduce yourself efficiently — 268
   State the purpose up front — 270
   Don't say you're sorry — 270
   Use slides to reinforce key points — 271
   Put it all together to create a great first impression — 274
   Stick the landing to avoid a poor last impression — 275
   Leave time for discussion, summary, call to action, and next steps — 275
   End on time — 276
   Don't end on an insincere slide — 277
   Key Takeaways — 280

Conclusion — 283

   Put it all together — 284
   Go forth and present! — 291

   Notes — 293
   Further Reading — 301
   Index — 305
   About the Authors — 319

Foreword

Presentations are how business decisions get made. Leading a large team means keeping many moving parts in sync—no small feat. To drive corporate strategy, you must align stakeholders, influence C-suite executives, and clearly communicate the strategy to your team. And in the business world, that often means presentations. Like it or not, it's the language of consultants, business leaders, and managers to shape strategy, coordinate stakeholders, and drive action.

As managing partner at the consulting firm Arica and throughout my many years as a leader at Capital One, I used presentations for all of these critical activities and more. Over the course of my career, I've had the opportunity to shape the corporate strategy of a Fortune 100 company, lead a team of over 5,000 associates across the globe, and help many corporate boards drive significant change in their organizations. If there is one thing I've learned in my career, it's that the ability to clearly and succinctly communicate your thoughts is critical in driving success. This is true for driving business outcomes as well as advancing your career.

But when presentations go wrong, they really go wrong. Cluttered slides, lost messages, and ineffective meetings consume time and lead to bad decisions. Having worked for massive and fast-moving organizations, I know it's exceedingly challenging to digest all of the risks, problems, and opportunities flying at you every day. You need presentations that help leaders understand the issues, choose the best ideas, and make the right decisions.

John solved these problems for my team, and I've used his lessons throughout my career. John was my de facto chief strategist multiple times in my career. John's superpower? He distills complex ideas into compelling and insightful presentations. However, it wasn't just John's ability to do that on his own that impressed me. It was how John transferred that skill, making my entire leadership team more innovative and more strategic. Thanks to his expertise and efforts, we described problems more accurately, identified business opportunities more easily, and communicated team objectives more clearly.

When John and Justin launched their presentation training and coaching business, I witnessed them having an impact across other companies and industries. Presentation skills are critical to success for any business, and it was no surprise that there was incredible demand for their services.

I also wasn't surprised when they decided to put their practices in a book. Many presentation books focus on one aspect, like public speaking, or a unique domain, like TED Talks. *Presentation Pitfalls* walks business professionals through the entire process of writing compelling storylines, building engaging slides, and confidently delivering their message. The book is practical—full of step-by-step processes, worksheets, checklists, and examples. But the book is also fun—full of stories and humor that make it an easy read.

When I read *Presentation Pitfalls*, I recognized the powerful advice that reflects the practices that have worked for me through the years. And it clued me in to traps I've fallen into (and occasionally still do). If you use presentations to drive action, *Presentation Pitfalls* should be required reading for you and your team. Even experienced executives will learn how to take their game to the next level. By the way, I still have John's "Don slide" from Chapter 1 hanging on my wall.

Great presentations inspire action. If yours are falling flat, John and Justin can help turn things around. Share this book with your team. You'll be surprised by the impact it will have.

Don Busick
Managing Partner, Arica
Former EVP of Enterprise Digital
Products and Platforms at Capital One

Figure 0.1 Scissor kicking to success
Source: Jack Metcalfe of Australia Competing in the High Jump at the 1936 Berlin Olympic Games / National Library of Australia / Public Domain

Introduction

Present your way to a promotion, a new job, new customers, or startup funding.

"I can't believe they just got promoted again!" How many times have you heard that phrase? Or said that phrase? Or muttered that phrase under your breath? Even if you're happy for a promoted coworker, it's easy to wonder, "What do they have that I don't?"

The promotion process is opaque at most companies. In some organizations, managers determine performance ratings and promotions through a cross-calibration process, where they meet to discuss and rate their associates' performance. This improves the odds that associates receive a fair performance rating rather than leaving it to their boss's discretion. While ensuring associates get a fair performance rating is important, this process can be painful. We sat through approximately 250 cross-calibration conversations for almost 2,500 associates in our careers. If you've never experienced one, trust us, they're no fun.

At the end of each cross-calibration, leaders discussed promotion candidates. While it might not feel like it, the difference between a good and an excellent rating is a relatively small step. Getting promoted to the next level is clearing a high bar, like in Figure 0.1.

In promotion discussions, we noticed a pattern in the associate feedback. Rarely did the debate focus on technical skills, subject-matter expertise, or results—when associates were up for promotion, they've already demonstrated those strengths. Instead, the competency gaps that typically held associates back were communication, influence, or the mystical "leadership presence."

Guess what? You demonstrate all these competencies through your ability to design and deliver effective presentations. Presentations are more than just slides. They encompass your speech, body language, audience interaction, emotional impact, and chosen medium.

While this book focuses on presentation design and delivery, the techniques apply broadly to all communications, including emails, memos, and hallway conversations.

To that end, we aim to help you get that promotion, land the next client, greenlight a big idea, or get your startup funded. So, if you haven't invested in your presentation skills, you might be missing the skill that puts you over the top.

If Figure 0.1 doesn't look like a typical high jump, it's because of a tectonic shift in the high-jump technique in the 1970s. Dick Fosbury struggled with conventional approaches like the scissor kick and developed a new style where he jumped with his back to the bar. The innovative "Fosbury flop" allowed him to set world records, and by the 1980 Olympics, all but a few athletes were using it.

Because people talk all day, it's natural to think you're good at communicating. But that is the equivalent of scissor kicking. The Fosbury flop is more challenging but more effective and requires practice. With this book, we'll take your presentation game to the next level.

Elevate your career with effective presentation skills

Your boss hired you for job-specific skills like strategy, analytics, tech, project management, or product management. Being excellent at those skills should lead to a promotion, right? Not without excellent communication skills.

Communication is the lens through which others judge your competencies.

If you're a brilliant analyst but can't communicate your insights effectively, no one thinks you're brilliant. If you're a talented software engineer and can't explain your buy/build/partner proposal, no one trusts your recommendation. If you're a creative product manager and can't connect your features roadmap to customer value … well, you get the point.

Presentations are a critical opportunity to familiarize stakeholders with your strategy, get feedback, and gain buy-in. That buy-in leads to the results that get you on the promotion shortlist. Improving presentation skills drives promotion along (at least) four dimensions:

- **Showcasing the work:** Your boss and others who influence your promotion are busy people. They can't know everything you and your team accomplished. Presentations let you capture and communicate results efficiently. There are other ways to share accomplishments with the boss, but they rarely carry as much weight as a formal presentation.

- **Getting visibility with leaders and a sneak peek at their strategy:** When you have a knack for writing presentations, your boss and your boss's boss will ask for help with their strategy presentations. You'll gain early insight into the strategy, spot opportunities to contribute, and demonstrate your strategic-thinking skills by actively shaping its direction. Being in the room with the leadership team means they know who you are and have seen you do good work. That's important when those same leaders decide who to promote.

- **Learning how to do the boss's job:** Did we mention how busy leaders are? If you lighten their workload by ghostwriting their presentations or helping set their strategy, you demonstrate your potential. Creating presentations for your boss often leads to an invitation to the meeting where your boss is presenting. That's an opportunity to observe how to perform in high-pressure meetings. Promoting you to that level is much easier once leaders see you doing next-level tasks.

- **Magnifying results and core job skills:** You get a paycheck to deliver company value, and presentations advance every stage of the projects and processes that deliver value. Presentations such as business cases, stakeholder socialization decks, and implementation plans harness teamwork to drive results. Presentations are the language of leadership—communicating strategy and culture gets the team on the same page. Sharing results in a logical, graphical presentation is an opportunity to convey the skills and thinking it took to achieve those results.

If you're not a manager (yet), teach others your expertise to improve their performance while practicing presentation skills. Host a workshop or mentor others to spread best practices, allowing your leaders to see you demonstrate leadership skills. We taught over 10,000 associates presentation skills while working at Capital One.

Take a systematic approach to improving presentation skills

The four-part framework in Figure 0.2 summarizes the presentation design principles we teach in our workshops.

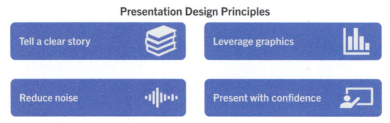

Figure 0.2 Agenda for a career-changing workshop
Source: John Polk & Associates

We hit on these themes throughout the book:

1. **Tell a clear story.** Compelling storytelling makes your presentations more engaging and memorable. Stories make complex topics easier to understand and illustrate how analytical insights apply in the real world.

2. **Leverage graphics.** Text-heavy, bullet-point-only slides are why people complain about "death by PowerPoint." Well-designed data visualizations, frameworks, images, and icons ensure your presentations are engaging, understandable, and memorable.

3. **Reduce noise.** When communicating, reducing noise lets the message shine through. Audio noise includes the barking dog and ringing doorbells in your home office. Visual noise includes typos, grammar issues, having too many words, and unaligned objects.

4. **Present with confidence.** It's hard for the audience to have trust in you and your ideas if you're nervous when presenting. Demonstrating confidence builds the audience's trust in the recommendations and your ability to deliver results.

Accept that presentations are the work

You haven't done the work until you've done the presentation.
John Polk, conversation with every analyst

John says this hyperbole to analysts when they share their spreadsheets to answer a business problem. To most analysts, the work is the spreadsheet, the dashboard, or the code. The presentation is the annoying work John makes them do.

But no one knows about your brilliant insights until you communicate them. So yes, the spreadsheets are the work, but the presentation turns that work into motivation and action. Presentations are how most companies drive action with the key stakeholders. Presentations differ in focus and have different names depending on the stakeholder:

- Sales presentations acquire new customers.
- Strategy presentations drive action.
- Town hall meetings motivate associates.
- Business cases secure executives' approval.
- Pitch decks generate new investors.
- Earnings calls report results to shareholders.
- Audit/review meetings give quality assurance or regulators confidence in policies, processes, and controls.

Raise the bar on presentations in your organization

Many of our clients are strategy and analysis leaders. They typically rely on presentations more than other leaders to communicate insights and turn strategy into action. Because of our engineering backgrounds, we look at the world and think, "How can we make it more effective and efficient?"

Effectiveness is about getting the results. Presentations are how new projects, products, and businesses secure funding. Data serves as the foundation for business decisions. And the act of creating a clear presentation improves the underlying strategy.

Efficiency is about spending less time to get those results. Thorough preparation and a clear vision reduce iterations. Software tips and tricks save time. And standard templates and slide libraries make it easier to get it right the first time.

In short, the tools and techniques in this book will help you get the resources you need to turn your ideas into reality.

> ### The irony of writing about presentations
>
> *Writing about music is like*
> *dancing about architecture.*[1]
>
> Martin Mull, attributed
>
> While perhaps not as absurd, there is a limitation to how much you can learn by reading about presentations. We bridge that gap with stories, frameworks, checklists, examples, and step-by-step techniques. But there's no substitute for observing great presenters and practicing the techniques we discuss to improve your presentation skills.

Avoid presentation pitfalls

Presenters fall into metaphorical pits every day, whether due to a lack of training, poor habits, or bad advice. In the Atari game *Pitfall!* (Figure 0.3), players swing on vines to avoid the water pit filled with crocodiles and the trap with the giant scorpion to reach the treasure.

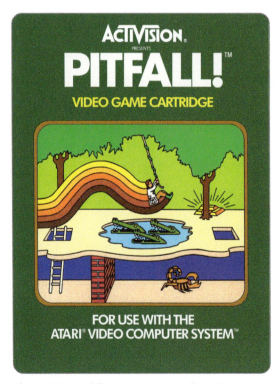

Figure 0.3 Avoiding nonpresentation pits
Source: Activision / Wikimedia Commons

We've adopted pitfalls and traps as the book's theme. Working with clients to design, develop, and deliver their presentations, we help them avoid 10 common traps:

1. **The Frankenstein Trap:** Using preexisting content or combining content from multiple slide creators in a way that misses the mark for the audience, purpose, or setting
2. **The Bury the Lede Trap:** Failing to present recommendations or other critical points early
3. **The Black Hole Trap:** Building slides so dense that the audience can't or won't digest them
4. **The Just the Facts Trap:** Ignoring the emotional and visual components of influencing
5. **The Expert Trap:** Failing to translate your knowledge in a way nonexperts can understand
6. **The Piece of Cake Trap:** Letting typos, grammar issues, and unprofessional slides reduce your credibility
7. **The Lipstick on a Pig Trap:** Relying on overly designed slides without a foundation of robust content
8. **The Under (or Over) Confidence Trap:** Letting fear of public speaking hurt your delivery or letting overconfidence lead to mistakes
9. **The Virtual Fatigue Trap:** Not adapting your presentation to the virtual world
10. **The First and Last Impression Trap:** Losing the audience with a poor opening and not sticking the landing

These are the potential presentation pitfalls—because people naturally learn from mistakes, we're exploring what can go wrong and how to avoid it. In this book, you'll learn the "vines" that help you avoid these pitfalls to get the "treasure"—engaging the audience to influence and drive action. And by driving action, you get the results that lead to promotion, or a new job, or new customers, or … you get the idea.

> ## How to read this book
>
> Each chapter starts with a title and subtitle, naming a common presentation pitfall and providing a concise summary of how to avoid the trap. A short pitfall description leads to a summary of ways to counteract it. Each chapter has headings that recommend strategies, tools, and techniques to enhance presentation skills.
>
> Sidebars include stories, advice, advanced techniques, and sometimes presentation-software-specific recommendations. If a sidebar isn't relevant to your situation, skip it. Key takeaways end each chapter, summarizing the most important strategies, tools, and techniques.
>
> > [Chapter Title] **The Frankenstein Trap**
> >
> > [Chapter Subtitle] **Assess the audience, purpose, and setting every time to avoid creating an inconsistent presentation that misses the mark.**
> >
> > [Recommendations] **Follow the Platinum Rule of Presentations**
> >
> > ...
> >
> > [Sidebar] **Planning to plan**
> >
> > ...
> >
> > **Key Takeaways**
>
> For those seeking a particular topic, look in the table of contents or the index. The table of contents lists each chapter along with its subheading.
>
> The chapters can be read in any order, though we arranged them in the rough order you'll need them as you build and deliver your presentation.

Note: Portions of this introduction were first published in the article "You've Visualized Your Data, Now Actualize Your Promotion" by John Polk in *Nightingale,* Journal of the Data Visualization Society, July 27, 2021.

Note: Portions of this book first appeared in "Communicating Your Analysis" by John Polk, in *Data & Analytics for Instructional Designers* by Megan Torrance, copyright ASTD DBA the Association for Talent Development (ATD), 2023. Reproduced with the permission of John Polk and ATD.

Figure 1.1 Frankenstein's monster with his trademark bolts and scars
Source: Universal Pictures / Piqsels / Public Domain

1

The Frankenstein Trap

Assess the audience, purpose, and setting every time to avoid creating an inconsistent presentation that misses the mark.

In Mary Shelley's book, Victor Frankenstein creates "the monster" portrayed in Figure 1.1 from spare body parts stitched together and reanimated through lightning. Was his creation a success?

- **The case for yes:** Dr. Frankenstein's goal was to create life from spare body parts. Yup, he did that. Success!
- **The case for no:** Villagers took up pitchforks and torches. People died. Failure!

Whichever side you take, most agree that Frankenstein's monster was not a handsome fellow. Otherwise, he'd be called "Frankenstein's gentleman." He had a giant scar on his forehead, his arms were different lengths, and bolts stuck out of his neck.

The same thing happens when pulling slides from multiple decks or different creators to build a new deck. The deck ends up with different fonts, styles, or vibes. Or worse, slides come from various templates, creating unintended consequences when merged.

Presentation software attempts to "help" by reformatting pasted slides—and inadvertently changes project status from green to yellow! True story.

Presenters fall into the Frankenstein Trap when they use preexisting content or combine content from multiple creators in a way that misses the mark. The Frankenstein Trap can occur from improper deck reuse or improper slide reuse. Deck reuse is presenting the same deck to different audiences. Slide reuse is pulling slides from one deck to use in another deck.

Here's how the deck-reuse version of the Frankenstein Trap often plays out:

> **Boss:** I need you to update the Operations vice president [VP] on Project JPA tomorrow.
>
> **You:** Sure, I can use the same update I gave to the Sales VP, and that meeting went great.

You just fell into the Frankenstein Trap! Here's the result of deck reuse:

> **Boss:** How'd the meeting with the Operations VP go?
>
> **You:** Actually, not so great. She had way more questions than the Sales VP. The Sales VP only wanted to hear the high-level details, and the Operations VP wanted to test all my assumptions. She didn't have the same background as the Sales VP, so I think she misunderstood a key recommendation. She also said she was worried about the impact of my recommendations on her team. She asked me to come back next week with an update on her concerns.

No one wants to create a new deck from scratch every time they present on the same topic, and we're not suggesting you do. But presentations land flat when you don't adjust for a new scenario.

In this example, different audiences cared about different things. The goal of the meeting with the Operations VP was to secure resources for your project, while the goal of the Sales VP meeting was to get input on how your project affects the Sales team. Also, you met the Sales VP in the office, but the Operations VP works remotely, so the meeting was over video.

Avoid the Frankenstein Trap by assessing the audience, purpose, and setting to inform design; understanding the presenter's style; and reusing slides effectively.

Follow the Platinum Rule of Presentations

To be successful with the Operations VP, follow the formula in Figure 1.2.

Figure 1.2 The Platinum Rule of Presentations
Source: John Polk & Associates

The Platinum Rule of Presentations guides the planning process even before opening presentation software. The audience comes first for a reason. Communication is about creating alignment with the audience. It's hard to influence without understanding their background and perspective. The purpose includes the key message for the audience to internalize and the presentation goals. Finally, the setting creates different demands and constraints. One reason virtual meetings are so terrible is that facilitators simply do what they did in person without adjusting to the virtual setting's challenges.

John learned this concept from his professor, Dr. Harold Kurstedt, who originally developed the Golden Rule of Presentations: **Audience + Purpose = Design**. John updated the formula to include the setting.

To be fair, when Dr. Kurstedt wrote the Golden Rule, the setting was always the same. Back then, all presentations happened in person, in conference rooms, with overhead projectors and transparencies—and if someone couldn't be in the room, you faxed them the deck. The term "deck" originally referred to a stack of transparencies displayed using an overhead projector. Technology has come a long way since then, with high-definition projectors, interactive whiteboards, and video meetings. But that doesn't seem like progress when you realize you don't have the correct cord to connect your laptop to the projector five minutes before the meeting starts!

If you've ever wondered what an overhead projector looks like, see Figure 1.3.

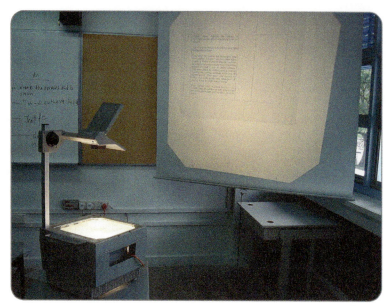

Figure 1.3 An overhead projector with a boring wall-of-text slide
Source: mailer_diablo / Wikimedia Commons / CC BY-SA 3.0

We're going to use the following terms throughout the book, so we want to define them clearly:

- **Presentation:** A talk, lecture, pitch, or discussion supported by visual content
- **Slide:** One page with text or graphics
- **Deck (a.k.a. slide deck):** The set of slides that together constitute a presentation's visual elements
- **Speech (a.k.a. delivery, voiceover, or talk track):** The words spoken when delivering a presentation

The key distinction is that a presentation represents the deck *and* the speech. Some presenters call just the deck a presentation.

When designing a presentation or any communication, you must know the audience, the purpose, and the setting to design the material effectively. It seems obvious, but how many times have you made these mistakes:

- Created a deck when you didn't know who would be in the room?
- Presented without knowing who the final decision-maker would be?

- Attended a meeting where you didn't know your role?
- Left a meeting with the decision you wanted but then realized you didn't ask for the needed resources?
- Attended a meeting where a key stakeholder was on the phone and couldn't hear everyone in the room?

We thought so. Using the Platinum Rule dramatically raises the odds of making the right impression and achieving your goal.

Before starting any presentation, answer the questions in Figure 1.4.

Platinum Rule Assessment

1. Audience	
Who is the decision-maker or target audience?	
What do they typically focus on?	
What context do they have?	
What have they asked for?	
What questions might they ask?	

3. Setting	
Who are the presenters?	
Will the audience be in person?	
How long is my time slot?	
What technology will I use?	
Do I need a preread or "live read"?	

2. Purpose	
What are my goals/outcomes?	
What should my audience learn, feel, and do?	
What do I need from my audience?	
What are the three most important takeaways?	

4. Design	
How formal should my presentation be?	
How much detail should I include?	
How "design-y" should my slides be?	
How can I build in interactivity?	

Figure 1.4 Answer these first or regret it later
Source: John Polk & Associates

Understand the audience, their backgrounds, and their concerns

As part of our scientific research on startup pitches, we've watched a few *Shark Tank* episodes (Figure 1.5). While it's clearly a heightened dramatization of entrepreneurship, that doesn't mean the participants' pitches and the sharks' critiques can't teach us business lessons. In many episodes, someone's pitch fails because the participants don't understand what's important to the sharks or their end customer.

Figure 1.5 So, a shark bit the tank?
Source: ABC / 1000logos.net

Presenters miss the mark when they don't deeply understand what the customer wants. We use "customer" in a broad sense. For a sales presentation, the customer is the person buying the product or service. For a pitch deck, it's the potential investor. If the entrepreneur doesn't know that Daymond John started his business in his mom's basement, they might skip sharing the business's emotional origin story. If the entrepreneur doesn't understand that Mark Cuban cares about how big the company could become, they won't give adequate attention to the three-year business scaling plan. Here are best practices for understanding and designing for the audience:

Distinguish among decision-makers and stakeholders. Many companies have consensus-driven cultures. We worked most of our careers in a consensus culture, and there were times when it felt like no one could say "yes" and anyone could say "no" to our ideas. That's why it's crucial to identify who the decision-maker is.

One driver of writer's block is the swirl created by thinking about all the different stakeholders you must please. Once you identify the decision-maker, design for their needs first, then consider what to add to address unique stakeholder needs. If it isn't clear who the decision-maker is, ask. If the answer includes multiple stakeholders, ask who will "write the check" for the investment. Depending on the situation, you might refer to the decision-maker as the client or customer. If it's a keynote or training presentation, think about a target audience member instead of a decision-maker.

In the rare case of multiple decision-makers, consider having individual meetings. Does this mean you have to make more than one deck? Probably. Or at least create variations targeting each decision-maker's unique needs.

Assess the audience's advocacy. After separating the audience into decision-makers and stakeholders, go deeper to assess their support level. Who are the advocates, neutrals, and detractors? Identifying detractors early creates an opportunity to socialize ideas with them before the meeting to understand their concerns. Then, address those concerns in the proposal. Joel DeLuca, author of *Political Savvy*, recommends "The 51 Percent Guide: When dealing with a new or controversial idea, ensure that those who have at least 51 percent of the influence in the discussion (1) already understand the idea and (2) are willing to explore it further."[1] If you haven't secured a majority of stakeholders' votes, you haven't set the decision meeting up for success. In most situations, stakeholders don't share voting power evenly.

Understand the audience's knowledge level. If the audience lacks context or foundational information, spend more time setting the stage and sharing essential background. Sending material early for a preread, including executive summaries, and adding background slides can help get the audience on equal footing.

The worksheet in Figure 1.6 assesses decision-makers' and stakeholders' advocacy and knowledge levels.

Audience Assessment Worksheet

Name	Decision-Making Role		Advocacy Level			Knowledge Level	
	Decision-Maker	Stakeholder	Advocating	Neutral	Detracting	Informed	Uninformed

Figure 1.6 Detractors are just advocates you haven't influenced yet
Source: John Polk & Associates

For scenarios other than decision meetings, replace the decision-maker with the target audience. Be specific about the persona you're trying to influence. We encourage presenters to name an actual person they are targeting. Assessing the audience's background knowledge is critical for determining how much context they need. And it's essential when adjusting a deck for a different audience. Finding a way to quickly get the audience on a level playing field is key to engaging the newbies without boring the experts.

Tailor content to the audience's natural concerns. Without an audience, you're just talking to yourself.

> *The great enemy of communication,*
> *we find, is the illusion of it.*[2]
> William H. Whyte, "Is Anybody Listening?"

Most presenters don't spend enough time understanding their audience to ensure their message is received.

The framework in Figure 1.7 uses the acronym PROD (people, results, options, details) to assess the audience and includes content suggestions for each category's likely concerns.

PROD Model of Audience Concerns

People	Results	Options	Details
Stakeholder opinions	Decisions	Ideas	Data and analytics
Change mgt. plan	Timelines	Brainstorming	Risk mgt. plan
Impact on customers and associates	Deliverables	Creativity	Process
	Output	Innovation	Financials
	Value		Appendixes

Figure 1.7 The correct way to PROD the audience
Source: John Polk & Associates

Tailor the presentation to align with the audience's focus and priorities:

- **People:** These leaders care about the impact proposals have on customers and associates. They are more likely to want to reach a consensus and will ask who else gave input on the recommendations. In addition, they often have questions about the impact proposals have on employees and customers.

- **Results:** These leaders can seem impatient. They want value, and they want it now! When presenting to a results-focused leader, highlight the value and delivery timeline. A timeline is helpful, not because these leaders want the project details but because they want to know when the value will hit the bottom line. They are prone to quick decision-making, so it's important to present recommendations before they jump to conclusions.

- **Options:** These leaders ask, "Did you consider this other idea?" This creates a challenging situation for two reasons. First, responding with "Yeah, we considered that idea" might come across as defensive. Second, it requires telling the leader why their idea isn't as good as your recommendation. It's better to meet with the options-focused leaders early in the project to get their thoughts on the options to consider and the decision criteria.

- **Details:** These leaders might be the most difficult to design for. When giving the details they crave, you overwhelm or bore the rest of the audience. Instead, offer details-focused leaders a premeeting to review the method and critical assumptions. Summarize the ideas and supporting data in the presentation body, then put the details in the appendix. It's gratifying to answer a detailed question with "Slide 22 in the appendix addresses that."

Of course, leaders are not one-dimensional. Most leaders tend to be results focused, but always look for a secondary focus. Many executives are results and people focused. The ability to drive results leads to promotions, and the more senior you get, the more you must drive results through others. If the leader has a background in analytics, they are likely details focused.

Get clarity on the customer's needs. The *Shark Tank* story illustrates a common risk: missing a core need. Customers and decision-makers are notoriously bad at declaring what they need. They think what is clear to them is clear to everyone. They ask questions to satisfy their human curiosity rather than to solve business problems. They assume all data is easy to get. They forget that performers are juggling multiple projects.

Validate the conditions of satisfaction with the customer. Clarify the request with the customer. Interview the customer to determine the "conditions of satisfaction"—in other words, the criteria you must meet for the customer to be satisfied with the deliverable. The checklist in Figure 1.8 includes questions to ask the customer to establish conditions of satisfaction for a hypothetical data-driven business case, following the classic rhetoric framework used in journalism.

Conditions of Satisfaction Checklist

Who
- Who is the decision-maker?
- What stakeholders should I talk to before the presentation?
- What resources can I leverage?

What
- What presentation style do you prefer—e.g., decision meeting, town hall, TED Talk?
- What is the scope—e.g., our department or company-wide?
- What data sources do you want to leverage?
- What's the quality requirement—e.g., quick and dirty or CEO-worthy?

When
- When is the presentation?
- How much time do we have to present?
- At what stages do you want to review the analysis and deck?

Where
- What's the location for the presentation?
- Is the setting in person, virtual, or hybrid?

Why
- What business problem are we trying to solve?
- What will you do with the results of my analysis?

How
- Do you have preferences for the problem-solving methodology?
- Are there specific solution options you want to consider?

Figure 1.8 Questions to discuss with the customer to avoid surprises
Source: John Polk & Associates

In a perfect world, write down the answers to these questions and ask the customer to sign off. Of course, that only helps if you remember to go back to the list. With big projects, there are weeks or months between the request and the delivery. Review the original agreement to ensure you delivered all components. Justin worked with a leader who was notorious for keeping hard copies of every project proposal. During project reviews months later, he would retrieve the original proposal to compare side by side with the latest updates. If you work for a leader who keeps receipts, you may want to put the original agreement in the appendix.

Research key stakeholders. When presenting to a decision-maker for the first time, it's hard to know how they like to receive information or what questions they will ask. One option is to check out the decision-maker and unknown stakeholders on LinkedIn. In addition to finding clues about their natural concern areas, you'll find points of common interest in their background to make a personal connection. Better still, ask someone who presented to this decision-maker previously. Ask how it went and what questions the decision-maker asked.

John used to facilitate a decision forum for a senior leader we'll call "Don." Over time, John noticed Don asked similar questions to everyone who presented. So, John wrote them down and created a checklist with questions for presenters to be prepared to address.

John sold that list for $1,000 a pop! Kidding. This intel is gold for anyone presenting to a leader for the first time. Figure 1.9 is the "Don slide" at no extra cost!

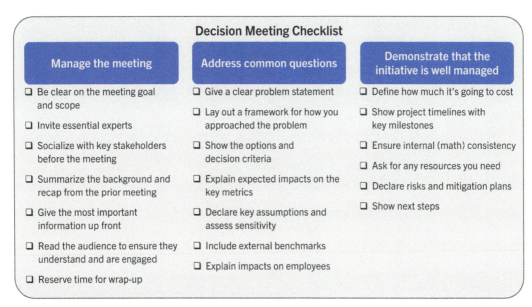

Figure 1.9 The secrets to a successful decision meeting
Source: John Polk & Associates

20   The Frankenstein Trap

It's a checklist for setting up decision meetings for success. If you facilitate meetings, do you have a Don slide? Do you know what your Don wants to see in a decision meeting? If you're a leader, have you clarified to your teams what you want to see in their presentations?

Clarify the purpose

While this seems obvious, many presenters aren't transparent with the audience (or themselves) about their goals for the presentation. When the audience knows the purpose, they can more effectively assist you in achieving it. And for audience members who don't like to think on the fly, ensure they know the purpose when they get the meeting invitation so they can prepare. Let's go deeper on assessing purpose.

Clarify what you want the audience to learn, feel, and do. When we ask presenters about their goals, they often say, "I want the audience to learn about my project," or "I want them to take the action I'm proposing." In both cases, they've given an incomplete answer. Even in a training class, the goal must go beyond learning to driving action. You need the audience to apply the concepts you teach, or the class was a waste of time. If you focus only on the action required, the audience might not understand the problem you're trying to solve, and they won't be able to adjust their actions when faced with implementation hurdles.

We like mnemonic devices, so we translated this framework to the 3Fs—facts, feelings, and follow-ups—shown in Figure 1.10.

Figure 1.10 The 3F framework
Source: John Polk & Associates

Before an important conversation, ask these questions:

- What are the **facts** you want the audience to learn?
- What are the **feelings** you want to inspire?
- What are the **follow-ups** you want the audience to take?

Most presenters think they understand the facts clearly. When asked to write and prioritize them, they realize it wasn't as clear as they thought. This simple exercise forces presenters to be clear and concise.

Too often, presenters don't have an opinion about the emotion they want the audience to feel. We've spent our careers working with analysts who believe that logic and data should win all arguments. We wish that were true. Humans are emotional creatures, and emotion plays a huge role in influencing and driving action. At a minimum, you want the audience to feel confident in the recommendations and your ability to implement them.

Every meeting should have clear follow-ups. How will you measure the meeting's success? The fact that so many meetings don't have clear decisions, requests, or actions gave rise to the phrase "Coulda been an email." If you don't know what you want to get out of a meeting, you won't get as much as you could have.

Ask for what you need. When in performer mode, it's easy to forget that success depends on getting resources and support from the customer. When negotiating conditions of satisfaction with the customer, you might need help getting access to stakeholders, or you might need a data analyst to pull data. When delivering the recommendation, you might need help from the customer to socialize the decision or assign a project manager to implement it.

Determine the three most important things you want the audience to remember. This is often the most challenging question to answer in the planning stage. It is also the most important. It's hard to answer in the planning stage because you might not know, especially if you don't have all the data yet. If it's hard to answer after building the slides, it's a sign that the strategy or story isn't clear.

Sometimes, this exercise is challenging because presenters have too many "important" things they want to cover. We don't like the phrase "less is more" because we think it leads to bad behavior in presentation design. But we agree with the core concept—if you hit the audience with too many ideas, they won't remember any.

Humans are lazy, forgetful, and distracted. Be clear about the key points and use thoughtful repetition to ensure the audience remembers those points. We worked with a leader who started presentations with "Here are the three things I want you to remember." This framework applies across scenarios:

- **Pitch deck or business case**
  - **Issue:** There is a significant problem (or opportunity) in the world.
  - **Action:** Here's a brilliant solution to that problem (or a way to take advantage of the opportunity).
  - **Impact:** Investing in this recommendation will make a bunch of money and make the world a better place.
- **Decision meeting**
  - **Issue:** To solve the problem, the team assessed several options against the decision criteria.
  - **Action:** The recommended actions focus on the most effective solutions.
  - **Impact:** Implementing these recommendations improves key metrics.
- **Product roadmap**
  - **Issue:** The roadmap outlines new functionality that addresses customer needs.
  - **Action:** The prioritized items best align with the decision criteria, and it's possible to trade off items or increase the investment.
  - **Impact:** Delivering these items improves key metrics.

> ### Planning to plan
>
> Presenters run into trouble when they don't plan enough, but it is possible to plan too much. Here's John's exchange with his daughter one Sunday:
>
> > **Daughter:** What are you doing?
> >
> > **John:** Preparing an agenda for a meeting I have tomorrow.
> >
> > **Daughter:** What's your meeting about?
> >
> > **John:** Planning for another meeting.
> >
> > **Daughter:** Your job sounds boring.
> >
> > **John:** (*silence*)
>
> The moral of the story is "Plan meetings to deliver the goals, but don't go overboard."

Adjust for the unique challenges of the setting

Misunderstanding the unique needs of your setting can sink a presentation. What works in one setting may not work in another. Consider these settings:

- **Conference room:** This intimate setting enables fluid audience interaction and calls for a conversational tone. It supports an action-oriented, results-focused discussion. It's also easy to have rapport-building conversations on breaks.

- **Auditorium:** Presenting to a large audience requires a confident delivery supported with simple, attention-grabbing visuals. Tell stories, project your voice, and use gestures to maintain engagement.

- **Hallway encounter:** "Success occurs when opportunity meets preparation."[3] Zig Ziglar's quotation reminds us that you must craft your elevator pitch before you're in the elevator with the CEO. Preparation also helps deliver the message concisely while respecting the time constraints of busy colleagues.

- **Virtual meetings:** Because it's so easy for a virtual audience to get distracted, double down on engaging visuals and interactive activities.

As you assess the setting, also consider these factors:

- **Audience location:** Whether the audience is in person, virtual, or hybrid influences the choice of technology and delivery style.
- **Time slot:** A short presentation requires a focused message, while a longer one allows for greater depth and discussion.
- **Technology:** When used effectively, presentation tools can bridge the natural gaps in virtual and hybrid environments.

Determine the design based on the audience, purpose, and setting assessment

The point of assessing the audience, purpose, and setting is to make design decisions. The framework in Figure 1.11 highlights three common presentation types and the common design aspects that can vary.

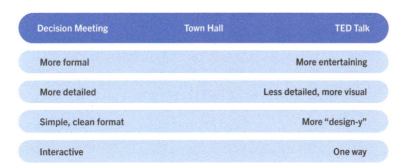

Figure 1.11 TED isn't invited to your decision meeting
Source: John Polk & Associates

We use "decision meeting" to encompass a wide range of business-focused meetings. These include business case meetings to evaluate a proposal, sales meetings to showcase products and services with prospects, and pitch meetings to secure funding for a new business. A TED Talk is a recorded presentation with powerful storytelling and simple but engaging graphics. TED is a nonprofit whose mission is to share ideas worth spreading. In town hall meetings, leaders present to their teams to share strategy, roll out new programs, celebrate successes, and reinforce the culture.

The light blue elements represent typical design choices for each style. A decision meeting is more formal, with more detailed slides and a simple format. Decision meetings are naturally interactive—telling the boss to hold all questions until the end is unwise!

But that doesn't mean that design aspects more associated with a TED Talk have no place in a decision meeting. More entertaining elements, like stories and engaging visuals, are still compelling in a decision meeting. Town hall meetings often mix aspects from both sides of the framework.

In the earlier deck-reuse scenario where your boss asked you to update the Operations VP, if you revisit the Platinum Rule assessment from Figure 1.4, you can make design updates to improve your chances of success, like the following:

- Update the associate impact slide to focus on the Operations VP's team rather than the Sales team.
- Add more details, including appendixes with the grounding for key assumptions.
- Schedule the meeting as a video call to see facial reactions.

We've taught hundreds of workshops and never used the same material twice. (You'd think we'd have it down by now!) In addition to regularly improving the content, we go deeper into the most important topics for each audience, prioritizing content within time constraints or redesigning exercises to work in different settings. Use the Platinum Rule assessment as a checklist for your next presentation. It saves time and, more importantly, increases the chances of success.

> ### The answer to all life's questions: "It depends!"
>
> Experts (even us) often give advice with absolute certainty. It's comforting to seek and share advice that works in all situations. However, for most presentation design questions, the right answer is "it depends." This is the heart of the Platinum Rule. Here are some common pieces of generic presentation design advice and when they might not be appropriate:
>
> - **Generalization 1: Less is more.** Using fewer words is the antidote to the wall-of-text problem. However, complex concepts require relevant detail. And presented slides are often forwarded to people who couldn't make the meeting and don't have the benefit of the voiceover.
>
> *(continued)*

- **Generalization 2: Limit the presentation to X slides.** An executive we worked with had a rule: "If your deck has more than 10 slides, I'll stop at slide 10." While this encourages brevity, we often see presenters cram 20 slides of content into 10, making slides overly dense. Presenting dense slides overwhelms the audience and leads to more questions.

- **Generalization 3: Make the smallest text X-point font.** This is usually targeted at large-audience presentations, like town halls or TED Talks, where the words need to be big enough for people in the back to read. However, large fonts take up too much real estate for decision meetings.

- **Generalization 4: Avoid animations.** Like many rules, this advice comes from misuse. When overdone, animation is distracting and unprofessional. When done right, animation can engage the audience and enable them to digest complex slides easily.

We return to these themes and share more nuanced versions throughout the book. The nuance typically involves different choices for different situations. Most business presentations support decision-making, making it a common scenario throughout the book. When our recommendations seem in conflict with those of other experts in the field, it's often because they focus on different scenarios. The goal of business presentations is to drive action. To drive action, you must influence, and to influence, you must engage, as illustrated in Figure 1.12. If a design choice isn't intended to engage, influence, or drive action, it's superfluous.

Figure 1.12 The presentation chain reaction
Source: John Polk & Associates

"It depends" isn't a cop-out, just an acknowledgment that there are few absolutes. We love getting pushback on our advice because it forces us to be explicit about the design principles. The core of effective design starts with understanding the audience, purpose, and setting, then making intentional design choices that engage, influence, and drive action.

Design decks for others to present

A variation on the Frankenstein Trap occurs when you create slides for someone else to present. Without effective collaboration, you might create a mismatch between your slide style and the presenter's delivery style. To solve this, we add a fourth variable, presenter, to the formula, as shown in Figure 1.13.

Figure 1.13 The Platinum (Plus) Rule of Presentations
Source: John Polk & Associates

If your writing style doesn't match the presenter's style, the presenter won't come across as authentic. We've resisted the urge to upgrade our formula to the Titanium Rule (we're running out of precious metals), but if you write for others, there are additional considerations:

- **Work through the Platinum Rule assessment with the presenter.** This ensures alignment and minimizes rework.

- **Ask the presenter about their preferred tone, style, and slide density.** Better yet, watch them present to learn their style. Note style preferences that are different from yours.

- **Understand the presenter's quirks.** If your presenter hates animation, don't use animation (even though they're wrong).

Similar challenges arise when building slides for multiple presenters to deliver, like for sales presentations. In this situation, you can't design to one specific presenter's style. But it's difficult for presenters who weren't involved in the deck's creation to authentically present it. Here are strategies for assisting presenters who weren't involved in developing the content:

- **Write speaker notes.** These can be bulleted talking points or a full-blown script. Chapter 8, "The Under (or Over) Confidence Trap," discusses in detail how to effectively use speaker notes.

- **Create a flexible design and set customization rules.** Build slide variations for different audiences and purposes. Then, let presenters choose variations and hide irrelevant content to personalize the deck for their customers and presentation styles.

- **Help presenters develop authentic speeches.** Presentations come alive when presenters share relevant, engaging stories. It's more powerful to say "A customer I worked with got these results" rather than "Here's a case study from our marketing department."

- **Make presenters practice.** Have presenters practice with the deck creator and their peers. In addition to getting feedback, they'll see best practices they can steal.

- **Make a best-practices video.** Record the best presenter delivering the presentation and share it with other presenters. Highlight best practices, optional content, and even places where the best presenter could have been better.

Reuse slides safely

Reusing slides and collaborating on decks are everyday realities in most workplaces. A typical Frankenstein deck follows the process in Figure 1.14.

Figure 1.14 Why Frankenstein's monster's bolts are showing
Source: John Polk & Associates

As can happen with deck reuse, presenters can become so focused on reducing effort that they don't consider the changes necessary to make the slides effective for the new audience, purpose, or setting. A better way to Frankenstein (which we just verbed) is the process in Figure 1.15.

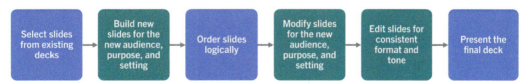

Figure 1.15 How to create a handsome monster
Source: John Polk & Associates

> ## Hunsaker wisdom: Whose shoes are you still tying?
>
> A few years ago, Justin's 10-year-old son was sitting on the stairs while Justin knelt in front of him to tie his shoes. It was a picturesque father-and-son moment, recreated in Figure 1.16.
>
>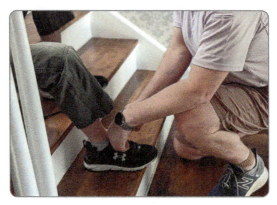
>
> **Figure 1.16** Justin's shoe-tying prowess
> Source: Courtesy of Kathryn Trapp
>
> "When are you going to learn to tie your shoes?" Justin asked casually, not wanting to spoil the moment. They'd had this conversation before, and Justin didn't want it to become a big deal.
>
> "You know, Dad, it's hard. Sandals and Velcro are sooo much easier," his son replied matter-of-factly. As Justin finished the last bow, his son smiled and, with a quick thanks, jumped up and ran outside to play on the swing.
>
> As Justin watched him, he had an epiphany. The problem wasn't his son—it was him. The solution was simple: he needed to stop tying his son's shoes.
>
> Later, when it was time to put his son's shoes on again, Justin sat with him while he labored to tie his laces. The next day, his son tied his shoes without asking for help. It was like magic.
>
> How often do you tie other people's shoes at work? In the moment, it's often easier to tie shoes than to teach skills. However, you're holding your team back by not addressing the underlying opportunity. When it comes to presentation skills, teach your team how to tie their own shoes.
>
> _____
>
> Note: Portions of this sidebar were first published in "Whose Shoes Are You Still Tying?" Justin Hunsaker, John Polk & Associates' blog, 6/11/2023.

Using the improved process, build new slides and modify existing slides to meet the new audience, purpose, and setting. Also, edit slides for consistent format and tone, particularly when different creators contribute slides. Here are other strategies for avoiding the Frankenstein look:

Appoint a deck conductor. We worked for an executive who created a 200-slide (no exaggeration) strategy deck once per quarter. John had the "pleasure" of being the deck conductor for those decks. The deck conductor is a project manager for a large deck build and is often the primary creator or editor. The deck conductor coordinates with information suppliers and deck jockeys. Deck jockeys take data and information to create professional-looking slides. A good deck conductor has the skills of a designer, storyteller, mind reader, managing editor, and librarian.

Manage "the conn." The conn is a nautical term that denotes the act of controlling the ship's movements. When the conn-holder is unclear, it can lead to version control problems, where multiple people edit the same slide or one creator overwrites another's changes. At worst, the result is a "camel deck"—a nod to the joke that "a camel is a horse developed by a committee."

Use collaboration tools. Most presentation software enables multiple creators to work on the same deck simultaneously. The ability for multiple performers to edit the same deck at the same time has obvious benefits. But collaboration tools have downsides:

- Anyone can edit slides, even without subject-matter expertise.
- The deck conductor or presenter might not notice last-minute changes.
- All slide creators and editors can see the whole deck, which is problematic for sensitive topics like budget presentations or reorganizations.

Teach slide jockeys how to use the presentation software. While building those 200-slide strategy decks, the team spent countless hours fixing other people's bad slides (unless they were our boss's slides, in which case the team called them "less than perfect" slides). This is why John started teaching presentation design. Rather than continue to fix slides after slide owners created them, John put together a workshop on how to create slides. In Lean thinking, reformatting slides to meet a standard is a non-value-added task. The effort invested in teaching performers to build professional slides from the start will save 10 times the effort later.

Set standards for common style and formatting choices. Grammar-and-style books don't set rules for every design decision. In these cases, use design best practices, set a standard, and ask all creators to stick to it. Also, remind deck creators about the grammar and punctuation rules they often miss.

Warning: This stuff can seem boring or picky, especially when explaining it to your team. But it's far more boring to review and correct other people's slides when they don't know the standards. Here are style and formatting choices where there's no "right" way to do it, leading to inconsistency. We share our approach and rationale for the following elements:

- **Date formats:** For compactness, we use numbers for the month, day, and year (e.g., 1/1/01). Use the four-digit year if regularly working with data that's over 100 years old. For charts, we use the three-letter month abbreviations (e.g., Jan) and put the year underneath.

- **Number formats:** For consistency, we use commas for the 1,000s. Also, don't use the two-decimal default unless that's the correct number of significant digits for the analysis.

- **Big-number abbreviations:** Our approach uses "k" for thousands because "K" technically refers to Kelvin. For millions, we prefer "M" instead of the accountant's "MM," which comes from Roman numerals. For billions and trillions, we use "B" and "T."

- **Chart title locations:** Centering makes titles stand out, but left alignment has a modern appeal. Where do the units and any big-number abbreviations (B, M, k) go? The easiest option is to include them in the chart title in parentheses or the axis label if your software doesn't add a label automatically.

- **Product and project names:** Apple declares it an "iPad" (known as camel case) and not an "Ipad" or "IPAD" or "i-Pad"? Make sure everyone knows any nonstandard spelling or punctuation.

- **Commas:** There is great debate among grammar nerds about the Oxford comma, the comma before the "and" in a list like "red, white, and blue." Your choices are always use it, never use it, or use it only if necessary to avoid confusion. Strunk & White, *The Chicago Manual of Style*, and the authors of *Presentation Pitfalls* recommend the Oxford comma (see what we did there?).

- **Dashes:** For decks, we prefer the em dash with spaces before and after, following *The Associated Press Stylebook*. However, since this is a book, we formatted dashes without spaces, in line with *The Chicago Manual of Style*.

- **Abbreviations:** We avoid abbreviations except when necessary to fit text into a tight space. When using abbreviations, be consistent. For example, in charts, we abbreviate "quarter" as "Q" and put the quarter in front of the year (1Q01).

- **Word wrapping:** When reviewing text, ensure word wraps don't separate clauses or phrases or create a runt (a.k.a. orphan), a single, short word on the last line. Figure 1.17 shows common word-wrapping issues and their solutions. Use Shift+Enter to insert a soft line break—it doesn't start a new bullet point and preserves hanging indents and line spacing.

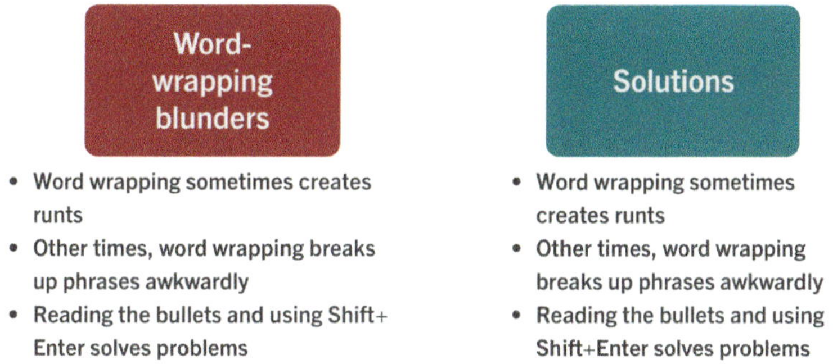

Word-wrapping blunders	Solutions
• Word wrapping sometimes creates runts • Other times, word wrapping breaks up phrases awkwardly • Reading the bullets and using Shift+ Enter solves problems	• Word wrapping sometimes creates runts • Other times, word wrapping breaks up phrases awkwardly • Reading the bullets and using Shift+Enter solves problems

Figure 1.17 Word wrapping: trusty tool or tricky troublemaker?
Source: John Polk & Associates

Key Takeaways

Assess the audience, purpose, and setting every time to avoid creating an inconsistent presentation that misses the mark.

- ✓ Consider one customer, decision-maker, or target audience when designing a presentation. Then add content for other stakeholders' needs.
- ✓ Determine the audience's degree of support and knowledge level before the meeting. Avoid deadlocks with the 51 Percent Guide.
- ✓ Deliver content based on the PROD (people, results, options, details) audience assessment.
- ✓ Negotiate clear conditions of satisfaction with the customer and ask for the resources needed to be successful.
- ✓ Define the purpose, determining what the audience should learn, feel, and do (a.k.a. facts, feelings, and follow-ups).
- ✓ Be explicit about key takeaways and next steps and thoughtfully repeat them to help the audience remember.
- ✓ Plan for the unique challenges of the setting—for example, ensuring remote participants can actively engage.
- ✓ Tailor design choices to the audience, purpose, and setting, considering factors like formality, interactivity, and visual engagement.
- ✓ When building content for someone else, design for their style, not yours.
- ✓ Set clear expectations for the content you want to see in the meetings you lead.
- ✓ Reuse decks safely by building or modifying slides to meet the new audience, purpose, and setting while editing for consistent format and tone.

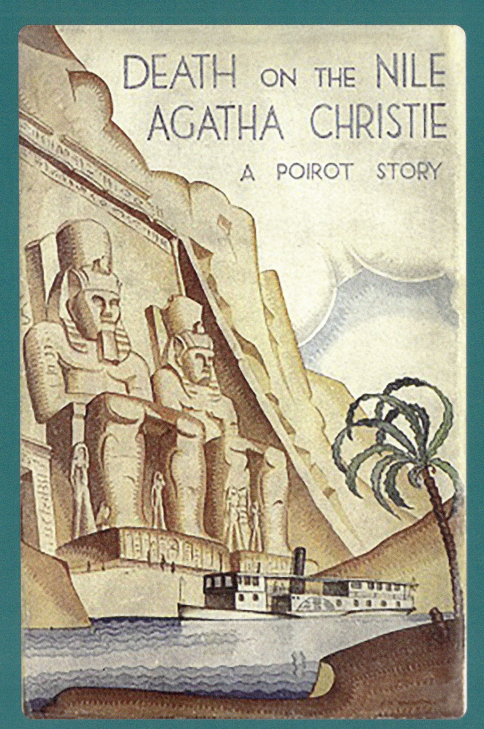

Figure 2.1 *Death on the Nile, Agatha Christie*
Source: Agatha Christie / Wikimedia Commons / Public Domain

2

The Bury the Lede Trap

Give the audience the most important information up front before they lose focus.

To bury the lede means starting a story with less important details and delaying the key message. Do you like to read mystery novels? While mystery novels, like the example in Figure 2.1, begin with the murder, they purposefully bury the lede about who committed the crime.

Now, imagine what your brain does as you read a mystery novel. With every clue, your brain guesses who the killer is. Authors use this to their advantage. They give you clues that point to multiple suspects, kill off prime suspects, introduce new suspects, and include red herrings—plot points that make you suspicious of an innocent character. In addition to interpreting the words for understanding, mystery readers spend mental energy trying to guess whodunit.

Presenters fall into the Bury the Lede Trap when they design presentations like mystery novels by saving recommendations or other critical points for a big reveal at the end. There are two problems with this approach. First, the audience spends mental energy guessing where you're going, which means they aren't listening to you. Second, because you haven't given them your solution to the problem, the audience might come up with their own solution. And when they don't come up with your solution, you must defend it and refute their solution. We've met a few people who like to read the last chapter of a mystery novel first. While this spoils the fun, it speaks to the human desire to want to know the solution up front.

Avoid the Bury the Lede Trap by spilling the beans—giving the most important information up front. In a presentation, spill the beans through effective presentation titles, storylines, slide titles, executive summaries, and agendas. Mind mapping and storyboarding techniques help spill the beans faster and more effectively. Now that we've spilled the beans, let's discuss each one.

Declare the subject and goal in your presentation title

The presentation title slide is the audience's first impression. A vague title will confuse and derail the meeting. It sounds obvious, but many people start with a generic title and then never go back to make it more precise. Or they copy an existing deck and don't revise the title for the new audience and goal. Presentation title slides should include defining elements:

- **Subject:** What's the main topic? Be precise.
- **Scope:** What aspects of the subject will you cover? When giving a presentation on bank statements to the Bank Operations leadership team, you might be tempted to label the deck "Statements." But when it gets forwarded to the Credit Card Statements team, they might think you're stepping on their toes. True story.
- **Meeting goal:** What do you want to achieve in this meeting? The audience has a different mindset if the subtitle includes "Idea Generation" versus "Project Launch."
- **Name:** Who did this work? Include the presenter's name or all contributors. Including your name lets people who weren't in the meeting track you down if they have questions.
- **Business unit:** What function does this work represent? For internal presentations, give the line of business or department name. When presenting to an external customer, your company logo might be sufficient.

- **Date:** When did this presentation take place? Without dating decks, you risk having someone assume the products, processes, or policies are current even after they've changed.

- **Draft (optional):** Is the deck finished yet? Labeling a deck as a draft lets any reviewer know it's not done yet. Don't forget to remove the draft label for the final deck. Another true story.

The callout boxes in Figure 2.2 highlight the key components of a clear presentation title slide.

Figure 2.2 A clear presentation starts with a clear title slide
Source: John Polk & Associates

Create a mind map to jump-start presentation planning

A mind map is a brain dump of all the ideas you might want to cover in a presentation. Whether you call it mind mapping or just "jotting down notes," you've used this technique before. However, most people don't use this technique every time they start planning a presentation, nor do they follow the complete structured process we teach. We promise this technique saves time and ensures you don't forget critical content.

Mind mapping is simple. Grab a piece of paper, think about the presentation topic, and write down everything that comes to mind. During mind mapping, alternate between flaring and focusing. When flaring, only generate options. Nothing dampens the mood more than when someone points out why someone else's idea won't work. When focusing, make choices. Also, knowing there will be focusing rounds lets the group enjoy flaring without constraints, confident there will be an opportunity to critique and prioritize.

Let's illustrate mind mapping for a presentation about how to make a million dollars. Start with a brain dump, like in Figure 2.3.

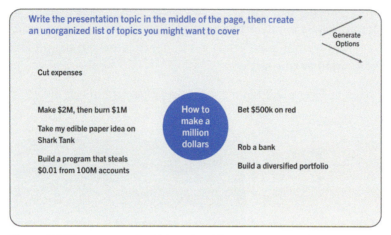

Figure 2.3 There are no bad ideas (at this stage, anyway)
Source: John Polk & Associates

Brainstorming rules apply. Go for quantity over quality. The goal at this stage is to be exhaustive. Don't judge ideas. Don't wordsmith. Include ideas that won't make the final presentation, like "Bet $500k on red," to push the boundaries.

Use the initial idea set to generate additional ideas, like in Figure 2.4. This is called "piggybacking."

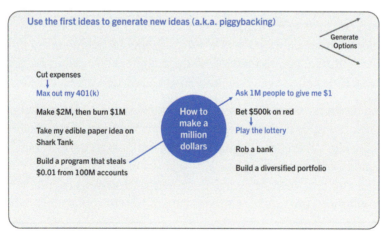

Figure 2.4 In brainstorming, it's not stealing; it's collaboration
Source: John Polk & Associates

The "Cut expenses" idea led to the "Max out my 401(k)" idea. While the goal here is quantity, generating more ideas also leads to better ideas. While asking one million people for a dollar isn't very practical, it's at least legal.

Use highlighters, circles, arrows, or colored text, like in Figure 2.5, to group related ideas.

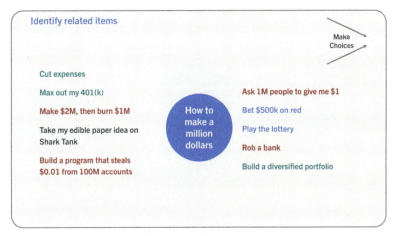

Figure 2.5 "Herd" the birds of a feather
Source: John Polk & Associates

Next, group similar ideas into categories and give each group a name. If the mind map is messy, rewrite it, like in Figure 2.6.

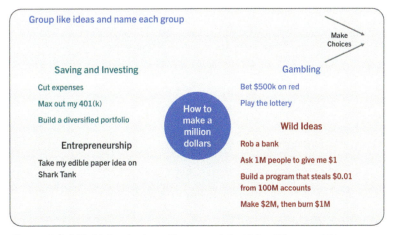

Figure 2.6 Affinitizing isn't really a word, but it's still a good idea
Source: John Polk & Associates

Categories, like Entrepreneurship and Wild Ideas, start to make explicit the hidden structure of the brainstorming inspiration. Organizing ideas into categories lets the mind see these ideas with fresh eyes. That leads to even more ideas, like in Figure 2.7.

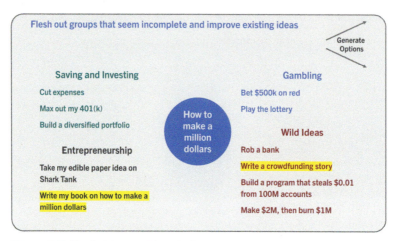

Figure 2.7 Single ideas get lonely, too
Source: John Polk & Associates

Having only one Entrepreneurship idea triggered the new idea to write a book. The long Wild Ideas list is beneficial for two reasons. First, it indicates that the mind map is exhaustive. Second, wild ideas can trigger innovative ideas. In this case, the impractical idea of asking one million people to give a dollar led to a crowdfunding idea. Finally, vote and prioritize the ideas, like in Figure 2.8.

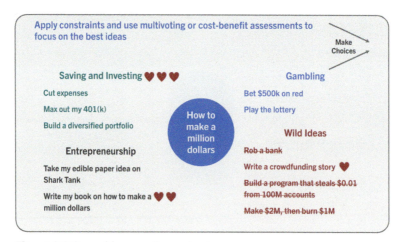

Figure 2.8 Some ideas really are bad
Source: John Polk & Associates

While generating wild ideas is fun and valuable, eventually, the ideas must connect to the real world. Eliminate ideas that don't meet constraints and prioritize ideas based on goals. In the real world, don't break the law, and don't try to do everything.

Plan and organize content with a storyboard

Storyboarding is a visual planning technique used in moviemaking. Movie producers hire an artist to illustrate each scene. Storyboarding shows actors where to stand, helps the lighting crew figure out how to light the scene, and keeps the boom operator out of the shot. The storyboard in Figure 2.9 comes from the scene in *The Sound of Music* where Julie Andrews teaches the children how to sing.

Figure 2.9 Storyboarding is as easy as "Do-Re-Mi"
Source: *The Sound of Music* (1965) / 20th Century Fox / Maurice Zuberano

The storyboard captures aspects of scenery, choreography, and camera angles. The actors can see where they stand relative to the other actors, and the camera operator can see which scenes, like the overhead maze shot, require a crane.

For presentation purposes, a storyboard is a slide-by-slide sketch of the deck. Our preferred method is to use one standard-sized sticky note per slide. Using your mind map, write a title and sketch the content for each slide. Focus on each slide's content in bullet-point form.

Then, sketch out visuals, like frameworks, charts, or images, like in Figure 2.10. It's OK at this stage to create simple bullet-point slides if you're unsure what visual to use. Finally, rearrange the sticky notes to refine the flow.

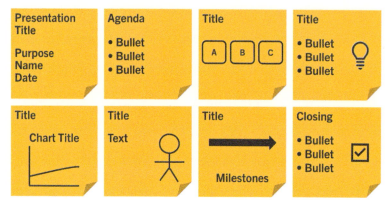

Figure 2.10 Sticky notes keep you focused on the story instead of fiddling with presentation software
Source: John Polk & Associates

As you storyboard, test the story for completeness, logic, and flow using these questions:

- What is the primary presentation point?
- What story flow effectively conveys the information?
- What does each slide need to say?
- What is the logical order for the slides?

There are ways to storyboard without sticky notes. Full-sized paper gives more real estate to work with but might encourage spending time on unnecessary details. Whiteboards let groups storyboard but make it difficult to rearrange slides. Digital whiteboards allow collaboration without being in the same room, but they aren't as easy as paper for creating sketches. Presentation software jump-starts slide creation but often puts the focus on slide design, distracting from story planning.

Unless you're a seasoned pro at storyboarding, practice with sticky notes first. Outlining functionality in presentation software is tempting but often derails progress. You think, "Oh. I have a slide I could use here. Let me find it." Then, 15 minutes later, you haven't found the slide and have lost the story flow. Or you waste time mocking up electronic sketches that would take seconds on paper. As a bonus, sticky notes are fun to crumple up, like in Figure 2.11.

Figure 2.11 A slide we never had to build
Source: Courtesy of Justin Hunsaker

Investing a little time in mind mapping and storyboarding saves you time and stress later. It saves time because you won't build so many slides that later get cut. It reduces stress because you realize you need data to support the core argument and can kick off data analysis sooner. These exercises also help overcome writer's block because it's impossible to be perfect when sketching on a sticky note. They help overcome procrastination because the process doesn't take a long time. Share the storyboard with your boss, peers, or advisers to get feedback early. Outlining the story primes the brain to think about the topic, allowing good ideas to emerge naturally while driving, walking, or dreaming. A client shared that creating a storyboard helped his leaders realize the project was too complicated, so they canceled it—the ultimate time-saver!

Avoid giving a history lesson

> *Let's start at the very beginning.*
> *A very good place to start.*[1]
> Rodgers and Hammerstein, "Do-Re-Mi"

The very beginning may be a very good place to start a singing lesson, but it's *not a* great place to start a presentation storyline. People naturally fall back on linear storytelling. We call the linear business storyline in Figure 2.12 the "history lesson."

Figure 2.12 Boring step-by-step story
Source: John Polk & Associates

Unfortunately, this storyline doesn't reveal the solution until the end, so the audience spends energy guessing where it's going. Your presentation is not a mystery novel!

If you're running short on time and have the audience flip to a later slide, it's a sign that your slides aren't in optimal order. A better way is to lead with the solution and then provide supporting information. The military coined the acronym BLUF to remind communicators to put the "bottom line up front."[2] There are two scenarios when it doesn't make sense to lead with the recommendation:

- The recommendation is counterintuitive or controversial.
- The purpose is to review the problem-solving approach.

In the first case, leading with the recommendation risks having the audience stop listening because they are spending mental energy organizing their argument to tell you how wrong you are. To prevent that, acknowledge early on that you know the recommendation is counterintuitive or controversial, so the audience keeps listening. Then, quickly share the critical data that led to that recommendation before delivering the answer.

In the second case, the audience's job is to review the sausage-making, so share the process steps, stakeholder inputs, data sources, key assumptions, and calculations.

Favor storylines that give the answer up front

For decades, people ascribed magical powers to the Egyptian pyramids and other pyramid-shaped objects, including the ability to preserve food! While *MythBusters* officially busted this myth, pyramids make powerful story archetypes.[3]

In her book *The Minto Pyramid Principle*, Barbara Minto describes an approach to structured thinking and writing that applies to presentations and documents, illustrated in Figure 2.13. We wrote this book leveraging the power of the Pyramid Principle! Minto worked as a consultant for McKinsey & Company, and this approach is how consultants typically build presentations.

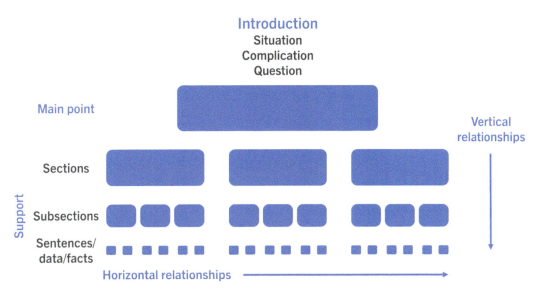

Figure 2.13 Pyramids: When the building (or story) needs to be on point
Source: Adapted from *The Minto Pyramid Principle* (1996) / Barbara Minto

The pyramid architecture includes the following:

- **Introduction:** Start with the situation, describing only the critical background information necessary for the audience to understand the presentation. Like a movie opening, the situation gives the time, place, players, and scope. The audience should accept the details of the situation as fact. The complication is the change in the situation that triggered the need for a presentation. The question arises naturally from the complication. A typical question is "What should we do about it?" Here's a sample introduction:
    - **Situation:** The Rock & Roll Hall of Fame in Cleveland, Ohio, is celebrating its 40th anniversary.
    - **Complication:** To commemorate, they decided to rank the best rock acts.
    - **Question:** Who is the greatest rock act of all time?
- **Main point (a.k.a. controlling idea):** Next, share the primary answer to the question. We sometimes call this "the answer to the case." Give the answer up front—don't save it for the end like the history lesson. Here's a sample main point: The Beatles are the greatest rock act of all time.

- **Support:** Include all the supporting details needed to convince the audience to agree with the main point and no more. In a deck, divide the content into sections, slides, and bullet points. In a white paper, divide the content into sections, paragraphs, and sentences. At the lowest pyramid level, give the data and facts supporting each slide's main point.

- **Vertical relationships:** Build hierarchical connections within the content. The three sections give the details behind the main point. Each subsection group gives the details for the section above it.

- **Horizontal relationships:** Establish the story flow. There are four ways to group horizontal relationships:
  - **Deductive:** Logical progression (major premise, minor premise, conclusion)
  - **Comparative:** Similarities and differences (first, second, third in importance)
  - **Chronological or cause and effect:** Time order (first, second, last)
  - **Structural:** Composition and relationship (first, second, third region)

Figure 2.14 shows the supporting content for the Beatles argument.

Figure 2.14 Ladies and gentlemen, live from the Great Pyramid! The Scarabs![4]
Data sources: Billboard / solobeatles.com / Forbes / Mental Floss; Source: John Polk & Associates

The supporting points give details for each blue box. These are vertical relationships. The horizontal relationship among the three blue boxes is chronological, from their time as the Beatles, through the solo years, to today.

There are two broad types of pyramid structures. Our Beatles argument uses the first structure, inductive reasoning. That means each of the three main supporting points independently supports the main point that the Beatles are the all-time greatest rock act. If you dismiss Paul McCartney's solo material as merely "Silly Love Songs," the argument can still stand on the first and third points.

The second pyramid structure uses deductive reasoning with a logic chain between the supporting points, like in Figure 2.15.

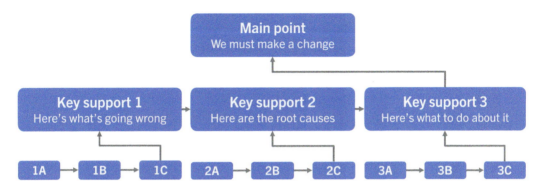

Figure 2.15 Elementary, my dear Watson!
Source: Adapted from *The Minto Pyramid Principle* (1996) / Barbara Minto

This example flows logically from the problem to the root causes to the solution. The 1A–3C branches represent the subcomponents of each key support. Let's apply this structure to the staffing decision shown in Figure 2.16.

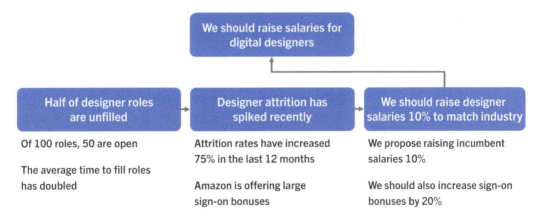

Figure 2.16 Did ancient designers have to "think outside the pyramid"?
Source: John Polk & Associates

Favor storylines that give the answer up front   49

When presenting your argument, imagine a stakeholder saying, "I just read in *The Wall Street Journal* that Amazon is closing its local digital design shop." You have a problem. Because the root causes no longer apply, the audience is less likely to support the recommendations. That's not a flaw in the structure. It just means the root causes must be accurate and exhaustive.

While the blue boxes use deductive reasoning, the supporting points use inductive reasoning. It's OK to mix them.

People naturally create a pyramid structure when they digest information. They look for meaning in the idea sequence. And they look for connections between ideas as they hear them. Creating the pyramid for the audience makes it easier to understand and remember the key points.

Organizations use presentations to drive project phases: kickoff, interim update, and final recommendation. Figure 2.17 shows sample storylines for each phase.

Project Phase Storylines

Proposal/kickoff
1. There is a problem
2. The problem is significant and should be addressed now
3. We have a structured approach and a clear set of deliverables
4. Here are the critical next steps
5. We formed a team and agreed on expectations
6. Here's what we need from stakeholders
7. We will update on this schedule

Interim update
1. Here's a reminder of our problem and approach
2. We are making good progress
3. We delivered key outputs— e.g., process flows, root cause
4. Here are our insights so far
5. Here is where we need help
6. We have clear next steps

Recommendation
1. We have a solution to the problem
2. The answer creates value
3. We tested or presold the recommendation
4. We built an implementation plan
5. We understand the risks and created a mitigation plan
6. We need support in these areas to be successful

Figure 2.17 The good, the bad, and the over-budget
Source: John Polk & Associates

50   The Bury the Lede Trap

Include relevant content in a pitch deck or business case

In the introduction, we mentioned our goal: to help you get the resources you need to turn ideas into reality. That is every pitch's goal. A pitch deck asks investors to give money to fund a big idea. Many sales presentations fit this model, too. Sales decks ask prospects to invest money in a product or service to solve their problems.

Inside corporations, the same process happens. Presenters ask leaders for resources (like money, staff, equipment, or software) to develop new products or services, solve problems, or improve processes. An internal pitch deck is a business case. The goal of a business case is to drive a decision, typically around an investment. Since few decisions are cut and dried, the primary purpose of the business case is to get decision-makers comfortable with the assumptions that go into it.

Sequoia Capital, the investment firm, requests the 10 business plan components in Figure 2.18 from entrepreneurs seeking capital.[5] This is a smart move all leaders should emulate: tell people pitching their ideas what you expect to see in their pitch!

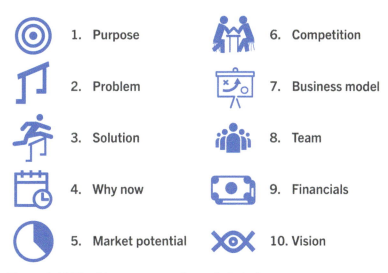

Figure 2.18 The 10 components for a pitch deck
Source: Adapted from Sequoia Capital

Let's discuss each component of the pitch or business case in turn:

1. **Purpose:** Why does your company, department, or team exist? Don't try to list all functions or features. The purpose is more critical in a startup pitch deck. In a business case, making the purpose explicit ensures that the pitch or business case is consistent with the mission. We have a client who starts every presentation with their corporate mission.

2. **Problem:** What is the pain customers face? How do customers deal with that pain now, and what do those solutions lack? Describe the problem in terms of the jobs that customers are trying to get done. The key to a good problem statement is to show the gap between the current and desired states using a metric that customers care about. The sample problem statement in Figure 2.19 highlights the key components.

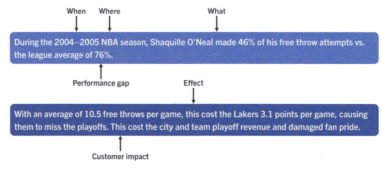

Figure 2.19 Can missed free throws cause a city to mourn?
Data source: NBA.com; Source: John Polk & Associates

For the record, we don't know if Shaq missed free throws in enough close games to cost the Lakers the playoffs. An effective problem statement is clearly articulated, solves a genuine business problem, and has a defined scope. Some business cases aren't designed to fix a problem but to take advantage of an opportunity.

3. **Solution:** How does the pitch or business case address customers' pain? Explain your value proposition (val prop). Dr. Alexander Osterwalder, in his book *Value Proposition Design*, developed the fill-in-the-blanks framework for writing a val prop in Figure 2.20.

Figure 2.20 Val prop (M)ad Libs
Source: Reproduced with permission from Dr. Alexander Osterwalder / Strategyzer AG / Ad-lib value proposition template / https://www.strategyzer.com/library/ad-lib-value-proposition-template, last accessed January 17, 2025

For most organizations, products and services are straightforward. What do you sell? What do you do for customers? For the customer segment, don't be afraid to define this narrowly. Having a targeted segment helps you better understand their needs and, in turn, develop better products and services that people outside that segment also value.

Companies typically use this framework for a customer-facing product, but it also works for internal or external services. The val prop framework for a "hypothetical" company we call "John Polk & Associates" is in Figure 2.21.

> Our presentation design workshops, coaching, and consulting services
> *products and services*
> help entrepreneurs and corporate strategy and analytics leaders
> *customer segment*
> who want to get resources to make their ideas a reality
> *jobs to be done*
> by simplifying and standardizing the pitch development process
> *verb (e.g., reducing)*   *customer pain*
> and leveraging the power of stories and visualizations to make ideas clear, concise, and compelling,
> *verb (e.g., increasing)*   *customer gain*
> unlike … we only have nice things to say about our competition

Figure 2.21 If you don't know your value, neither will your customers
Source: John Polk & Associates

In our first-draft val prop, we defined the jobs to be done as "write presentations." That's true for graphic designers and communications specialists. Clients don't think of presentations as their job but as a means to engage, influence, and drive action. In a pitch or business case, the job is to get resources to turn ideas into reality. Good val props also require customer-back thinking. What hurdles do customers face to get their jobs done? What new opportunities can you offer?

4. **Why now:** Why is now the right time for this solution? If you've ever been in a meeting and someone said, "We tried that before, and it didn't work," you've experienced the human need to understand "why now." The "why now" shows you've addressed why an idea didn't work before. You might have new technologies, lower costs, or reduced risk. Sometimes, the "why now" is because customers are now ready to adopt the new solution.

5. **Market potential:** Who are the customers, and how many are in the market? Depending on data availability, you might do a top-down or a bottom-up market assessment. The top-down approach says, "The US market is $400M,

and we believe we can capture 20% market share." The bottom-up approach says, "We can acquire 70M customers at scale worth $80M." In a business case, the market potential might be the number of customers affected by the solution. In some cases, the solution creates a new market.

> *If I had asked people what they wanted,*
> *they would have said faster horses.*[6]
> Henry Ford (dubiously attributed)

6. **Competition:** Who are the competitors? Include indirect competitors. Coke doesn't just compete with Pepsi; it also competes with Starbucks. Show that you have a plan to win. For a business case, the competition section might include options. What other ideas did you consider, and what were the decision criteria? When comparing a product to the competition's or a solution to the alternatives, don't just show the winning features—there are always tradeoffs.

7. **Business model:** How will you increase revenue or reduce costs? How will you price the solution? Are you selling to businesses or consumers? What is the sales model? Do you need to hire a sales force? For a business case, how does this idea impact business economics?

8. **Team:** Who is on the team, and what is their expertise? The goal is to give investors or decision-makers confidence that the team can pull off the idea. Who else do you need to expand or implement the idea?

9. **Financials:** What is the cost/benefit of the pitch or business case? Define how you'll make money; include profit and loss, balance sheet, and cash flow. What risks do you face, and how will you address them? In many organizations, financials are the business case—and the business case is only the spreadsheet. However, the other nine components are necessary to bring the numbers to life. Financial projections, like all forecasts, are based on models.

> *All models are wrong, but some are useful.*[7]
> George E. P. Box, "Science and Statistics"

Two strategies can ensure the model is less wrong. First, perform sensitivity analysis. All models use assumptions. Vary the key assumptions and review the results. After identifying the assumptions that produce the widest variability in model outcomes, invest in better grounding those assumptions. Rapid testing helps quickly improve key assumptions and is central to the "fail fast" philosophy of design thinking and Agile methodologies. Second, create a monitoring plan. Determine success criteria ahead of time. If you don't, you'll be tempted to rationalize subpar results. Then, put a safety net in place in case you're wrong. How and when would you pull the plug? What risk mitigation can you put in place to limit the impact of a bad decision?

10. **Vision:** What can the solution achieve in three to five years if all goes well? Where is the market heading? What follow-on products or projects are possible? Consider product extensions (e.g., introducing mint Oreos), new add-on services (e.g., selling credit monitoring with a credit report), and market expansions (e.g., entering Canada). Internally, what other departments or processes could benefit from your idea? Sometimes, the infrastructure that solves one problem can solve different problems or create new opportunities. Amazon Web Services (AWS) started as a solution to an internal problem. As of Q1 FY 2024, AWS made up 17% of Amazon's revenue and 66% of its operating income.[8]

Emphasize the main point of the slide in the title

The most powerful improvement to a presentation is using sentence titles that give the main point of each slide. Let us say that again:

> The most powerful improvement
> to a presentation is using sentence titles
> that give the main point of each slide.
>
> John and Justin, *Presentation Pitfalls*

If you disagree with that statement, you're not alone. Of all the concepts we teach, this gets the most pushback. But stay with us—science is on our side.

During one of our workshops, a woman stood up, pounded the table, and said, "I don't get this sentence title thing! I was trained from birth to use subject titles." While that might be a slight exaggeration, her frustration was genuine. We didn't learn this approach until graduate school. Our kids created presentations in elementary school through college, and no teacher has ever taught them to use sentence titles. It's our education system's greatest failing (another slight exaggeration).

Before diving deeper, it's helpful to start with definitions for the common slide elements in Figure 2.22.

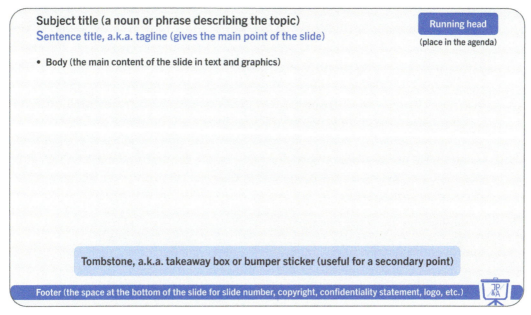

Figure 2.22 Slide nomenclature
Source: John Polk & Associates

We'll discuss each element eventually but focus on sentence titles here. Sentence titles are the slide's prime real estate and should always capture the audience's attention. So much goodness flows from writing precise but concise sentence titles. Here are the benefits for the presenter:

- **Improved clarity for the strategy and the story:** Writing sentence titles when sketching out the deck forces clarity on the story early. As you build content, there's a natural iteration between the slide title and body. We typically brain-dump content in bullet-point form, then write a sentence title, then refine the content based on the title, then refine the title based on the content, then ... you get the point. Struggling with clear sentence titles might indicate an unclear strategy. Writing clear sentence titles forces you to distill and refine the strategy.

- **Help in remembering the key point you want to make on each slide:** Have you ever had that moment where you click to the next slide, and your mind goes blank? You don't have to remember if you've written a sentence title with the slide's main point! Simply paraphrase the title to give the main point without reading the exact text to the audience. That is typically enough to get your mind unstuck.

- **Increased comprehensibility when you're not there to present:** We work with many people who consider themselves better talkers than writers, so they use simple bullet-point slides with subject titles and then focus on their speech. Even if that's effective for you, decks get forwarded. With the minimal text approach, the reader of the forwarded deck has no chance to understand it. Conversely, well-crafted sentence titles do the heavy lifting for conveying the story and key points clearly. A deck with sentence titles is also easier to review when the decision-maker arrives 25 minutes late for a 30-minute meeting. In this scenario, quickly hit the key points in the slide titles and then spend a few minutes on critical slides.

Here are the benefits for the audience:

- **Improved understanding:** Without a clear title, the audience must interpret the message on their own. Without a written conclusion, there's a risk that the audience will come to a different one. In our workshops, participants practice writing sentence titles for a sample chart, often highlighting 5–10 different themes. They focus on different time ranges or different trend segments. Some summarize the change over time as an absolute, while some list it as a percentage. All of these are valid, but choose the one that is relevant to your presentation.

- **Ability to refocus after "zoning out":** It's a distracting world. Texts, emails, and instant messages compete for the audience's attention. In a virtual world, it's easy for the audience to convince themselves they can check email while listening. General estimates put attention span at 10–15 minutes, and although the studies aren't conclusive, the most significant impact on attention span is likely the presenter's skill.[9] There's no rewind button on a live speech. When the audience tunes out (and they all do eventually), sentence titles help them catch up when they tune back in.

- **Increased retention:** Science supports sentence titles. Studies compared student recall when the main point was in the title versus the first bullet point. In one study, the test scores for the student group taught from the sentence title slides were 37% higher than those taught from subject-title slides![10]

When subject titles go bad

When John and his wife dropped their daughter off at college, the parent orientation session included the slide in Figure 2.23.

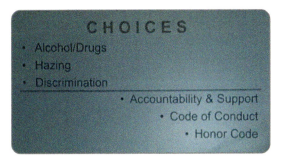

Figure 2.23 Bad choices
Source: Anonymous, courtesy of John Polk

When John saw this slide, he thought, "You're giving my daughter a choice between alcohol and drugs?!" That's the day his crusade for sentence titles got real!

Craft compelling, concise, and complete sentence titles

Writing compelling sentence titles takes practice and iteration. Here's a secret—when drafting a new slide, we don't always start with a sentence title. We sometimes start with a subject title. Then, we sketch out the slide. Then, we write a mediocre sentence title. Then, we finish the slide. Finally, we write a killer sentence title. Here are additional tips for writing effective sentence titles:

- **Make it "so what."** Give the main point of the slide or the bottom line. If you could say only one thing to encapsulate the slide, what would it be? The most common feedback we give presenters is to include the "so what" in a strong sentence title.

- **Make it precise.** Focus only on the slide's main point. Make it action oriented. Highlight the compelling data.

- **Make it concise.** Keep titles to one or two lines. Any longer, and it's hard for the audience to take it all in. No, you can't shrink the font to make a long title fit. If you can't get it down to two lines, that's a clue the content belongs on two slides.

- **Make it a complete sentence.** Technically, we shouldn't have to write "complete sentence"—if it's not complete, it's just a phrase. In grammar terms, a sentence has a subject (noun) and a predicate (verb). Here are titles written by workshop participants that don't pass the sentence test:

    - "Kentucky employment in coal mining over a decade"—this lacks a verb and a "so what" conclusion.
    - "Coal mining jobs down 80% in the last decade"—this has a "so what" conclusion but lacks a verb. The participant dropped the verb to be concise, leaving a newspaper headline, not a complete sentence.

- **Ensure slide content supports the title.** This should go without saying, but don't count on it happening naturally. This is a vertical logic test, consistent with the Pyramid Principle.

- **Read all titles without looking at the content.** Ensure the story is clear and flows well. If not, rewrite the titles or reorder the slides. This is a horizontal logic test. If the audience couldn't see the slide body, could they understand the key points?

- **Look in the slide content.** Even if you're not used to writing sentence titles, you've thought about the slide's most important point. Perhaps you put it in the first bullet point, the speaker notes, or the tombstone. Why hide it? Give it the prominence it deserves as a sentence title.

Figure 2.24 shows sample slide titles from bad to great.

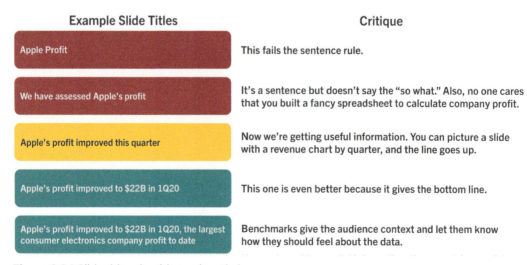

Figure 2.24 Slide titles should stand on their own

Data source: "List of Largest Corporate Profits and Losses," Wikipedia, https://en.wikipedia.org/wiki/List_of_largest_corporate_profits_and_losses (last modified January 9, 2025); Source: John Polk & Associates

When writing a title summarizing data, include the components in Figure 2.25.

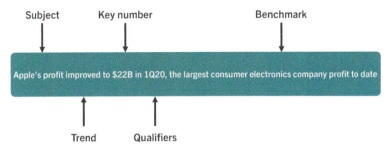

Figure 2.25 Titles can be precise and concise
Source: John Polk & Associates

Benchmarks are the element most often left out of sentence titles. Benchmarks tell the audience how they should feel about the number. "The largest consumer electronics company profit to date" grabs attention. "Up 0.01% over last year" says nothing to see here. Typical benchmarks include forecasts, prior time periods, all-time highs or lows, other products, competitors, or industry averages.

Writing a sentence title can be challenging without data. The framework we use to summarize everything in our eight-hour workshop appears in Figure 2.26.

Presentation Design Principles

Tell a clear story

- Assess the audience, purpose, and setting to determine the design
- Create a compelling story
- Put important things first

Leverage graphics

- Support the story with data and charts
- Use frameworks, images, and icons to convey ideas

Reduce noise

- Leverage a standard template with a simple, elegant design
- Write professionally
- Use the fewest words required

Present with confidence

- Prepare and practice
- Show confidence with voice and body
- Read the audience as you present

Figure 2.26 Brilliant advice we cover throughout the book
Source: John Polk & Associates

Craft compelling, concise, and complete sentence titles 61

A framework with four boxes and 11 bullet points is challenging content to summarize in one sentence. Figure 2.27 illustrates three approaches.

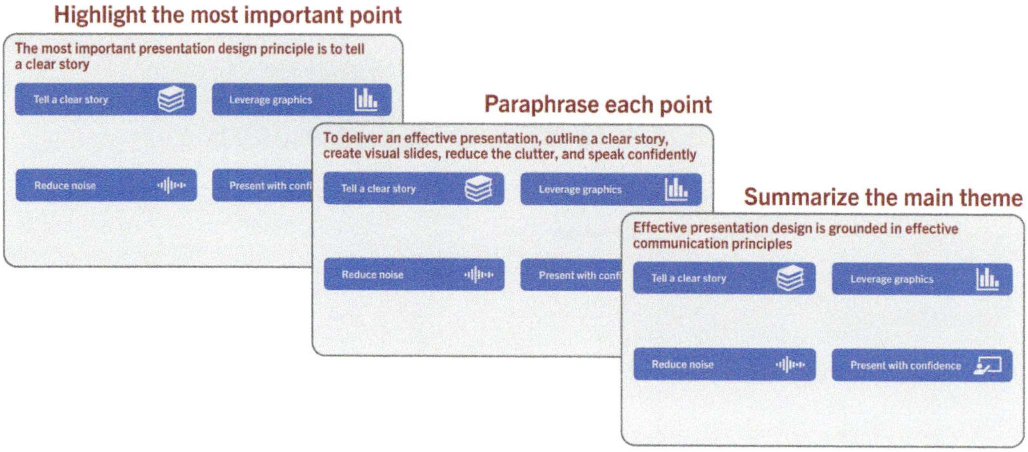

Figure 2.27 Three ways to title a slide
Source: John Polk & Associates

Each approach has tradeoffs:

- **Highlight the most important point.** It's like saying, "If you remember nothing else, remember this." This approach elevated storytelling above the other content.
- **Paraphrase each of the main points.** This is comprehensive but avoids pure repetition. If the points are equally important, include them all in the title for this approach.
- **Summarize the overarching theme.** Create a connection from your content to a broader theme. This approach highlighted the connection between communication and presentations.

There are a handful of exceptions to the sentence title rule:

- Cover slide
- Agenda
- Outline
- Executive summary
- Summary

But even in those cases, you *could* write a sentence title that gives the main point of the presentation.

> ### Sentence titles and science fairs
>
> When John's daughter was in middle school, she earned a trip to the state science fair. She asked for feedback on her deck the night before she presented. Procrastination is not a best practice. To avoid overwhelming her with feedback, John decided to focus on sentence titles. Here's how the conversation went:
>
> > **John:** This is an excellent deck. The one thing I'd change is to write sentence titles that give each slide's main point.
> >
> > **Daughter:** I don't want to do that.
> >
> > **John:** No, really. It's the one thing that will noticeably improve your slides and help the audience follow the story. I'm kind of an expert on this.
> >
> > (She is not impressed.)
> >
> > **Daughter:** But they gave us a template, and the template didn't use sentence titles.
> >
> > **John:** Interesting. Please show me the template.
> >
> > (She pulls up the template and shows him the sample scatter plot slide without a sentence title. Then he flips through the other slides.)
> >
> > **John:** You're right. This slide doesn't have a sentence title, but all the other slides do, and I created them!
>
> Unbeknownst to John, the person who created the science fair template worked at the same company as him. She based the science fair template on the company template that John built! She added a sample scatter plot slide and didn't write a complete-sentence title for that slide. Small world.
>
> John eventually convinced his daughter to add sentence titles, and she took first place. This demonstrates the value of sentence titles. Oh, and also his daughter's hard work.

Presenters often ask if it's OK to use a question as a sentence title. The answer is "Yes, but…" Presenters sometimes use questions for titles, like "What is the vision?" That's simply a wordier way to write the subject title "Vision." However, it is appropriate to use a question when the goal is to generate discussion, solve problems, or brainstorm. In that case, don't bias the group by giving an answer in the title. In those cases, it's appropriate to make the discussion question the title.

In organizations with a subject-title approach, use sentence titles underneath the subject titles. The downside is that it takes up more real estate and is one more object to maintain across slides. We typically don't use subject titles, sentence titles, and running heads in the same deck—that's just too much going on at the top of each slide.

John coached a client who resisted using sentence titles in his pitch deck. John stopped arguing, even though he hadn't convinced the client. Halfway through the deck, the client had a slide with a sentence title. John asked why there was a sentence title here and nowhere else. The client said, "I always got the same question on this slide, so I thought I should put the answer at the top." John pointed out, "Don't *all* your slides deserve that clarity?" Yes, all your slides deserve a sentence title.

Write an executive summary, even if you don't present it

We have a love-hate relationship with executive summaries. Let's start with the hate. We hate an executive summary that is a wall of text. We hate an executive summary that tries to drive a meeting on one bullet-point-only slide when there are thoughtful, visual slides that better support the discussion. We hate the awkward attempt to talk to a slide while the audience reads the text like a Word document.

Now for the love. We love it when writing an executive summary helps presenters get their story straight. We love it when an executive summary clearly highlights the presentation's key takeaways. We love it when a forwarded deck has an executive summary that helps us understand the content without the deck creator there to present it. And we love it when it lets us get the main points without reading the whole deck.

We encourage presenters to write an executive summary, even if the final deck doesn't require one. Writing an executive summary improves the presentation by forcing you to determine the key points and validate the logical flow. The longer the presentation, the more valuable it is to include the executive summary in the deck. However, executive summaries don't fit well with short presentations, town halls, or TED-style presentations.

There are two seemingly contradictory best practices for writing an effective executive summary—write it first or write it last.

- **Write it first.** This creates a word-based storyboard. Just don't use this as an excuse to skip the sticky note storyboard. A well-written executive summary has bullet points that are good candidates for slide titles.
- **Write it last.** After writing slide titles that are complete sentences, copy the slide titles onto one slide to create a draft executive summary. Then, check the

flow and edit. If there's a better way to phrase an executive-summary point, update the related slide title. It might also become clear where the deck needs additional content to support the argument.

Because we get the "write it first" benefit from storyboarding, we typically write our executive summaries last. When building an executive summary or writing an introduction, pretend the time allotment was cut to five minutes. This forces you to include only the information the audience cares most about. As a bonus, you'll be prepared when a busy executive cuts your time to five minutes.

With both methods, don't forget to apply good slide design practices:

- **Frame it.** Choose a story structure, like "problem, root causes, solution," to create high-level categories with sub-bullet points.
- **Visualize it.** Use icons or a graphical framework.
- **Make it precise.** Remove any noncritical words, phrases, or bullet points.

Upcoming chapters discuss each practice in greater detail.

Guide the audience with agendas, bumpers, and running heads

Surprizes [sic] are foolish things.
The pleasure is not enhanced, and
the inconvenience is often considerable.[11]

Jane Austen, *Emma*

During a presentation, the audience has questions running through their minds. "Why are we here?" "What are we talking about?" "How does this topic fit into the overall picture?" "What else do we have to cover?" Please don't make the audience figure this out on their own. Agendas, bumper slides, and running heads answer these questions for the audience.

List presentation topics with an agenda. Unlike an executive summary, an agenda doesn't give the main points, just the main topics. It's like the map in the amusement park that shows where the major attractions are located. Use simple visual objects to make the agenda engaging. Adding time estimates to an agenda reduces the audience's natural anxiety. "When will we get to the topic I care about?" "When do we get a break?" "When will this presentation be done?" Figure 2.28 shows simple agenda layouts.

Figure 2.28 Agenda slides for a meeting about "Text"
Source: John Polk & Associates

Break up sections with bumper slides. For longer presentations, add bumper slides (a.k.a. section or chapter breaks) to reorient the audience within the high-level story. Bumper slides match the agenda, with one bumper per agenda topic. A bumper slide acts like a "downloading" progress bar, giving the audience the same endorphin boost as crossing something off a to-do list: "One more topic down!" Bumper slides also recapture the attention of any audience members who tuned out on the prior topic. Figure 2.29 shows sample bumper slides.

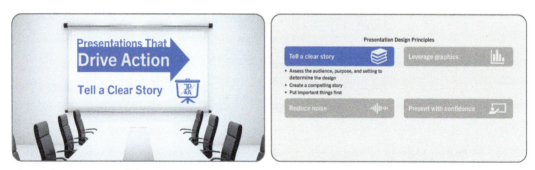

Figure 2.29 Bumper slide examples
Sources: (conference room) vasabii / Adobe Stock Photos / (slides) John Polk & Associates

Using the full-screen image from the cover slide grabs the audience's attention and gives the module a mini-presentation vibe within the broader presentation. Using the four-box framework creates a natural reminder of the key points. In later sections, the bumper adds new bullet points and grays out the prior ones. The dark backgrounds on the bumpers in Figure 2.30 overtly signal a transition.

Figure 2.30 Dark background bumper slide examples
Source: John Polk & Associates

Consider running heads to orient the audience. Often called "breadcrumbs," running heads, like the elements in the upper-right corner of the three slides in Figure 2.31, create a "You Are Here" effect by listing the section title or showing the section icon on each content slide.

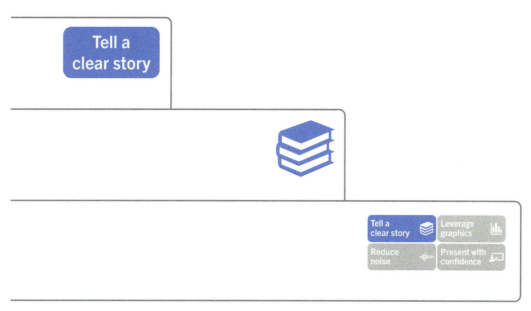

Figure 2.31 Running head examples
Source: John Polk & Associates

The first approach is a simple box with text. This is the easiest to create and maintain and the easiest for the audience to understand. The second approach uses a simple icon. This is more visual but risks the audience forgetting the icon's meaning. The third approach repeats the core framework in miniature and highlights the current section. This combines the best of the previous approaches (text plus icon) and adds a "You Are

Here" element. The downsides are that they are harder to create and maintain, and the tiny text is harder to read.

Confession: We don't use running heads for our workshop material. They require extra effort to create and maintain, increasing the risk of mistakes, like leaving a running head off or putting the wrong one on a slide. However, if you think the audience might get lost, they are worth the effort.

Key Takeaways

Give the audience the most important information up front before they lose focus.

- ✓ Make the subject, scope, purpose, date, and name clear on the title slide.
- ✓ Use mind mapping and storyboarding to sketch the story before building the slides.
- ✓ Choose a storyline that leads with the recommendations. Avoid giving your audience a history lesson.
- ✓ For business cases and pitch decks, use the Sequoia framework to structure content.
- ✓ Craft compelling and concise slide titles that convey the main point.
- ✓ Test slide titles for vertical logic. Ensure the title summarizes the body and the body supports the title.
- ✓ Test slide titles for horizontal logic by reading only the titles. Ensure the story is clear and the titles logically flow to the conclusion.
- ✓ Write an executive summary to communicate key points concisely and ensure the story flows logically, but don't drive the whole meeting from the summary.
- ✓ For longer presentations, orient the audience to the story flow with agenda slides, bumper slides, or running heads.

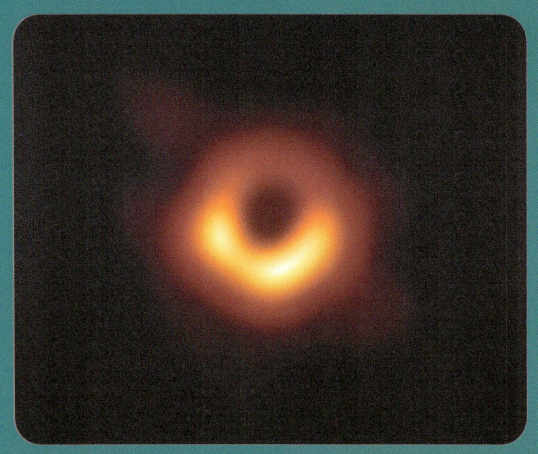

Figure 3.1 The first image of a black hole
Source: Event Horizon Telescope Collaboration / NASA / Public Domain

3

The Black Hole Trap

"Graphicalize" slides and eliminate unessential content to avoid overwhelming the audience with too much information.

Black holes, like in Figure 3.1, form when a star collapses, creating objects with massive amounts of matter jammed into a relatively small volume. Black holes are so dense that gravity prevents light from escaping.

Presenters fall into the Black Hole Trap when they build slides and decks so densely that the audience can't or won't digest them. Many presentations are like black holes, where presenters jam too much information into too little time with too many words on every slide. These presentations become so dense that the audience tunes out, and no information can escape!

Black hole presentations have a poor signal-to-noise ratio. In electrical or audio engineering, the signal-to-noise ratio compares the amount of information getting through to the amount of background noise. Imagine listening to a baseball game on a car AM radio. The signal includes the announcer's voice, the bat's crack, and the crowd's roar. The noise includes the hum of the engine, the crackle from the lightning storm outside, and the static as the car drives farther away from the radio station. Optimizing the signal-to-noise ratio is such an important concept that we considered naming this book after it.

In a presentation, noise is anything on the slides or in your speech that doesn't align with the core message, including having too many words, misaligned objects, or unprofessional designs.

To illustrate what a slide in a black hole presentation looks like, let's describe how they form, using a bad wall-of-text slide in Figure 3.2.

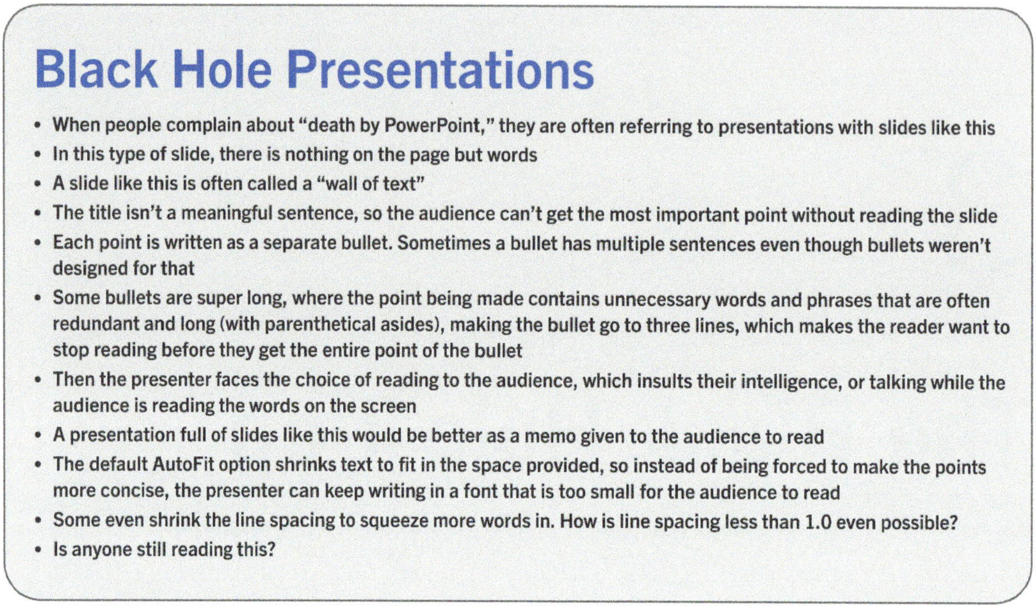

Black Hole Presentations

- When people complain about "death by PowerPoint," they are often referring to presentations with slides like this
- In this type of slide, there is nothing on the page but words
- A slide like this is often called a "wall of text"
- The title isn't a meaningful sentence, so the audience can't get the most important point without reading the slide
- Each point is written as a separate bullet. Sometimes a bullet has multiple sentences even though bullets weren't designed for that
- Some bullets are super long, where the point being made contains unnecessary words and phrases that are often redundant and long (with parenthetical asides), making the bullet go to three lines, which makes the reader want to stop reading before they get the entire point of the bullet
- Then the presenter faces the choice of reading to the audience, which insults their intelligence, or talking while the audience is reading the words on the screen
- A presentation full of slides like this would be better as a memo given to the audience to read
- The default AutoFit option shrinks text to fit in the space provided, so instead of being forced to make the points more concise, the presenter can keep writing in a font that is too small for the audience to read
- Some even shrink the line spacing to squeeze more words in. How is line spacing less than 1.0 even possible?
- Is anyone still reading this?

Figure 3.2 Every bad presentation you've ever seen
Source: John Polk & Associates

How hard was it to read that slide? How far did you get before you stopped reading? The presenter's job is to make it easy for the audience, but black hole presentations increase the audience's cognitive load. Bullet-point-only slides are unengaging even when they aren't this dense.

Avoid the Black Hole Trap by making slides graphical through data visualization, tables, images, and icons while eliminating content that's not necessary to make key points.

Understand the causes of poor signal-to-noise ratio

Presenters create black hole presentations for three reasons: lack of will, skill, or kill.

- **Lack of will**

> *I have made this [letter] longer than usual because
> I have not had time to make it shorter.*[1]
> Blaise Pascal, letter to a friend (translated)

Choosing the most efficient and effective way to make your point takes time. It's faster to dump initial thoughts on a slide and move on. But that shifts the communication burden to the audience.

- **Lack of skill**

> *It's easy to make things hard.*
> *It's hard to make things easy.*[2]
> James Abbott,
> The Executive Guide to Low Cost Call Centers

We don't know if James was the first to say this, but he's the first person to say it to us. Creating a logical storyline and distilling complex concepts into easy-to-digest diagrams or summaries requires strategic thinking. Leveraging data to support your ideas requires analytical skills. Building clear and concise text requires writing skills, including grammar, style, and word dieting. Creating professional slides requires presentation software skills. Delivering presentations requires public speaking skills.

- **Lack of kill**

> *Murder your darlings.*[3]
> Arthur Quiller-Couch,
> On the Art of Writing

The failure here is one of prioritization. To experts, every fact in their domain is essential. To the audience, only the facts required to accept an argument are necessary. Experts find complex concepts easy to comprehend, so they don't take the time to simplify them for nonexperts.

As the story evolves, some slides no longer support the story. Because of the time spent creating those slides, deleting them causes physical pain even when that's the best thing for the presentation. People are naturally risk averse and include slides "just in case there's a question on that." This highlights how hard it is to objectively edit your work.

Another dense-deck driver is the desire to have the material readable and understandable without the presenter needing to be there to present it. It's a fact of life in business that decks get forwarded, which makes this style reasonable. However, that's not an excuse to overwhelm the audience with words.

Visualize the data

Naturally, charts (a.k.a. graphs) are the first way to graphicalize—it's in the name. No, graphicalize isn't a real word, but we're making it our mission to get it in the dictionary. We're looking at you, Webster!

Analyze your data, find patterns, translate them into actionable insights, and visualize them in a chart. Figure 3.3 is a guide to the most common chart types and when to use them.

Figure 3.3 Common chart types and their uses
Source: John Polk & Associates

Chapter 4, "The Just the Facts Trap," discusses common mistakes when visualizing data. For a deeper discussion of chart types and when to use them, check out *Effective Data Visualization* by Stephanie Evergreen.

Organize with useful tables

When you have data, copying the spreadsheet directly into the deck is tempting. But that's a numeric wall of text! You're flooding the audience with lots of numbers, forcing them to look for insights. Yes, a 36-line profit-and-loss (P&L) spreadsheet pasted into the deck as a picture is awful, but not *all* tables are awful. Here are effective table strategies:

- **Features table:** This graphic compares your product to the competitors' products on the key features customers care about, in order of importance. The product with the most check marks wins unless the check marks are for lower-ranked features. Similarly, an options table compares solutions to a problem against the most impactful decision criteria, as in Figure 3.4.

Features	Proposal	Option 2	Option 3
Feature 1	✓		✓
Feature 2	✓	✓	
Feature 3	✓	✓	
Feature 4	✓		
Feature 5			✓

Figure 3.4 Check out these features!
Source: John Polk & Associates

If the differences are more nuanced than yes/no assessments, Harvey balls represent a five-point scale, with circles filled in to varying degrees. The table in Figure 3.5 compares different call center models.

Criteria	Silo	Superagent	Combo
Ability to tailor	◐	●	◕
Feasibility	◕	○	○
Efficiency	○	●	◕
Scalability	◐	○	●
Customer experience	◔	●	◕

● Denotes the option fully satisfies the criteria

Figure 3.5 Features table with Harvey balls
Source: John Polk & Associates

The fully darkened circle means that the option fully satisfies that criterion. The empty circle means that the option doesn't satisfy that criterion. The other circles indicate gradations in between.

- **Heat map:** The colorful table in Figure 3.6 assesses business risk or process/project status using the stoplight colors—red, yellow, and green. Process 3 is struggling on multiple dimensions, and multiple processes are underperforming on Metric 1 and Metric 5.

Features	Process 1	Process 2	Process 3
Metric 1	yellow	yellow	red
Metric 2	green	green	red
Metric 3	green	green	yellow
Metric 4	green	green	green
Metric 5	red	green	red

Figure 3.6 Turn up the heat
Source: John Polk & Associates

Because the green cells create a large contiguous area, they draw the audience's attention. To focus the audience's attention on the problem areas, remove the green, like in Figure 3.7.

Features	Process 1	Process 2	Process 3
Metric 1	yellow	yellow	red
Metric 2			red
Metric 3			yellow
Metric 4			
Metric 5	red		red

Figure 3.7 Hot spots, not hot messes
Source: John Polk & Associates

The monochrome heat map in Figure 3.8 translates the stoplight colors to light, medium, and dark blue. This option focuses on intensity and is an accessible alternative if anyone in the audience has a red/green color deficiency.

Features	Process 1	Process 2	Process 3
Metric 1			
Metric 2			
Metric 3			
Metric 4			
Metric 5			

Figure 3.8 A cool heat-map design
Source: John Polk & Associates

- **Combination table:** To portray mixed data types, combine previous table styles across rows, as in Figure 3.9. Because each Beatle feature is measured differently, we use images, data, and icons for different rows. The heat-map colors let the audience quickly translate the data to a high/medium/low assessment.

Features	Paul	John	George	Ringo
Hairstyle	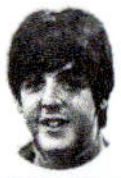	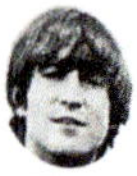	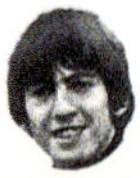	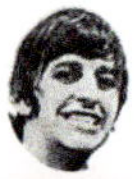
American favorite	45%	27%	17%	11%
Beatles songs written	73.6	84.5	22.2	2.7
Married Yoko		✓		

Figure 3.9 Combination tables can even include the kitchen sink
Data sources: YouGov / Chicago Tribune; Source: EMI / Wikimedia Commons / Public Domain

- **Annotated table:** If the purpose is to review finances, you may have to show the P&L statement. A typical P&L comparing two years of performance is in Figure 3.10.

So many numbers! Except for the bold headline statistics, there's nothing to tell the audience where to look or what to conclude.

Profit & Lost Statement

	Prior Year	Current Year
Total Revenue	$10,000,000	$11,000,000
Less Cost of Goods Sold	$4,141,000	$4,750,000
Gross Profit	$5,859,000	$6,250,000
Gross Profit Margin	58.6%	56.8%
Less Expenses		
Accounting & Legal Fees	$203,000	$205,000
Marketing	$222,000	$220,000
Depreciation	$153,000	$150,000
Utilities	$37,000	$44,000
Insurance	$195,000	$195,000
Interest & Finance Fees	$179,000	$180,000
Office Rental	$901,000	$633,000
Maintenance	$132,000	$120,000
Salary & Benefits	$1,735,000	$1,915,000
Other Expenses	$66,000	$71,000
Total Expenses	$3,823,000	$3,733,000
Net Profit	$2,036,000	$2,517,000
Net Profit Margin	20%	23%

Figure 3.10 Wall-of-numbers P&L
Source: John Polk & Associates

Solve this problem by adding percentage change and notes columns, as in Figure 3.11. Apply conditional formatting to focus attention on significant metric shifts with accent colors. Green indicates favorable variances of 10% or more, while red indicates unfavorable variances. The notes column explains why key metrics changed significantly.

Profit & Loss Statement

	Prior Year	Current Year	% Change	Notes
Total Revenue	$10,000,000	$11,000,000	10%	Revenue increased as the economy improved
Less Cost of Goods Sold	$4,141,000	$4,750,000	15%	COGS impacted by supply chain issues
Gross Profit	$5,859,000	$6,250,000	7%	
Gross Profit Margin	58.6%	56.8%	-3.0%	
Less Expenses				
Accounting & Legal Fees	$203,000	$205,000	1%	
Marketing	$222,000	$220,000	-1%	
Depreciation	$153,000	$150,000	-2%	
Utilities	$37,000	$44,000	19%	Utilities driven by energy price increases
Insurance	$195,000	$195,000	0%	
Interest & Finance Fees	$179,000	$180,000	1%	
Office Rental	$901,000	$633,000	-30%	Rental fees reduced due to work-from-home policy
Maintenance	$132,000	$120,000	-9%	
Salary & Benefits	$1,735,000	$1,915,000	10%	Salaries increased to combat attrition
Other Expenses	$66,000	$71,000	8%	
Total Expenses	$3,823,000	$3,733,000	-2%	
Net Profit	$2,036,000	$2,517,000	24%	

Figure 3.11 Annotated P&L, the CliffsNotes version
Source: John Polk & Associates

The P&L is still dense, but the audience can focus on the line items with notes. Detail-oriented audience members appreciate the clear insights and the opportunity to look at all the numbers to their hearts' content.

Include relevant images

A picture is worth ten thousand words.[4]
Arthur Brisbane, *New Orleans Item*

This quotation is the origin of the phrase "A picture is worth a thousand words." Reading to gain information is hard, while looking at images is easy. People have interpreted visual information throughout history, but text interpretation began only after the invention of written language around 3200 BCE.

Consider two mediums where images shoulder more of the communication burden than text: children's picture books and TED Talks. In a picture book, the images take up most of the page, and the text is short, simple, and often repetitive. The goal is to engage the child through the images and then tell the story, all while teaching language by matching the text to the picture. A picture book with no text is open to interpretation and more challenging to "read" than a picture book with short text. Think about the last time you tried to follow product instructions that only had pictures. Any great TED Talk uses images to illustrate the key points the speaker is presenting. However, the information comes from the speaker's words. If you review a TED Talk's slides without listening to the talk, you won't get much information.

Images are engaging because they grab attention and elicit emotion. And images don't distract the audience from the speech as much as text can. Asking the audience to read and listen at the same time requires multitasking skills that even the most engaged audience can't manage.

Many presenters make poor design choices when using images. The challenges fall into two categories: choosing the right image and effectively designing picture-based slides. Let's take each in turn.

Choose the right image. Because many presenters have learned that a picture is worth a thousand words and that bullet-heavy slides are bad, they go to a free stock photo site and grab the first vaguely related image they find. Or they grab a generic image of businesspeople business-ing or science people science-ing, like in Figure 3.12.

Here's what to look for when choosing images:

- **Use images that illustrate the point.** It's not effective to use images just because they're not words. The photo of well-dressed professionals around a conference table won't help the audience understand key points. Choosing a generic stock photo that doesn't relate to the topic makes the audience try to

 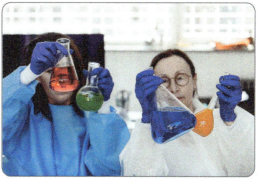

Figure 3.12 Businesspeople business-ing and science people science-ing
Sources: (left) Yan Krukau / (right) Kaboompics.com / Pexels

guess a connection that isn't there. When stock photos use actors, the real professionals know. In the business photo, the team has missed the memo on digital collaboration tools (probably buried under all that paper). The science photo looks like an ad for food coloring. Although this issue appears in most of the decks we review, *well-chosen* images are effective. If a challenging project is almost done, show the light at the end of the tunnel; if a team needs encouragement to get organized, show some ducks in a row, like in Figure 3.13.

- **Be consistent.** Choose images from the same photographer or source with the same design style. Avoid mixing cartoon illustrations with photos.

- **Choose professional-looking images.** Many free sources offer amateurish photos. While amateur photographers can take professional-looking photos, there are a lot of bad photos out there. Look for a high-resolution image with visual harmony, a concept discussed in Chapter 7, "The Lipstick on a Pig Trap."

Figure 3.13 Light at the end of the tunnel and ducks in a row
Source: Courtesy of John Polk

- **Keep it simple but bold.** Choose images that focus attention on a primary object. Remove distracting elements. John took the photo in Figure 3.14 of the Hotel Marqués de Riscal, designed by Frank Gehry.

Figure 3.14 Hotel Marqués de Riscal, Rioja, Spain
Source: Courtesy of John Polk

The composition focuses primarily on the hotel and its undulating roof pattern. The image has bold colors and a focal point that draws attention. The clouds create an interesting background without drawing attention away from the hotel.

Design effective image-based slides. Having a cool image won't matter if you botch the slide design. You don't need Adobe Photoshop to design effective image-based slides, but you do need to know how to compose and modify images. Here are image composition tricks for different slide types:

- **For slides with no words, let the image fill the entire slide.** Most slides should have consistent white-space margins at the edges. However, having margins around an image is less powerful. A full-screen image creates an immersive experience for the audience. It's analogous to watching an IMAX movie. In contrast, an image with wide margins is like watching an old film in the standard aspect ratio on a widescreen TV with black bars on the sides. While the comparison in Figure 3.15 is no IMAX screen, you get the idea. Ensure the image edges don't contain essential elements in case the screen cuts them off.

Figure 3.15 Spilling the (coffee) beans
Source: Alin Luna / Pexels

- **For slides with few words, overlay the text on a full-screen image.** Don't give up the widescreen effect when including text, as in Figure 3.16. The trick is to choose images with a clear space, like the light blue sky, to overlay words. Choose a font color with sufficient contrast.

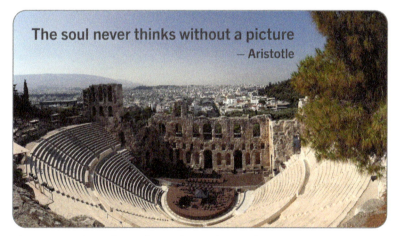

Figure 3.16 The Odeon of Herodes Atticus, Athens, Greece
Source: Courtesy of John Polk

- **For images without a clear space, size and crop the image to leave open space for the text.** Avoid stretching a picture in one direction. We call this the Silly Putty effect—like pressing Silly Putty onto a newspaper to copy an image and then stretch it. The leadership team won't be thrilled if their photos end up stretched wide in the town hall. If the camera adds 10 pounds, stretching a photo adds 20! Instead, keep the photo aspect ratio the same and size it to hit three sides of the slide, leaving room for text on the fourth side. For a comparison, see Figure 3.17. Then, put the text on a nonwhite background. When using photos of people, their eyes should look at the center of the slide toward the words rather than staring off into space.

Figure 3.17 Roman Emperor Hadrian, National Archaeological Museum in Athens, Greece
Source: Courtesy of John Polk

- **Minimize the number of images on a page.** One relevant image is better than multiple generic images. Keep it simple—one key point needs *only* one key image. Use two images to make contrasting points, like before-and-after views.

- **Use collages for inclusiveness.** The photo collage is an exception to the one-image rule. Collages visually convey that "we did a lot of this" or "many people took part." Town hall collages often show different teams volunteering in the community to recognize them. The audience scans the images for their team's volunteer day spent building a house for Habitat for Humanity rather than "reading" each image. When designing collages, size and crop images for consistent height or width, as in Figure 3.18. We made each flower the same height, then chose images to fill out the width. The collage without borders has a cleaner look. However, when images come from different sources, borders create separation among the inconsistent backgrounds.

Figure 3.18 A bouquet of flower images
Sources: (clockwise from upper left) Evie Shaffer / Carol Vázquez / Skylar Kang / Min An / Kaboompics.com / Kaboompics.com / Pexels

82   The Black Hole Trap

- **Crop images to shapes where appropriate.** Sometimes, a square image is square in the unhip sense. Use the Crop to Shape tool to transform images into any geometric shape. A classic technique is to turn square headshots into circles for a team slide or a LinkedIn profile, like in Figure 3.19.

Figure 3.19 Early LinkedIn adopter
Sources: (skyline) LinkedInBackground.com / CC0 1.0 / (headshot) Leonardo da Vinci / Wikimedia Commons / Public Domain

- **Combine images with other visual designs.** Images can work in concert with frameworks and charts. The mountain overlaid on the chart reinforces the upward trend in mountain climbing equipment in Figure 3.20.

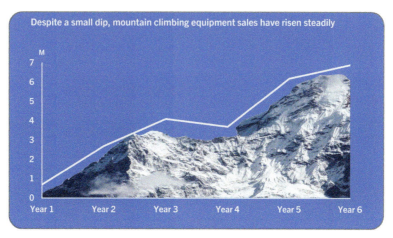

Figure 3.20 Sales climbing to a new peak
Source: Ama Dablam / Pixabay

To create this design, find an image to illustrate the data, remove the background, and crop and size the picture to fit the page and the chart.

Include relevant images   83

- **For busy images, use filters to focus attention.** If the image has a lot going on, use filters or artistic effects to focus attention and mute any distracting elements. We use the image from Athens in Figure 3.21 to illustrate how to work with busy images.

Figure 3.21 Monastiraki Square, Athens, Greece
Source: Courtesy of John Polk

We love how the main tile pattern curves, but the people are a distraction. One way to draw attention to the curved tile path is to use a color selector tool (a.k.a. eyedropper) to change the background color under the text to match the tile. The next strategy is to change the saturation, as shown in Figure 3.22. Setting the color saturation to 0% creates a black-and-white image, reducing the distractions from brightly colored clothing. Amping up the color saturation to 300% makes the tiles surrounding the path in the foreground look like confetti, drawing the audience's eyes to the tile path's beginning. In both cases, we changed the text background to match the color in the image we wanted to emphasize.

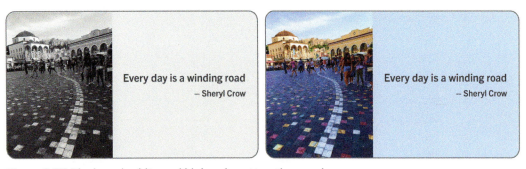

Figure 3.22 Black-and-white and high-color saturation versions
Source: Courtesy of John Polk

The final strategy is to use an artistic effect, as in Figure 3.23. In addition to the benefits of going black and white, this effect makes the distracting people in front look like an artistic blob rather than individual people.

Figure 3.23 Artistic effect version
Source: Courtesy of John Polk

- **For screenshots, use a device image.** When illustrating digital content for a user manual or a noninteractive demo, putting screenshots on the relevant device lets the audience see the real-world application, as in Figure 3.24.

Figure 3.24 A LinkedIn demo on a cell phone
Source: Ravi Roshan / Pexels

Include relevant images 85

Show the setting where users interact with the content, like participating in our virtual training from a balcony, as in Figure 3.25.

Figure 3.25 Enjoying a workshop from home
Sources: (patio) paladin1212 / (screen) vasabii / Adobe Stock Photos

Incorporate icons to visualize concepts quickly

An icon is a simple rendering of a real-world object. The etymology of "icon" traces to the Greek word *eikenai*, meaning "to resemble." The best icons are universally recognized and designed for instant interpretation. That's why designers use them for software navigation, smartphone apps, and dashboard controls, like in Figure 3.26.

Figure 3.26 Bacon available only in the Limited Edition
Source: Courtesy of John Polk, re-creation of internet meme

86   The Black Hole Trap

Here's how to use icons effectively (note the similarity to our advice on choosing images):

Use icons that illustrate the point. Analogies are a powerful way to communicate. Icons can illustrate and reinforce analogies, even complex ones. For example, if a person is overwhelmed, they are like the plate spinner in Figure 3.27, running between projects and never finishing any.

Figure 3.27 Plate spinner icon (or is it?)

Choose icons that clearly represent the concept you're illustrating. Some in the audience might interpret this icon as a person being kidnapped by drones!

Be consistent. You wouldn't mix pastel colors with neon on the same page. Similarly, don't use icons with conflicting styles, like in Figure 3.28. Don't mix solid icons with outline icons. Don't vary the icon color unless you want to impart meaning. Don't mix icons with and without backgrounds.

Figure 3.28 Inconsistent icon styles

Choose professional icons. When icons look amateur, the deck looks amateur. Technically, Figure 3.29 is an icon, but it sure looks like clip art. Also, it looks like a mean kid trying to burn dollar signs with a magnifying glass, which isn't the analogy you're looking for (if it is, nailed it).

Figure 3.29 Icon or sneaky clip art?

Keep it simple. Choose the most straightforward icon that illustrates the point. Anything extra creates visual noise, distracting the audience. No one will be unsure if the object without radiation marks in Figure 3.30 is a light bulb. The noisy icon makes the audience uncertain whether to focus on the bulb, the bright light, or the electricity.

Figure 3.30 Simple icons are iconic—complicated icons are *ironic*

Choose solid icons where available. Consider the two soccer/football players in Figure 3.31. The solid icon has three parts: head, body, and ball. Simple enough. The outline icon has four parts because the kicking leg is drawn separately. Even worse, the brain sees each part as two elements—the outline and the internal white space. It's a small impact, to be sure, but small impacts add up. It's also harder to shrink or grow outline icons, which require modifying the border width to keep the icon balanced.

Figure 3.31 Is that a ball or another player's head?

Improve bulleted lists with engaging visual elements

We shouldn't have to say this anymore, but never, never, never create a plain wall-of-text or bulleted-list slide. No exceptions. Not even agenda slides or executive summaries. If you're having an adverse reaction to that statement, you might not have seen these simple tricks to graphicalize slides.

You've likely noticed that this book frequently uses bulleted lists. However, presentations are a different setting. In books, readers expect content in paragraphs, so bulleted lists are a clear, digestible alternative. Presenters overuse the default bulleted list. Instead, graphicalize content to take advantage of visual representation alternatives.

Adding graphical elements transforms bulleted lists from boring to engaging. Figure 3.32 uses offset circles for the numbering and rectangles for the text.

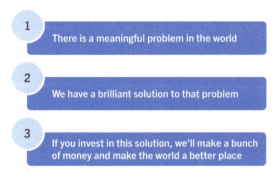

Figure 3.32 Graphically numbered list
Source: John Polk & Associates

Figure 3.33 includes a city skyline image for even more graphicalization.

Figure 3.33 Richmond, Virginia, skyline
Source: Courtesy of John Polk

The sunset reflected off the building creates an interesting effect without being too distracting. A simple hack creates the cutout effect around the circles. To get this effect, bring the circle to the front and give it a thick shape outline that is the same color as the slide background.

Company logos are another way to graphicalize slides. Logos also boost the slide's credibility. Figure 3.34 replaces the accolade-givers' names with their logos.

Figure 3.34 Logos acting like the *Good Housekeeping* Seal of Approval
Source: John Polk & Associates

Put slides on a word diet

Perfection is achieved
not when there is nothing more to add
but when there is nothing left to take away.
Antoine de Saint-Exupéry, L'Avion (translated)

"Having too many words" is the number-one design pet peeve we've collected from workshop participants. A photo of our favorite version of that peeve is in Figure 3.35.

Years ago, John asked an analyst on his team to ghostwrite an email on a project the analyst was leading. While editing the email, John realized he could cut out at least half the words without changing the meaning. Because they had a great relationship, John used this draft email to playfully highlight the importance of word dieting. John copied all the words he cut from the draft email and pasted them into a new email with this

Figure 3.35 Sticky note wisdom
Source: Courtesy of John Polk

90 The Black Hole Trap

note: "Thanks for drafting the email. Here are the words I didn't need to tell the story, so I'm sending them back to you to use in future emails." Here are strategies for using the fewest words necessary to clarify your points:

Just cut. Experts have so much knowledge and pride in that knowledge that they want the audience to know it all too. But too much information buries what's most important. It's painful to cut content because it feels like throwing away hard work. Accept that this is a necessary step in the process. Here are ways to cut fat without cutting muscle:

- **Cut the least important bullet points.** Sometimes, you just have to let go! When people say, "Less is more," this is what they mean. With every added point, you risk the audience tuning out and reading none. Or being distracted by a less critical point. Prioritize bullet points and cut from the bottom. Some make better talking points.

- **Edit multiline bullet points with the fewest words on the last line.** If cutting one or two words saves a whole line, why wouldn't you? Some may call that a lazy edit. We call it high leverage!

- **Shorten wordy phrases.** Many common phrases have way more words than necessary to convey the message. Spot these phrases and convert them to their simpler equivalents:

    - In order to = to
    - This is a process that = this process
    - Because of the fact that = because
    - In the not-too-distant future = soon
    - On a going-forward basis = (use nothing; without a time machine, everything is on a going-forward basis!)

- **Avoid tautologies and redundancy.** When redundancy doesn't just lie in repetition (Department of Redundancy Department) but derives from the words' definitions, you have a tautology. "General consensus" is our favorite tautology. "Consensus" means "general agreement," so "general consensus" means "general, general agreement." Other common tautologies include the following:

    - Adequate enough
    - Advance warning
    - End result
    - Estimated forecast
    - Future plans
    - Merge together
    - New innovation
    - Past history
    - Reply back
    - Unexpected surprise

These suggestions may save only a word or two, but those extra words add up when you ask the audience to digest slides. And that effort is multiplied by the number of people in the audience.

Choose efficient styles. Presenters often make style choices unconsciously. While not a matter of right or wrong, some style choices convey the message with fewer words. Here are efficient style choices:

- **Use active voice.** Business writers often use passive voice, hiding the person or thing doing the action. For example, "The computer was turned on" is passive voice, and the reader doesn't know who turned it on. Adding the doer at the end—"The computer was turned on by Bob"—solves this problem, but it's inefficient. It's more direct to say, "Bob turned on the PC."

- **Use positive statements rather than negative ones.** Saying "it was hot" saves a word versus saying "it was not cold."

- **Put adjectives first.** "Data distribution" has one fewer word than "distribution of data." Search for words like "of," "with," and "for" to identify this opportunity. Don't apply this rule to common phrases like "turn of phrase" or "piece of cake."

- **Choose rich verbs.** "They drove to the store" contains more information than "they went to the store" with the same word count. This technique works for other parts of speech, but verbs are the biggest opportunity.

- **Promote words repeated at the beginning of all bullet points to an introductory phrase.** Consider the following bulleted list:
    - Bruce Springsteen has the greatest B-sides of any artist ("Pink Cadillac" and "Jersey Girl" were B-sides!)
    - Bruce Springsteen has the longest concerts of any artist (his longest concert lasted over four hours)
    - Bruce Springsteen supports local food banks at his concerts

    Improve the list by promoting "Bruce Springsteen" above the list.

    Bruce Springsteen:
    - Has the greatest B-sides of any artist
    - Has the longest concerts of any artist
    - Supports local food banks at his concerts

    Cut parenthetical phrases and use them as voiceover when presenting. Note: This doesn't follow *The Associated Press Stylebook* or *The Chicago Manual of Style* for vertical lists, which recommend a full-sentence introduction and a colon. However, presentation slides are for a different setting where vertical lists can complete the sentence that begins in the header.

Separate the presentation deck from the "slideument."[5] Garr Reynolds coined this portmanteau for a deck that is a combination of presentation slides and a handout document. Without the burden of having to be understandable to someone not in the room, the deck can focus on key points and effective visuals. While having separate documents isn't practical for every decision meeting, it makes it easy to avoid the Black Hole Trap.

Use an appendix, but avoid "appendicitis"

The ultimate word diet is to eliminate a slide. Cut the slide if it addresses a noncritical point or answers a question the audience is unlikely to ask. While cutting a slide is hard, moving it to an appendix helps get over that feeling of loss or wasted effort. When John worked with a group on a 200-slide strategy presentation, his boss labeled a wall "Slides That We Once Thought Were Brilliant, but We Were Wrong." The group posted all the slides that no longer fit the story on this memorial wall. While this was driven by the punchiness that comes from working long hours, it served a valuable purpose. It recognized the work that went into developing the slides and acknowledged that the effort wasn't wasted—it got us to a better presentation.

Alternatively, if you don't plan to distribute the deck, hide any slides that aren't necessary now but could be useful for a different audience or purpose. We do this all the time for our training decks. When distributing the deck, consciously decide whether to share hidden slides.

A poorly managed appendix is a lot like appendicitis: swollen and painful. Here's how to perform a much-needed "appendectomy" and make it a functional addition rather than useless padding:

Consider removing the appendix. Most presentations don't need an appendix. Remember the Platinum Rule. Appendixes are most valuable in these circumstances:

- The **audience** wants to know if you've done your homework or they will ask a lot of questions, including off-topic ones.
- The **purpose** is to make a real-time decision; an appendix could avoid a follow-up.
- The **setting** enables moving quickly between the main story and the appendix.

Don't let the appendix remain a slag heap. In mining, the slag heap is the rock pile left over after extracting the valuable metal, like in Figure 3.36. A deck slag heap collects slides you once thought were brilliant—but you know better now, and you're still not emotionally ready to hit delete. Slag heaps are helpful when building the deck. However, they aren't helpful to the audience.

Figure 3.36 Looking for that perfect slide from last year's deck
Source: Man Gathering Good Coal from the Slag Heaps at Nanty Glo, Pennsylvania (1937) / Den Shahn / Congress.gov / Public Domain

Don't share unfinished slides. While the quality bar for appendix slides is lower, don't show the audience confusing, noisy, or unprofessional slides. Even worse is unintentionally sharing the draft slide with a recommendation different from the final proposal. Appendix slides are often denser because they are designed for reference, not presentation.

Organize it. Don't just dump slides in the appendix. Instead, arrange them in a logical order. Typically, order appendix slides by where they fit in the main story as if you hadn't cut them. If the appendix has many slides, consider adding a table of contents to make it easier to find a specific slide. Adding links to the table of contents makes it easy to access content quickly.

Animate complex slides

This step is last for a reason. Animation is a fine strategy for making complex slides easier to digest during the presentation. But if you use animation as an excuse to skip the previous steps, you'll be worse off. Fundamentally, animations should be for one of these reasons:

- Chunking up an information-dense slide—for example, showing one bullet-point group at a time
- Focusing the audience's attention on a particular object—for example, having an arrow fly in
- Supporting the slide message or reinforcing an analogy—for example, using a bouncing animation for a ball

We've worked with leaders who forbid animation because they believe it's not worth the extra effort and the risk when it's done wrong. We understand but disagree. Here's how to use animation effectively:

Keep it simple. Don't try to wow the audience with ever-changing entrance animations. At least 95% of our animations are the simple fade entrance. Splits, checkerboards, and paper-airplane effects should never have been invented. They are cheesy and unprofessional. Motion is the most overt way to draw the audience's attention.

Reveal the hierarchy's top level first. Let's say, hypothetically, that we have a four-box framework with bullet points to summarize the key concepts in our Presentations That Drive Action workshop. Figure 3.37 shows two ways to start: reveal the first box and its bullet points or the four boxes without any bullet points.

Figure 3.37 Don't keep the audience guessing about your framework
Source: John Polk & Associates

In the first example, the audience will notice the white space and know there's more framework to come. So, instead of listening, they'll wonder, "Are there any other hidden blue boxes?"

Animate complex slides   95

To prevent that, start with all the blue boxes and no bullet points. Explain the framework, then reveal the bullet points, one group at a time, like in Figure 3.38.

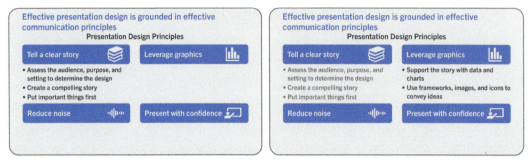

Figure 3.38 Multistep animation with de-emphasized light gray text
Source: John Polk & Associates

Notice we wrote "group." In most cases, revealing one bullet point at a time is tedious and potentially insulting to the audience. An exception to this rule is funny top 10 lists for town halls, where revealing one bullet point at a time lands each joke. To discourage the audience from rereading the first group when discussing the second group, dim the first group by making it light gray.

Go easy on slide transitions. Animations occur within a slide, while transitions occur between slides. Transitions suffer from the same challenges as animations. Most of our slides use simple fade or push transitions. The push transition is overt and can recapture the audience's attention.

We have two exceptions. The first exception is using a transition to reinforce an analogy. A presenter used the shatter transition when talking about breaking the glass ceiling. The second exception is the morph transition. This feature creates animated transitions between objects, text, or images that transform from one version to another. For example, shapes can grow larger, and text can transform. Use morph to smoothly transition from a "before" to an "after" view or to zoom in on a critical part of a slide.

Transitions and animations can lag over video. Perfecting animations and transitions takes effort. Make wise decisions about where to spend your time.

Avoid the MBR paradox

When multiple black holes merge, they create a *supermassive* black hole millions of times more massive than the Sun. The typical monthly business review (MBR) is like a supermassive black hole.

MBRs start with good intentions: "Let's assess the business's health and review it monthly to decide where we need to take action to improve the business." Here's when and how those good intentions usually go wrong:

- **Before the MBR, disjointed data collection leads to rushed, unfocused presentations.** All the departments gather data. The IT systems take five days to make the data available each month. Then, analysts take five days to pull data from multiple systems that don't talk to each other to create dashboards. The MBR deck conductor takes the weekend to compile and reformat slides in a race to hold the MBR on the 14th business day, the only day the VP is available.

    Because the team doesn't spend enough time determining the key performance indicators (KPIs), they waste time gathering metrics that aren't critical to assessing business health. Given the time crunch, there isn't enough time to evaluate the data and charts to tell the whole story. The content isn't filtered to focus on the critical issues and opportunities. The dashboards don't use sentence titles because no one had time to figure out the "so what" for each slide.

- **During the MBR, the meeting lacks focus, up-to-date data, and clear next steps.** The meeting starts late since the senior leaders all have back-to-back meetings. The business areas want to cover every metric, including irrelevant ones, hoping to impress the VP. Some business areas cover their charts in excruciating detail. Others ignore the charts to tell long, boring anecdotes. Eventually, someone suggests that the data must be wrong. Often, red metrics are no longer red because so much time has passed since the analysts pulled the data. A debate breaks out about how to calculate a key metric. The VP asks a question about root causes that the existing data can't answer. The final speaker has only five minutes to present their content because the earlier speakers took more than their allotted time. Everyone comments on how long the deck is. The VP tells the deck conductor to shorten the deck despite asking for additional analysis.

    Without effective facilitation, no one reviewed the action items from the previous MBR. No one agreed to take explicit actions to solve an issue or take advantage of an opportunity based on the data presented.

- **After the MBR, analysts address questions by adding more charts and data.** Analysts must work on the unanswered questions from the MBR, postponing their high-priority projects. They add new charts and tables to the next MBR, which they must now produce monthly. The deck conductor shifts the slide format from one chart to four charts per slide to make the deck "shorter."

Boom! That's how a supermassive-black-hole MBR forms! It's a paradox: efforts to improve the MBR process often lead to adding more charts and data, making the MBR worse. Your job titles, business units, and processing times may differ, but the results are the same. Here are several strategies to improve MBRs:

- **Shorten data collection.** Enable systems to talk to each other and declare one source of truth. Integrating systems ensures seamless data flow and reduces redundancy, improving accuracy and consistency. Establishing a single source of truth eliminates discrepancies and data debates.

- **Automate data collection and visualization.** Automating visualization ensures consistency and claws back time for data analysis. Schedule the work time required to translate data into useful information. This ensures there's time to ask questions and fix any problems with the data.

- **Make the MBR deck shorter.** Use business intelligence software to create dashboards. When built effectively, interactive dashboards address typical MBR goals. Create hierarchies in the data to focus the conversation on KPIs first. Make sure those performance indicators are actually "key." Then, drill down on driver metrics for those out-of-tolerance KPIs. Avoid the supermassive-black-hole problem by building filters and drilldowns into dashboards to make them interactive, rather than creating multiple charts with presentation software. Enable views by business area, region, supervisor, or other relevant divisions. Design for the screen rather than the printed page.

- **Make the MBR meeting shorter.** Manage attendance. Leaders often invite their experts to answer questions during an MBR, which leads to an ever-expanding invite list. When people come to meetings, they ask questions and give opinions, extending the time required to work through each business area. Use color to highlight issues. Then, don't talk about green metrics unless they indicate a new business opportunity. Create a slide for metrics definitions and sources to quickly resolve debates about how to calculate a metric. Add a "Key Takeaways" section on each slide, as in Figure 3.39. The takeaways are the equivalent of "so what" sentence titles for each chart.

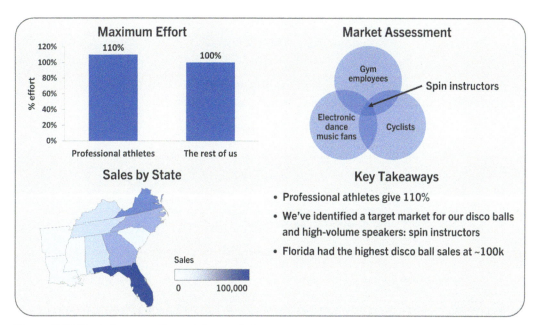

Figure 3.39 Key takeaways for a niche market
Source: John Polk & Associates

- **Make the MBR action oriented.** Clarify the MBR purpose. Naming the meeting a "review" doesn't set it up for success. If it were the "monthly take action to improve the business" (MTAIB) meeting, participants would focus more on the actions required to turn around red metrics. Create an overview of metrics requiring discussion and action to focus the meeting on the hot spots. Enable real-time root cause analysis through interactivity, like filters and drilldowns. Bring the best dashboard jockey into the MBR to answer questions in the meeting, avoiding the monthlong follow-up analysis cycle.

Key Takeaways

Graphicalize slides and eliminate unessential content to avoid overwhelming the audience with too much information.

- ✓ Turn data into actionable insights by analyzing patterns and creating visualizations. Choose the correct chart for the data relationship.

- ✓ Build options tables, heat maps, or annotated tables to avoid the table equivalent of the wall of text.

- ✓ Choose large, bold images to illustrate key points. Avoid generic stock photos.

- ✓ Represent concepts with simple, relevant icons to convey meaning quickly.

- ✓ Improve bulleted lists with graphical elements, images, logos, and icons.

- ✓ Word diet slides by choosing efficient writing styles, shortening wordy phrases, and cutting less important points.

- ✓ Include an appendix for reference material to address questions tangential to the core story.

- ✓ Organize appendix slides thoughtfully and clear out unfinished slides to avoid "appendicitis."

- ✓ Chunk up dense slides with simple animation to focus the audience's attention.

- ✓ Design business reviews to be action oriented by analyzing the data before the meeting and adding a key takeaways section for each slide. (How meta to suggest using a key takeaways section in a key takeaways section!)

Figure 4.1 Sgt. Joe Friday eschewing emotion
Source: Jack Webb on Dragnet (1957) / NBCUniversal Media LLC / Wikimedia Commons / Public Domain

4

The Just the Facts Trap

Balance logic and data with emotions, stories, and focus to influence the audience.

> *Just the facts, ma'am.*[1]
> Sgt. Joe Friday (attributed), Dragnet

As with many famous quotations, Sgt. Friday (Figure 4.1) never said that phrase. Instead, he said, "All we want are the facts, ma'am." The misattributed phrase came from a comedy record, *St. George and the Dragonet*, by Stan Freberg. In Freberg's *Dragnet* satire, Sgt. Wednesday says, "I just want to get the facts, ma'am." Over time, the phrase was shortened, and the revised phrase was attributed back to Sgt. Friday. Thanks to snopes.com for fact-checking this one.

Regardless of the quotation's actual phrasing, the question remains: Why does Sgt. Friday want just the facts? Sgt. Friday is a detective who believes facts are the only things that matter when trying to understand what happened. Having spent much of our careers in analytics, we wish facts were the only thing that mattered, but that's not the case. As the headlines in Figure 4.2 attest, emotion plays a huge role in decision-making.

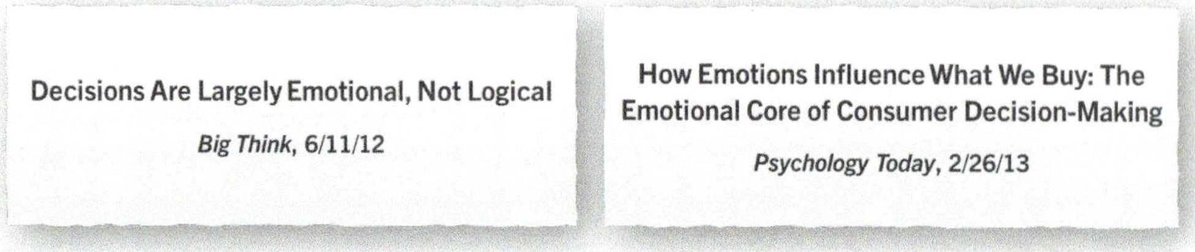

Decisions Are Largely Emotional, Not Logical
Big Think, 6/11/12

How Emotions Influence What We Buy: The Emotional Core of Consumer Decision-Making
Psychology Today, 2/26/13

Figure 4.2 People are emotional animals
Source: *Big Think / Psychology Today*[2]

Presenters fall into the Just the Facts Trap when they ignore the emotional and visual components of influencing. Not only do "just the facts" presentations ignore emotion's role in decision-making, but they are also boring. And boring presentations lead the audience to tune out. All the facts in the world won't convince an audience that isn't paying attention. Don't get us wrong—facts are fantastic. Ground presentations in data and analytics, but don't give *just* the facts.

Avoid the Just the Facts Trap by effectively pairing memorable stories and anecdotes with data visualizations to balance emotional and intellectual influence. Direct the audience's attention with preattentive attributes.

Use stories to illustrate key points

Imagine cave people sitting around the fire, roasting saber-toothed-tiger ribs. It might look like Figure 4.3 but with more animal-skin clothing (sorry, there are no photos from that era, only cave paintings).

The hunters tell the story of the hunt: tracking the saber-toothed tiger, avoiding its *saber* teeth, and taking it down. One storytelling goal is to entertain, but the more important goal is to teach the next generation of hunters how to hunt before they face a saber-toothed tiger.

Written language hadn't been invented, so they had only spoken language to communicate. The spoken language had at least a 5,000-year head start on the written language. Storytelling is in our DNA.[3] If the hunters couldn't explain clearly *and* memorably how to spear the saber-toothed tiger, the next generation of hunters wouldn't survive.

Stories are how we teach. Stories are how we communicate what's important. Stories are how we bring data to life.

[Editor's note: The authors' understanding of cave-people life may have been influenced by watching *The Flintstones* in their youth.]

Figure 4.3 Telling stories around a campfire
Source: Laura_O / Pixabay

Here are natural places to use stories in presentations based on your role:

- **Entrepreneur:** Tell the story about how you encountered a problem in the world that you needed to solve. Include images that make the problem visceral.

- **Leader:** Recount the hurdles your team member overcame to fix an issue for a big customer. Include the thank-you letter from the customer.

- **Analyst:** Share a customer anecdote that illustrates the problem your analysis uncovered. Play a call center recording to bring the voice of the customer into the room.

- **Product manager:** Describe how a new product feature increased profit for a small business. Highlight feedback with direct quotations from clients.

- **Software engineer:** Explain how the top item on the roadmap delivered functionality that solves a major pain point for a high-value client. Share the roadmap that includes the next big functionality delivery.

There's a natural tension between the benefits of storytelling and the benefits of "spilling the beans" from Chapter 2, "The Bury the Lede Trap." You should do both. For example, use story archetypes that give the answer up front, like the Pyramid Principle. Then, use anecdotes to support and explain key concepts.

Design for the audience's preferences by leveraging the PROD framework from Chapter 1, "The Frankenstein Trap." Leaders who focus on people appreciate beginning with a narrative. In contrast, results-oriented leaders want to get straight to the point and then use stories to back it up. Leaders who value exploring options want to ensure you assess all practical ideas. Use stories and analogies to summarize the potential solutions. Detail-oriented leaders want to concentrate on the facts first. But they also know that stories can bring data to life. Start with the data, then use storytelling to bring it to life. In settings like training or town halls, kicking off with a story works for all audiences.

Structure anecdotes

In a behavioral job interview (a.k.a. situational interview), interviewers ask candidates to "tell me about a time when you" led a large project, or dealt with an interpersonal conflict, or had to make up a structured story in a behavioral interview.

The STARC method (updated from STAR) gives candidates a story structure to ace the interview.[4] We modified this approach to work with structured anecdotes:

- **Situation:** The story's time and place, the protagonist (typically you), and other relevant "characters"

- **Trouble (originally Task):** The conflict, problem, or challenge, which often involves fear and naturally grabs the audience's attention

- **Action:** How you addressed the trouble with your brilliant solution

- **Results:** The consequences of the action, how it fixed the trouble, and the benefits achieved

- **Connection:** The moral of the story or insight gained

Make stories memorable

In our cave-person fireside scenario, remembering the story had life-and-death stakes. Boring stories aren't memorable. When was the last time you memorized a procedure or owner's manual? On the other hand, how many stories from your life can you tell from memory? Remember that boring story you heard the other day? Of course you don't.

For stories to drive action, the audience must remember them. In their book *Made to Stick*, Chip and Dan Heath lay out the SUCCESs model shown in Figure 4.4 to make stories memorable.

Figure 4.4 The SUCCESs model for sticky stories
Source: Adapted from Made to Stick (2007) / Chip and Dan Heath / Reproduced with the permission of Chip and Dan Heath

The dark blue boxes represent the story elements that make them memorable. The light blue box highlights the power of stories to illustrate ideas. You don't need to include every SUCCESs element in every story, but the more elements you hit, the more memorable the story will be. Presenters often avoid detail and emotions in business settings. That's a mistake. You can paint a mental picture without rambling and capture emotions without ignoring facts.

A SUCCESs story

John tells this story to illustrate the SUCCESs model:

When I was working in corporate America, my boss invited me for a mountain bike ride the morning before a 100-person off-site event. I'm a road cyclist, but I figured, "It's just like riding a bike," so I agreed. The bike I borrowed had clip-in pedals, but I had cycling shoes that fit.

Our route was a picturesque single-track trail next to the Potomac River. Early in the ride, we stopped to let two hikers pass. After they passed, my boss hopped on his bike and took off.

(continued)

I clipped in with one foot, pushed off, and ... couldn't quite get my other foot clipped in.

Without momentum, I slowly fell over sideways onto the steep riverbank and began sliding toward the chilly waters. My life didn't flash before my eyes, but I did have time to wonder how fast I'd sink, clipped to a mountain bike!

Thankfully, I stopped sliding before hitting the water. The hikers heard me fall and returned to see if I was OK. Except for bruises and embarrassment, I was fine.

When I got back on the trail, my boss was so far down the path that I couldn't see him. I hammered it to catch up and told him about my near-death experience.

That afternoon, I presented to the off-site attendees about an Agile transformation project I helped design. With the completed design and leadership buy-in, we were ready to roll out the changes to our teams.

At the end of my speech, I shared my mountain bike adventure (Figure 4.5). Then I connected it to the project: "As leaders, we are like my boss. We're excited about this change, and we've taken off down the path. But some people on our teams are still trying to get clipped in. They were excited about the ride but are now sliding down the hill. As leaders, we must look back and help them get back on their bikes."

Figure 4.5 Not John on a mountain bike
Source: Mason Dahl / Unsplash

(continued)

Let's assess John's story against the SUCCESs model:

- **Simple:** Most people have ridden a bike, so they can understand the mechanics at play.

- **Unexpected:** The main twist is the moment John starts sliding down the riverbank. It's also an unexpected move to make fun of your boss in front of 100 leaders! Cognitive psychologist Carmen Simon notes that surprise causes the body to release endorphins.[5] That endorphin release creates a positive feeling in your audience members associated with you and your story.

- **Concrete:** John gave details about the single-track path next to a river so the audience could picture themselves in the story. The details about bike pedals and clip-in shoes set up John's fall, using the dramatic principle known as "Chekov's gun":

  > *If, in the first act, you have hung a pistol on the wall,*
  > *then in the following one, it should be fired.*[6]
  >
  > Anton Chekhov, "Reminiscences of A. P. Chekhov" (attributed)

- **Credible:** John didn't use any data or expert opinion in this story, although he did in the rest of the presentation. Giving concrete details also boosts the story's credibility.

- **Emotional:** Fear, panic, and embarrassment all played a part in this story. The feeling of being left behind is a powerful emotion. The unexpected twist also heightens emotion.

Don't show the sausage-making

Chapter 2, "The Bury the Lede Trap," mentioned the history lesson. You poured your heart and soul into this project and want everyone to know it. Sorry, but decision-makers don't care how you made the sausage. They care that the recommendation is grounded. They don't want to hear how much time you spent cleaning dirty data, how you brilliantly manipulated the spreadsheet to find brilliant insights, or how many hours you spent in meetings socializing the recommendation with stakeholders.

> *It is the consistency of the information that*
> *matters for a good story, not its completeness.*[7]
>
> Daniel Kahneman, *Thinking, Fast and Slow*

Connecting story elements with "then" and "next" tells a history lesson. Connecting story elements with "therefore," "however," and "but" allows the audience to see the logical and emotional connections between story elements. Tell the story effectively, and customers will love the recommendation and intuitively understand how much work went into it. Well, bosses rarely appreciate *all* the hard work.

Don't leave data up for interpretation

Chapter 3, "The Black Hole Trap," discussed data visualization as a way to graphicalize slides. However, that only works if you interpret the data *and* make that interpretation clear to the audience. Here are common data visualization mistakes:

Mistake 1: Using a column chart instead of a line chart to show a trend. If you want to show a trend, use a line chart. Compare the column and line charts in Figure 4.6. Yes, the audience can observe a trend by looking at the top of the columns, but the line chart is designed for trends. Two things happen when the audience tries to assess a trend on a column chart. First, the weight of the columns' ink draws the audience's eyes to the center of each column rather than the top. Second, with two or more series, as the audience follows the gray series' trend, their eyes run into the blue series.

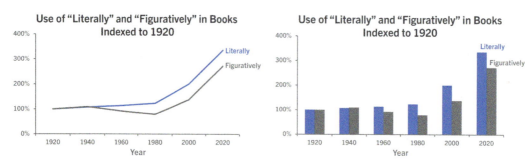

Figure 4.6 Two ways to show a trend, one good
Data source: Google Ngram Viewer; Source: John Polk & Associates

Mistake 2: Letting charting software rotate x-axis labels diagonally instead of using a horizontal bar chart. Anytime audience members tilt their heads to read, you've made a suboptimal design choice. Even with the extra space that diagonal labels create, the software cut off our labels in Figure 4.7, which is problematic when three titles start with "Monty Python." If the category titles are too long, convert to a horizontal bar chart. Technically, all bar charts are horizontal; vertical bar charts are called column charts.

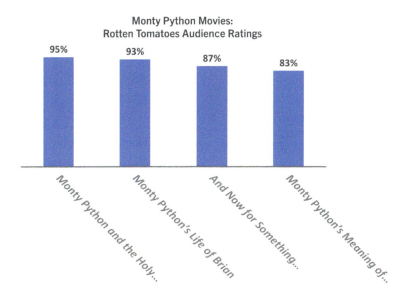

Figure 4.7 Monty Python and the Holy what?
Data source: rottentomatoes.com; Source: John Polk & Associates

Mistake 3: Not sorting categories in a bar or column chart. Unless the x-axis is time, sorting data by size makes it easier to interpret a chart, like in Figure 4.8. Sorting bar and column charts by length is a natural way to show league tables, where the ranking is top to bottom, like for sports conference rankings.

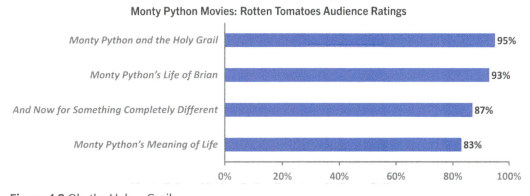

Figure 4.8 Oh, the Holy … Grail
Data source: rottentomatoes.com; Source: John Polk & Associates

Mistake 4: Expecting the audience to compare sizes of stacked column segments. In a stacked column chart, the audience can measure the bottom segments only against the y-axis and compare them to each other. We've counted the M&M's our kids ate each day by color in Figure 4.9. It's impossible to accurately assess the variation in the nonbrown M&M's because each segment starts at a different height. Add data labels to let the audience know how big the upper segments are. Or skip the stacked column and use multiple charts.

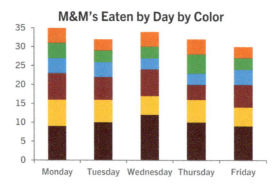

Figure 4.9 Mmm, stacked column chart
Source: John Polk & Associates

Mistake 5: Not identifying all the drivers in a waterfall chart. Waterfall charts are the perfect visual for explaining variance, like budget versus actual, or for showing the drivers of a change, like a call volume increase. A waterfall is a stacked column chart with the bottom segments hidden, as in Figure 4.10. The "floating" segments size the variance drivers. When assessing variance, it's easy to miss drivers, especially if positive and negative drivers cancel each other out. This first waterfall quantifies two drivers that increased cost and one that reduced cost. We jokingly call waterfall charts that go up "geysers."

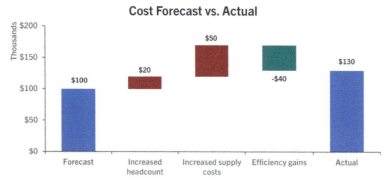

Figure 4.10 Waterfall (or geyser?) chart
Source: John Polk & Associates

Additional research found three more drivers, two that increased cost and one that decreased it, shown in Figure 4.11. Those costs sum to zero, but understanding these additional drivers creates opportunities for new actions. In this case, the driver reducing cost is a bad thing—there are fewer customers to service. If you don't understand all the drivers, the cost-improvement strategy will be less effective.

Figure 4.11 Comprehensive waterfall chart
Source: John Polk & Associates

Here are additional best practices for waterfalls:

- Group all the increasing categories first, then all the decreasing categories.
- Put the categories in size order within the up and down groups, largest to smallest.
- Combine small categories to minimize the number of columns.
- When data applies to multiple categories, specify which category gets the credit.

Mistake 6: Choosing a 3D chart for 2D data. Imagine the software engineer who first figured out how to code a 3D chart. "Hey, boss. Isn't this cool?!" Maybe at the time it was cool. However, that third dimension is unnecessary, and it makes it harder to interpret the chart, as in Figure 4.12. Compare the 2007 and 2008 columns. Your eye might compare the back of the 2007 column to the front of the 2008 column, unintentionally

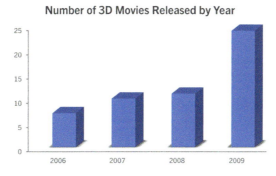

Figure 4.12 "Cool" 3D chart
Source: John Polk & Associates

Don't leave data up for interpretation 113

reducing the gap between them. By the looks of the shadow at the base of each column, this chart was created on the equator at noon during an equinox.

Mistake 7: Confusing correlation and causation. The simple scatter plot in Figure 4.13 shows a correlation between two datasets.

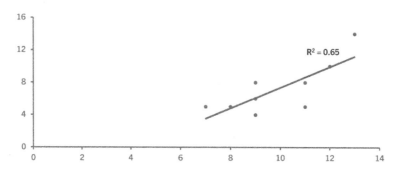

Figure 4.13 Scatter plot showing a correlation
Source: John Polk & Associates

For the statistics geeks, this correlation has an $R^2 = 0.65$. However, correlations can occur randomly. The scatter plot in Figure 4.14 uses real data to show the relationship between letters in the winning word of the Scripps National Spelling Bee and the number of people killed by venomous spiders between 1999 and 2009. Correlating enough datasets produces spurious correlations—precisely what Tyler Vigen does on his Spurious Correlations website.

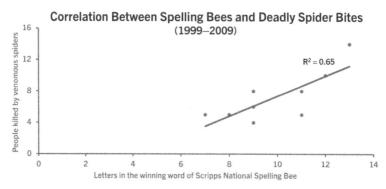

Figure 4.14 Spiders are more likely to attack when frustrated by their inability to spell long words
Data source: Tyler Vigen / Spurious Correlations / CC BY 4.0; Source: John Polk & Associates

114 The Just the Facts Trap

Mistake 8: Creating a "spaghetti chart" instead of a slopegraph. A slopegraph is simply a line chart showing only the start and end points. This removes the noise from a typical line chart, especially if there are more than three series with crisscrossing lines. We call crisscrossing line charts "spaghetti charts." Of course, the trend between the start and end points is sometimes important. Instead, use a line chart if the trend is a hockey stick or cliff shape. The line chart in Figure 4.15 shows the Washington and New England National Football League teams' win percentages from 1991 until 2019. There's not as much crisscrossing as in a typical spaghetti chart, but the jagged ups and downs from year to year distract the audience.

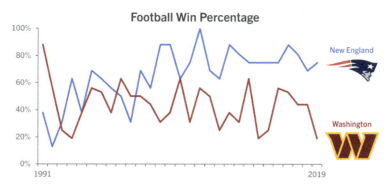

Figure 4.15 Noisy spaghetti chart
Data source: Wikipedia; Sources: (logos) National Football League and respective NFL teams / John Polk & Associates

Converting the same data to a slopegraph in Figure 4.16 makes it easier to see how the cheating New England Patriots overtook a once proud Washington franchise.

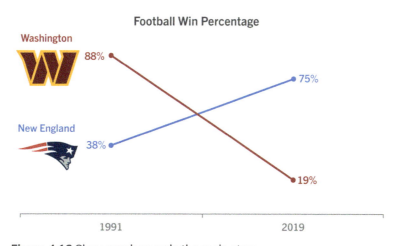

Figure 4.16 Slopegraph reveals the main story
Data source: Wikipedia; Sources: (logos) National Football League and respective NFL teams / John Polk & Associates

Mistake 9: Putting charts with different scales side by side. Audiences naturally compare column size across two charts placed side by side. If the scales are different, audiences may draw an incorrect conclusion. Most charting software automatically scales the y-axis based on the data range. This encourages misleading comparisons across side-by-side charts. In Figure 4.17, year 1's February data point appears similar in size to year 2's April data point.

Figure 4.17 Auto-scale fail
Source: John Polk & Associates

Avoid incorrect comparisons by setting the axes to the same scale, as in Figure 4.18, which shows that year 1's data is all lower than year 2's. This problem is common in supermassive black hole MBRs, discussed in Chapter 3, "The Black Hole Trap."

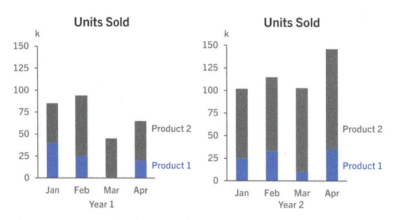

Figure 4.18 Manual scales prevail
Source: John Polk & Associates

Mistake 10: Using dual-axis charts. Having multiple axes can confuse the audience. The dual-axis chart in Figure 4.19 shows Legendary Pokémon height and weight.

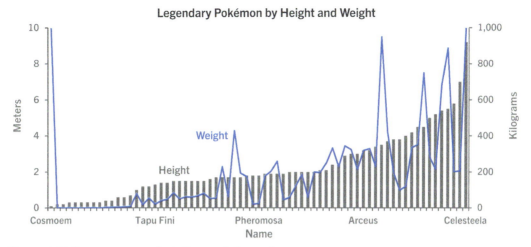

Figure 4.19 Cosmoem—really tall or really heavy?
Data source: Rounak Banik / kaggle.com; Source: John Polk & Associates

One challenge with dual-axis charts is the visual noise from overlapping lines and columns. The second challenge is ensuring the audience understands which axis relates to which data series. Labeling the series helps, but it's still easy to mix up.

Another challenge occurs when designers use a dual-axis chart to show a relationship. In this example, as height increases, weight also increases. But the outliers draw attention, especially the high weight data points. These outliers visually argue against the correlation between height and weight. You may wonder why the shortest Legendary Pokémon, Cosmoem, weighs about 1,000 kg. Cosmoem is based on a protostar, a superdense baby star. Instead, put two charts side by side, like in Figure 4.20.

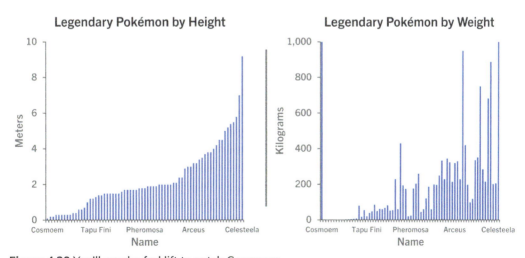

Figure 4.20 You'll need a forklift to catch Cosmoem
Data source: Rounak Banik / kaggle.com; Source: John Polk & Associates

Notice that this violates the prior guidance about using consistent scales. This is less of an issue here, given that the charts have different units with dramatically different scales. Adding the gray divider line as a break blocks the audience from reading from the Meters scale across to the Kilograms scale. Or, if the goal is to show correlation, use a scatter plot, like Figure 4.21.

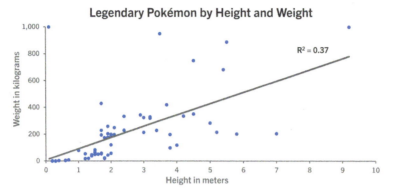

Figure 4.21 Does the keto diet work for Pokémon?
Data source: Rounak Banik / kaggle.com; Source: John Polk & Associates

Turns out Pokémon height and weight are not highly correlated after all. Had you used the previous charts and voiced over the correlation confidently, most audiences would have believed you.

A dual-axis chart is appropriate in Figure 4.22 because it displays the same data but with two different measurement systems.

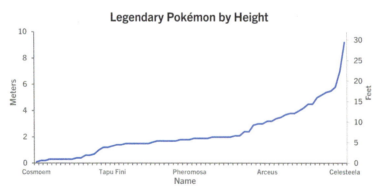

Figure 4.22 Parlez-vous metric?
Data source: Rounak Banik / kaggle.com; Source: John Polk & Associates

118 The Just the Facts Trap

Audience members naturally read the axis with their familiar measurement system. We put "Feet" on the right side to make it more difficult for Americans to read since they refuse to move to the superior metric system!

Mistake 11: Not starting the y-axis at zero. Which company's stock from Figure 4.23 would you rather have bought in January?

Figure 4.23 Past performance is not a guarantee of future results
Source: John Polk & Associates

The chart with the steeper slope must be the better-performing stock! Not so fast. Seeing the y-axes included in Figure 4.24 clearly reveals the same data with a different scale. The chart with the steeper slope doesn't start at $0.

Figure 4.24 Cheating exposed
Source: John Polk & Associates

Failing to start the y-axis at zero exaggerates the chart trend. An exception to this rule is when variations within a small range are meaningful, as in the system uptime chart in Figure 4.25, where the data varies from 98 to 100%. If the y-axis started at zero, the line would be nearly flat, obscuring any meaningful trend. In this case, set the y-axis from 90 to 100%, but add a note that the axis doesn't start at zero, or visually break the axis. Similarly, if the data stays below a certain percentage, extending the y-axis up to 100% is unnecessary.

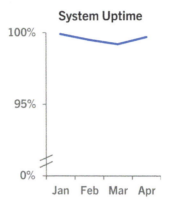

Figure 4.25 Not cheating
Source: John Polk & Associates

Some chart designers remove the y-axis to give a cleaner look. When designers use data labels, the audience doesn't need the y-axis to interpret the data. However, without the y-axis, the audience can't verify that the scale starts at zero. It's also harder to ensure consistency—invariably, other chart designers include the y-axis by default.

Mistake 12: Burying shocking statistics in a chart. Sometimes, a single number creates a powerful argument through its shock value, like in Figure 4.26.

Figure 4.26 Terawatt hour? Sounds big
Data source: Bitcoin Energy Consumption Index, Digiconomist, https://digiconomist.net/bitcoin-energy-consumption (last accessed July 4, 2024); Source: John Polk & Associates

This is a "big-number slide" in both senses—a big number and a big font. Notice how cranking up the font size on the big number draws your eye in the same way other visual objects, like the icon, grab attention. Were you shocked? When you saw the statistic that Bitcoin mining uses 172 terawatts of energy per year, it sounded big, but you likely had no idea how big.

Adding a comparison in Figure 4.27 makes it easier to understand. Even people with no energy expertise know that Poland, a midsized European country, uses a lot of energy.

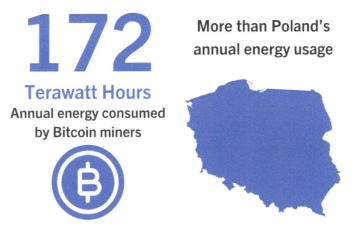

Figure 4.27 Big Bitcoin energy
Data sources: Bitcoin Energy Consumption Index, Digiconomist, https://digiconomist.net/bitcoin-energy-consumption (last accessed July 4, 2024) / Wikipedia; Source: John Polk & Associates

The graphic in Figure 4.28 uses multiple big numbers to illustrate that the Beatles weren't just a one-hit wonder (see what we did there?).

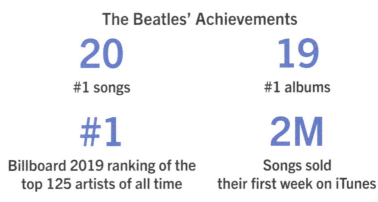

Figure 4.28 Big numbers everywhere!
Data sources: Billboard / Mental Floss; Source: John Polk & Associates

Don't leave data up for interpretation   121

The waffle chart in Figure 4.29 is an effective way to visualize the scale of a big or small number.

Figure 4.29 Mmm, waffle chart
Data source: NCAA; Source: John Polk & Associates

The two blue squares appear at the end, so the audience must first scan the 98 gray boxes as their eyes move left to right and top to bottom, reinforcing how slim a college athlete's chances are of turning pro. The waffle chart in Figure 4.30 uses icons to represent the athletes.

Figure 4.30 Sports chaos
Data source: NCAA; Source: John Polk & Associates

Using icons from multiple sports reinforces the point that the data represents all sports, but it creates visual noise, making it harder for the eye to pick up the two blue icons. In this case, the noise reinforces how hard it is to turn pro.

Mistake 13: Creating "giraffe charts." When a chart is visually interesting but doesn't convey information relevant to the story, we call it a "giraffe chart." Sorry for the dis, giraffes (Figure 4.31). We didn't invent the term!

Mistake 14: Misusing pie or donut charts. Like their food counterparts, avoid pies and donuts. *Business Insider* declared pie charts "the Worst Chart in the World."[8] Cole Knaflic called pie charts "evil" in her book *Storytelling with Data*. John used her book as the textbook for the MBA course he taught. If you haven't read it, stop reading this and read her book first. We'll wait.

Figure 4.31 Giraffes that find you interesting to look at
Source: Andreas / Adobe Stock Photos

Cole (appropriately) softened her stance on pie charts. Pie and donut charts show parts of a whole, and people recognize that. If there are only two or three segments, a pie chart can avoid most of the issues that data viz professionals hate.

What's wrong with pies and donuts? Research shows that people likely interpret pie and donut charts, like in Figure 4.32, by assessing a combination of arc length and area.[9] But people have a tougher time comparing arc length or wedge area than side-by-side straight lines, like in a column chart.

Data labels can clarify comparison but require a choice between absolute values and percentages. Percentage data labels can be misleading when comparing multiple pie charts on the same slide. A wedge could be a larger percentage in one pie chart but represent a much smaller actual value than a wedge in another pie chart, simply because the total populations differ. Because each wedge needs a distinct color, pie charts often have a distracting rainbow of color. These charts use our default color palette, where red is the fifth color. The red color unintentionally draws attention to an insignificant category.

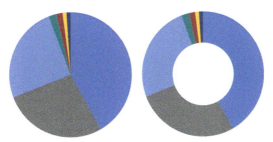

Figure 4.32 No thanks, I'm on a diet
Source: John Polk & Associates

Don't leave data up for interpretation   123

Pareto charts show parts of a whole without the baggage associated with pie charts. Let's compare the two chart styles with data on NFL mascots. Due to real estate challenges with the pie chart in Figure 4.33, we had to choose between category labels and team logos. Without the labels, some of the audience won't know the star logo is for the Cowboys and might think there is a "celestial bodies" category. And because the small categories cluster near 12 o'clock, the Jets logo is the first the audience sees rather than the last.

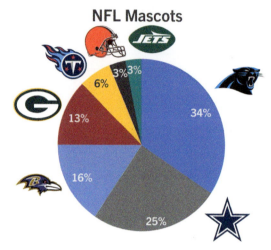

Figure 4.33 Mmm, mascot pie!
Sources: (logos) National Football League and respective NFL teams / John Polk & Associates

The Pareto chart in Figure 4.34 avoids these issues.

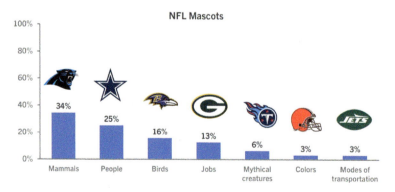

Figure 4.34 NFL mascot Pareto chart
Sources: (logos) National Football League and respective NFL teams / John Polk & Associates

The formal Pareto chart in Figure 4.35 includes the cumulative line.

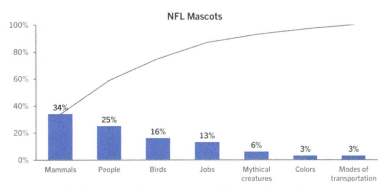

Figure 4.35 NFL mascot Pareto chart with cumulative line
Source: John Polk & Associates

John created the obnoxious pie chart in Figure 4.36 for his farewell email from corporate life.

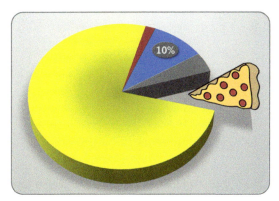

Figure 4.36 A purposefully noisy chart
(or Pac-Man eating pizza)
Source: Courtesy of John Polk

Use preattentive attributes to focus the audience's attention

Do you know this Sesame Street song? Here's the opening verse:

> One of these things is not like the others,
> One of these things just doesn't belong,
> Can you tell which thing is not like the others
> By the time I finish my song?[10]
> Joe Raposo, Jon Stone, and Bruce Hart, "One of These Things"

People naturally see patterns and notice when something breaks them. Preattentive attributes use differences in design elements, like orientation, size, shape, position, and hue, to draw the eye to specific parts of a visual. This is a subtle form of mind control—before the audience can consciously decide where to look, design choices guide their attention. Figure 4.37 illustrates the most common preattentive attributes. We learned this concept from Cole Knaflic, who adapted it from Stephen Few's book *Show Me the Numbers*.

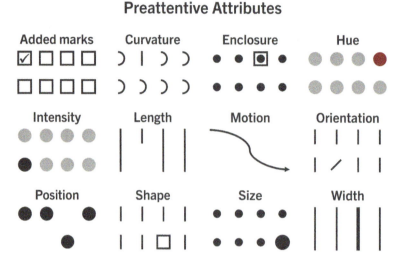

Figure 4.37 Look at me!
Source: Adapted from *Storytelling with Data* (2015) / Cole Nussbaumer Knaflic / Reproduced with permission of Cole Nussbaumer Knaflic

Preattentive attributes work for any slide object, not just charts. Most templates make the slide title the largest font on the slide. We also make our slide titles a distinct color. But preattentive attributes earn their keep in data visualization. Certain chart types incorporate preattentive attributes by design. Bar and column charts rely on people's ability to compare line lengths. We'll use the straightforward chart in Figure 4.38 to explore different preattentive-attribute applications.

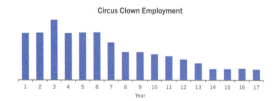

Figure 4.38 What's important?
Data source: Bureau of Clown Labor and Juggling Statistics (BCLJS), *2024 Annual Report on Balloon Animal Economics*; Source: John Polk & Associates

126   The Just the Facts Trap

We removed the y-axis and the data labels because we made up this data. Notice what happens as you digest the chart. Do you wonder why circus clown employment increased from years 1–3? Does your eye focus on the dramatic decrease in circus clown employment from years 6–14? Do you see that circus clown employment is flat from years 14–17 and hope things will soon look up for them? Each interpretation is legitimate, and you don't know which interpretation the audience will latch onto.

Preattentive attributes focus the audience's attention on the interpretation that reinforces your story. That won't prevent the audience from generating other conclusions, but they're more likely to consider your conclusion first. That keeps the audience in sync while you walk through the chart. Common preattentive attributes include the following:

- **Length:** Did your eye focus on the highest circus clown employment (year 3) in the clown employment chart? That's the preattentive attribute, length, in action.
- **Intensity:** Reducing the color intensity on the shorter columns in Figure 4.39 draws attention to the tallest column.

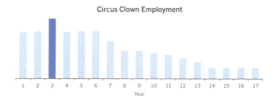

Figure 4.39 Good year to be a clown
Source: John Polk & Associates

- **Hue:** Making year 3 green also draws the eye to the highest column, as shown in Figure 4.40. Green reinforces that the peak year was positive for circus clowns. Hue is typically more attention-grabbing than intensity.

Figure 4.40 Great year to be a clown!
Source: John Polk & Associates

- **Added marks (indicator arrow):** A large green arrow highlights the peak clown employment in Figure 4.41. An arrow is a classic added mark, equivalent to a pointing finger signaling "look here!" The green arrow background aligns with the positive message and stands out from the blue columns.

Figure 4.41 Is it ever a "great" year to be a clown?
Source: John Polk & Associates

- **Added marks (trend arrow):** Adding a trend arrow in Figure 4.42 draws attention to the dramatic decrease in circus clown employment. A big number quantifies the drop.

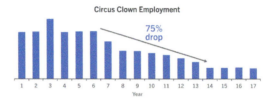

Figure 4.42 Hard to look for work in giant shoes
Source: John Polk & Associates

- **Added marks (bracket):** The bracket and label in Figure 4.43 call out the two-year recession. Brackets have a pointing effect, like arrows, and a grouping effect, like enclosures.

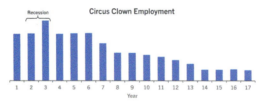

Figure 4.43 In a recession, audiences want cheap laughs
Source: John Polk & Associates

- **Enclosure:** The red box and label in Figure 4.44 call out the low employment over the last four years. Note that the label uses the recession as a reference point. When using a similar chart for a title-writing exercise in our workshop, participants often use the phrase "all-time low." Use that phrase only when you have data for "all time." In the earliest days of circus clowning, employment was likely lower than today.

Figure 4.44 Enclosures—where clowns belong (kidding)
Source: John Polk & Associates

- **Multiple attributes:** It's OK to combine attributes. However, applying too many attributes creates cognitive overload. Stacking hue, enclosure, and added marks in Figure 4.45 is just extra. It's equivalent to wearing a belt and suspenders. Leave that for the clowns.

Figure 4.45 A veritable circus of preattentive attributes
Source: John Polk & Associates

But don't misrepresent the facts

Often, there is implicit or explicit pressure to find data to support your boss's recommendation. Or you feel pressure to validate that your recommendation is getting positive results. This can lead you to "bend" the data to support your boss's hypothesis rather than leveraging data to seek the truth. In fact, acknowledging data limitations or uncertainties creates transparency and boosts your credibility. Numerous biases can show up in analyses. Here are a few common biases:

- **Confirmation bias:** Ignoring data that contradicts your hypothesis. Social media algorithms put confirmation bias on steroids. Clicking on a post supporting your opinions results in more posts supporting those opinions and fewer posts contradicting them.

- **Availability bias:** Only using easy-to-get data. Have you heard the joke about the absent-minded person looking for lost keys under a streetlight and the friend who offers to help them look?

    Absent-minded person: Can you help me look for my keys?

    Friend: Yes, I'm a good friend.

    (After looking for several minutes under the streetlight)

    Friend: Where did you last have your keys?

    Absent-minded person: Over there, in that dark alley.

    Friend: So, why are we looking over here?

    Absent-minded person: Because the light is better.

    The moral of the story is "Don't confuse the data that's already available or easy to get with the data that you need." Find the right data to solve the problem.

- **Confounding variables:** Failing to understand *all* drivers of a relationship. It is a statistical fact that violent crime rises when ice cream sales rise. Does that mean ice cream causes violent crime? Although we want to yell at someone for retiring Ben & Jerry's Chocolate Peanut Butter Cookie Dough ice cream, this phenomenon is correlation, not cause and effect. The confounding variable here is the summer heat. People are more likely to be outside around other people in warmer months. Heat makes people crave cold treats, and heat makes people irritable, leading to more violent crimes.

Influencing for good or evil

This chapter discussed tools to engage and focus the audience's attention. Storytelling brings data to life and tells the audience how to interpret it. It's like magic. However, magicians are maestros of misdirection, manipulating their audience's focus to conceal their sleight of hand. The aim should be for genuine understanding, not a smokescreen. Be a great storyteller—don't be a magician.

Unless you're Nolan Haims. He's a Microsoft PowerPoint MVP *and* a magician, but we know he'd never use his powers for evil.

Key Takeaways

Balance logic and data with emotions, stories, and focus to influence the audience.

- ✓ Tell anecdotes to illustrate the key points in the presentation.
- ✓ Structure stories using the STARC (situation, trouble, action, results, connection) method.
- ✓ Make stories memorable with the SUCCESs (simple, unexpected, concrete, credible, and emotional stories) model.
- ✓ Don't waste time presenting the process and hard work. Instead, focus on the key insights, recommendations, and results.
- ✓ Don't include data without an interpretation on the slide to focus the audience.
- ✓ Avoid pie charts and multi-axis charts.
- ✓ Set consistent scales for side-by-side charts and start the y-axis at zero to avoid misleading the audience.
- ✓ Include big-number slides to illustrate surprising statistics.
- ✓ Direct the audience's attention with preattentive attributes, like hue, size, and added marks.
- ✓ Don't misrepresent the facts! Avoid common decision-making mistakes, like confirmation bias, availability bias, and confounding variables.

Figure 5.1 Why they invented coffee
Source: Scholars at a Lecture (1736) / William Hogarth / Artvee.com / Public Domain

5

The Expert Trap

Use analogies, visuals, and frameworks to make complex concepts digestible for nonexperts.

We used to be lousy teachers, like the teacher reading from the book in Figure 5.1. Notice the confused listener in the bottom left? How about the yawning guy in the bottom right? What about the side conversation in the middle? We started teaching presentation design because we were good at presentation design, not teaching. To our students, we were the experts. Our approach was to tell people what to do and what to stop doing. Then, we'd give example slides that applied those principles.

While that was a natural approach to sharing expertise, and participants appreciated the training, it fell short on five dimensions:

- **Mistake 1: We thought we had the "right" answer.** In quantitative fields, most problems have one answer. When someone gets the correct answer, it's usually evident to everyone else. However, business problems rarely have just one answer, and the path to the result may differ for the audience. Showing your work is essential, or better yet, showing the specific steps the audience needs to arrive at the same conclusion.

- **Mistake 2: We didn't explain the "why" or the science behind the principles.** Because the company had a strong presentation culture, we sometimes said, "This is how we do things here, so you need to do it this way." However, people who don't understand the rationale or science behind the principles are less likely to adopt them. Or they misapply them.

- **Mistake 3: We didn't consistently demonstrate our principles on our slides.** We even used slides with long bulleted lists! We look back on those slides and cringe. So much for practicing what we preached!

- **Mistake 4: We didn't make people practice new skills.** Because John started the workshop as a two-hour session, the participants didn't have time to practice the skills we were teaching. It's easy to hear new information and think, "I got it." It's much harder to put that into practice—and that's where real learning happens.

- **Mistake 5: We assumed that what came easy to us would come easy to others.** We relied heavily on showing good, finished slides rather than detailing the steps involved in developing them. Unfortunately, showing participants a finished product doesn't mean they can create it. We've seen the *Mona Lisa*, but that doesn't mean we could paint a masterpiece.

Experts often make bad teachers because they forget about the process they took to become experts. They don't remember the struggles. They don't remember doing things the hard way before they learned the shortcut. They don't realize the rules of thumb, heuristics, and tricks of the trade they use aren't evident to nonexperts. And they forget that not everyone shares their passion for the topic.

Presenters fall into the Expert Trap when they fail to translate their knowledge in a way the audience can understand. Everyone has heard the phrase "You don't know what you don't know." If you've fallen into the Expert Trap, you don't know what the audience doesn't know. Sometimes, the trap shows up as a failure to simplify complex concepts. To explain complex concepts clearly to the audience, you must make hard things easy. The world is a complex place. Nonexperts don't have the patience for complexity and don't want to feel dumb.

Avoid the Expert Trap by providing the necessary background, reverse engineering processes, organizing content into frameworks, and applying analogies while using simple language.

Quickly give the background necessary to understand core concepts

Don't assume that the audience knows everything you do. Remember to use the Platinum Rule assessment to understand the audience's knowledge level. Experts often forget to share essential background information and context because they assume everyone knows it.

Explaining planetary motion to a nonexpert isn't possible if they don't understand Newton's laws of motion. What are the "laws" behind the concepts your audience might not understand? Couch this part of your presentation as level setting by saying, "To ensure we're all starting from the same baseline, here are the things you need to know to understand my proposal." Even if the audience is familiar with the background concepts, highlighting them assists learning. Activating the audience's existing knowledge makes it easier for them to remember the new ideas. Think of the existing ideas as a garden lattice, providing structure for the new ideas to grow like vines.

Early in our Presentations That Drive Action workshop, we ask participants to write down what they already know about effective presentations. This leverages the "lattice" process to activate participants' knowledge about presentations, which makes incorporating new concepts into their framework easier. However, the need to give background and set context isn't a license to share *all* the information you know about a topic.

Reverse engineer your expertise

Experts forget what it was like before they earned their expertise. They take steps that are second nature to them but unobvious to nonexperts. They use shortcuts and heuristics. But you can't skip steps when explaining complex concepts to nonexperts. By chunking up the process into discrete steps, the audience can deliberately step through the process that experts follow intuitively. The "Conclusion" chapter includes an example of this process, where we break down the steps to build a complex slide. Here are the steps we took to reverse engineer our process:

1. **Identify the inputs and outputs.** Using mind mapping and other brainstorming techniques, we listed the elements that went into creating the slide and the products at the end of the process. These are usually nouns.

2. **Functionally decompose the process.** Now that we understood the inputs and outputs, we defined the steps that transformed between them. We listed the steps, focusing on the order in which we performed them. The process steps are usually verbs.

3. **Analyze the steps.** Each step should be as clear, concise, and independent as possible. Many steps were self-explanatory, but others required decomposition into three to five substeps. When there were too many steps, we grouped related steps and restructured the original steps as substeps within the group.

4. **Validate, test, and document.** We wrote the "Conclusion" chapter and then found that we missed steps, while other steps needed more explanation. Embrace iterations.

Create frameworks

John stores his compact disc collection on the bookcase shown in Figure 5.2. This was once considered a state-of-the-art music catalog. (Yes, we mostly stream music now.) When he bought the bookcase, he carefully alphabetized the CDs by artist, with each artist's collection ordered by release year.

Figure 5.2 John's too many CDs and a budding music fan
Source: Courtesy of John and Marty Polk

But over the years, it was too much work to move whole rows of CDs to squeeze a new CD in the right spot, so he just stacked them up near the appropriate letter in front of the carefully alphabetized back row. With a large haul from a used-record store, he'd stack them on the floor, intending to sort them later. Of course, that never happened!

Now imagine that his adorable toddler pulled the CDs off the shelf (he did). Now, try to find a specific CD title. You force the audience to do that if you flood them with information without an organizing framework.

A framework is a simple structure representing a group of ideas, concepts, systems, or processes. Effective frameworks organize key concepts so the audience can understand, digest, and remember them. In addition, frameworks can define scope and hierarchy. The easiest way to create a framework is to organize ideas into three to five groups, create a summary name for each group, and then put those names in boxes with representative points underneath each box.

Suppose we want to create a list of the greatest songs recorded by the Beatles as a group or solo artists. The wall-of-text form is in Figure 5.3.

The Greatest Songs Recorded by the Beatles, Group or Solo

- In My Life
- Let It Be
- Maybe I'm Amazed
- Imagine
- Twist and Shout
- I Want to Hold Your Hand
- Something
- Rock and Roll Music
- What Is Life
- Roll Over Beethoven
- Photograph
- Please Mr. Postman

Figure 5.3 Hard-to-digest, wall-of-text list
Source: John Polk & Associates

We bet you got bored reading it and stopped after just a few songs. If we group the songs into three categories and arrange them in a logical order, we get Figure 5.4.

The Greatest Songs Recorded by the Beatles, Group or Solo

Written by Beatles	Covered by Beatles	Written by solo Beatles
I Want to Hold Your Hand	Please Mr. Postman	Imagine
In My Life	Rock and Roll Music	Maybe I'm Amazed
Let It Be	Roll Over Beethoven	Photograph
Something	Twist and Shout	What Is Life

Figure 5.4 Easier-to-digest, simple three-box framework
Source: John Polk & Associates

For the record, this is not our opinion on the best Beatles songs—we needed songs that would span three categories with an even number of bullet points per group.

Compare these two versions of the same information. Note how much easier your brain digests the one with a simple framework. In technical terms, the framework slide has a lighter cognitive load. Your brain can choose to dive into information it finds interesting, without having to digest the complete list.

Here's the kicker—not only is the framework easier to digest, but it also conveys more information!

We love working with startup founders on their pitch decks. Working with passionate founders dedicated to making their audacious ideas a reality is a vicarious thrill. Most founders have difficulty framing their core idea because they know all the great things their product or service does, and they don't want to leave anything out. In working with founders, we developed this framework of frameworks (meta, we know!).

Focus on one big idea. This framework is the easiest for the audience to understand. The one-big-idea framework in Figure 5.5 describes a new food-delivery app. The audience will quickly understand how your app works if they're familiar with Uber. Of course, Uber became the Uber of food delivery. But distilling your ideas down to one big idea is difficult. It's difficult because your ideas are rich and multifaceted. It's difficult because you're too close to your ideas. Focusing on one part of your idea feels like abandoning other parts. It's also challenging to get in the audience's mindset. But when you do, you'll see what aspect of your idea is most valuable to them.

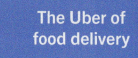

Figure 5.5 If only Uber delivered food
Source: John Polk & Associates

Sell one big benefit and ancillary benefits with a Ginsu framework. "In Japan, the hand can be used like a knife [*martial artist chops a board in half*]. But this method doesn't work with a tomato [*martial artist chops a tomato and makes a big mess*]." Thus began the Ginsu knife commercial. If you watched TV in the late 1970s, you remember this ad. If not, check it out on YouTube. In the Ginsu commercial, they kept piling on "free" items, like the serving fork, the spiralizer, and six steak knives. It was an early infomercial with the "but wait, there's more" approach.

The Ginsu framework in Figure 5.6 sells one primary benefit with additional but less significant benefits. Customers remember the phrase "really sharp knife," but they don't have to remember all the other benefits—just that there are other benefits.

Figure 5.6 But wait, there are more frameworks
Source: John Polk & Associates

Show equal ideas. This framework illustrates the benefits as equal or in a specific order. This is the approach for the greatest Beatles songs framework. The equal ideas framework is the most common, so use it sparingly. There are many other options to choose from. The framework in Figure 5.7 delineates three career change components. The equal ideas framework works well if there aren't too many boxes in the model. Beyond five boxes, you need a mnemonic device, like an acronym, to aid memory.

Figure 5.7 Some ideas are more equal than others
Source: John Polk & Associates

Add a unifying theme with an umbrella. This framework adds an overarching theme to the equal ideas framework. In Figure 5.8, the career change ecosystem label ties the equal ideas together and helps the audience remember them. If the audience remembers the umbrella idea, they can more easily remember the components under it.

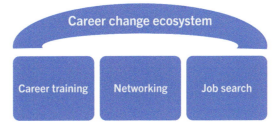

Figure 5.8 Protect your ideas from the elements
Source: John Polk & Associates

When building these "n-box" frameworks, choose a layout based on the number of boxes and the amount of text. Figure 5.9 shows a portion of our slide library illustrating

Figure 5.9 Several of the 54 simple n-box frameworks in our slide library
Source: John Polk & Associates

Create frameworks   139

horizontal, vertical, and grid framework layouts. Yes, it's possible to create these on the fly, but with a robust slide library, you won't have to.

These four frameworks are most valuable for grouping things. The Ginsu and umbrella frameworks convey simple hierarchy information. The following frameworks focus on hierarchy or the interrelationships between their components.

Sequence elements with chevrons (a.k.a. speedboats). This framework highlights the sequence of events. Use the framework in Figure 5.10 for project (or career) phasing.

Figure 5.10 Chevrons, which usually indicate progress
Source: John Polk & Associates

Highlight connections to a central concept with an atom model. This framework mimics how scientists depict atomic structures and shows a connection between multiple ideas and a central idea. In Figure 5.11, the central focus is the Beatles, who have influenced the connected bands.

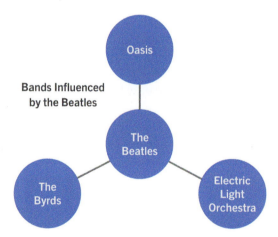

Figure 5.11 Atoms, which sometimes have weak bonds
Source: John Polk & Associates

Plot elements on a two-by-two matrix. This is a classic consulting framework. Use it to assess ideas or options against two criteria. Typical two-by-two matrixes map ideas in terms of risk and reward or cost and benefit, with each axis divided by high and low. The two-by-two boxes imply only four choices, but mapping continuous data works, too. Technology consulting firm Gartner uses the two-by-two matrix for their Magic Quadrants that map software solutions against the completeness of vision and ability to execute. Figure 5.12 illustrates a subjective assessment of four solo albums by ex-Beatles in terms of song quality and quantity.

Figure 5.12 They can't all be classics
Sources: (lower left) Boardwalk Records / (others) Apple Corps

Create frameworks

Portray overlap with a Venn diagram. This framework, named for mathematician John Venn, shows the overlap among categories. The overlap in the three circles in Figure 5.13—master's degree, executive coach, and Venn diagram maestro—can only represent Justin.

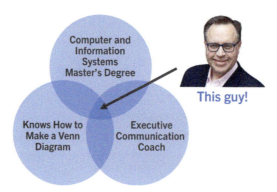

Figure 5.13 We'd like to have a diagram named after us
Sources: (headshot) Courtesy of Todd Rafalovich / John Polk & Associates

Use overlapping circles to portray a target (a.k.a. bullseye) diagram. This framework shows a central concept, with each outer ring being farther away on a dimension. The target framework in Figure 5.14 shows the change management model of circles of concern, influence, and control. It asks people to assess their concerns about an upcoming change or event. During a reorganization, you have *concerns* about changing roles, getting a new boss, or even the risk of job loss. The key to effectively working through any stressful change is focusing on areas of influence and control. You can *influence* your boss by telling them which new roles you could take on, and you can *control* whether your LinkedIn profile and résumé are current.

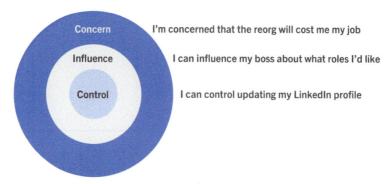

Figure 5.14 We'd all like more control
Source: Adapted from *The 7 Habits of Highly Effective People*, Stephen R. Covey, 1989

Bottom-aligning the circles creates more space for text inside, as in Figure 5.15.

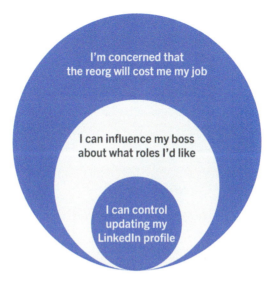

Figure 5.15 When your ability to control hits rock bottom
Source: John Polk & Associates

Set a foundation with a pyramid. This framework orders categories, with the bottom row being the foundation for all the other rows. A pyramid framework for building an actual pyramid is in Figure 5.16. Having a solid foundation is foundational, natch. The pyramid's layers build up to the capstone. The version with rectangles works better when there's too much text to fit in the top levels.

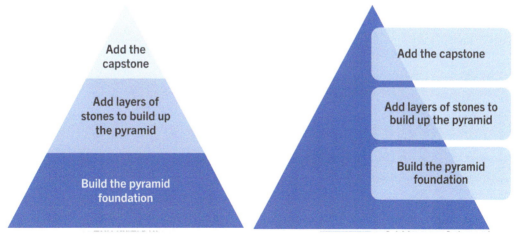

Figure 5.16 Meta pyramid frameworks
Source: John Polk & Associates

Create frameworks 143

Narrow a population with a funnel. An inverted pyramid is a funnel. This framework illustrates how a population gets smaller from top to bottom. The sales pipeline is a classic application for the funnel. The two funnel designs in Figure 5.17 show how online dating activity goes from swipes to partners. Adding ovals to the trapezoid segments creates a three-dimensional effect.

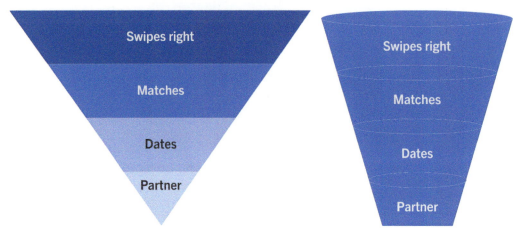

Figure 5.17 Optimistic dating funnel frameworks
Source: John Polk & Associates

One downside of the funnel diagram is that it implies a steady volume reduction moving down the funnel. To show the magnitude of the decrease at each step, use a tornado chart with actual data, as in Figure 5.18.

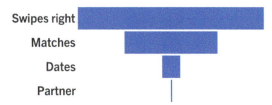

Figure 5.18 Dating tornado (great name for a reality TV show!) chart
Source: John Polk & Associates

Repeat steps with a cycle. Many processes repeat. Figure 5.19 illustrates the vicious cycle that can occur with pre-presentation nerves.

144 The Expert Trap

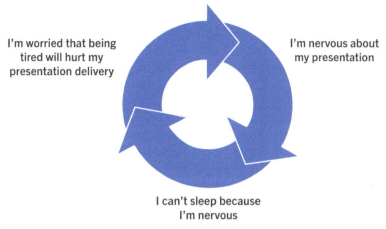

Figure 5.19 Nothing says "prepared" like three hours of sleep
Source: John Polk & Associates

Climb up or down stairsteps. This framework illustrates something getting better or worse over time. The framework in Figure 5.20 illustrates the challenges of the wine industry.

How to Make a Small Fortune in the Wine Business

Make a large fortune
　　Open a winery
　　　　Have a small fortune
　　　　　　Toast your success

Figure 5.20 If only we had a large fortune
Source: John Polk & Associates

The descending stairs illustrate a large fortune decreasing to a small fortune.

Illustrate tailwinds and headwinds with a force field. This framework shows the tailwinds and headwinds affecting a strategy. Figure 5.21 illustrates a force field framework for our new diet and exercise strategy.

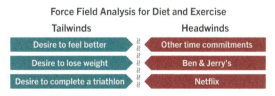

Figure 5.21 The tailwinds are losing
Source: John Polk & Associates

Create frameworks   145

Assessing the forces that can help or hurt a strategy is essential for two reasons. First, you can build strategies for taking advantage of tailwinds and overcoming headwinds in the plan. Second, acknowledging the risk before launch is better than using it as an excuse if a headwind undercuts the strategy.

Break down influencing factors with a driver tree. This framework decomposes the levers that can move the needle on an outcome. (How do you like the tree, lever, and needle mixed metaphor?) Imagine your boss asks you to increase profit. Sure, boss, I'll get right on that. Unfortunately, there's no physical "profit" lever to pull—you must understand what drives profit and pull those underlying levers. In the driver tree in Figure 5.22, profit splits into revenue and cost, each with subdrivers. How do you increase revenue? You could sell more units or raise prices. At each level, possible actions become more evident. Now, you can brainstorm ways to sell more units.

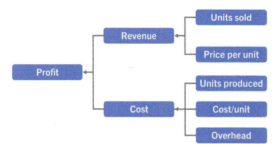

Figure 5.22 More profit coming up, boss!
Source: John Polk & Associates

Adjust across continuums with slider bars (a.k.a. stereo bars). This framework shows how options rate on one or more continuums. The term "stereo bars" comes from the sound mixer controls that let you increase or decrease different instruments in a recording or a stereo equalizer that adjusts bass, midrange, and treble volumes separately. Figure 5.23 shows the red, green, and blue values from the RGB model for a royal purple. We're not sure how practical this example is, but we ran out of Beatles-related ideas.

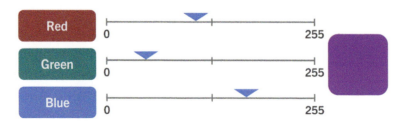

Figure 5.23 Mixing the perfect purple
Source: John Polk & Associates

146 The Expert Trap

Slider bars can also portray qualitative data—for example, to assess aspects of an option or product on a high/medium/low scale. If there are only two sliders, consider a two-by-two matrix. You could also add competitors, benchmarks, or goals.

Highlight priorities with strategic pillars. This framework highlights strategic priorities. Figure 5.24 illustrates a subset of the Fight Club rules. We almost didn't include this diagram because leaders overuse it. Overused analogies become clichés eventually—we're looking at you, puzzle pieces! But we couldn't resist the *Fight Club* reference.

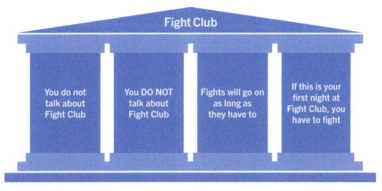

Figure 5.24 Gladiators were the first fight club
Source: Rules from *Fight Club* (1999) / 20th Century Fox

Weigh decisions with pros and cons. This framework is a fundamental part of decision-making. Choose the option with the best balance of pros versus cons and build risk mitigation strategies to manage the cons. Pros and cons lists can combine qualitative and quantitative data. Because the pros and cons evaluation step is called "weighing," the scale is an excellent analogy for visualizing pros and cons, like in the assessment of dog ownership in Figure 5.25. Fun fact: Benjamin Franklin invented the pros-and-cons list in 1772.[1]

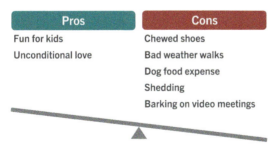

Figure 5.25 Pros and cons of getting a dog
Source: John Polk & Associates

For the record, we're dog lovers. We love other people's dogs.

Illustrate relationships with interrelated lists. The relationship between framework elements doesn't have to be complex. Illustrate before-and-after or cause-and-effect relationships with overlapping arrow pentagons. Figure 5.26 shows the cause-and-effect impact of common retirement-planning mistakes.

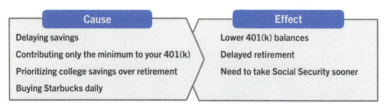

Figure 5.26 The best time to start saving is now
Source: John Polk & Associates

Make frameworks easy to digest

Everything should be made as simple as possible, but not simpler.[2]
Albert Einstein, attributed and paraphrased

An overloaded, confusing framework is no better than a wall-of-text slide. The framework must reinforce the key message. No matter which framework you choose, follow these tips:

Start with a mind map. Remember the mind map technique from Chapter 2, "The Bury the Lede Trap"? Mind maps work for frameworks, too. List every idea, group related items, and create a title for each category. The grouping step uses chunking to help the audience digest and memorize. Americans don't memorize their Social Security number as a nine-digit number. Instead, they memorize it as a three-digit number, a two-digit number, and a four-digit number.

Choose a framework type. Understanding the hierarchies and interrelationships among categories helps choose a framework. You can illustrate four categories as a four-box framework, a two-by-two, or four chevrons representing project phases.

Order categories and bullet points logically. Common ordering strategies include importance and timing. If there's no logical order, alphabetize them.

Break up long lists. If any category has too many bullet points, consider splitting it into two categories, grouping similar points, or creating another hierarchy level.

Make the framework MECE. When a framework is mutually exclusive and collectively exhaustive (MECE), it holds up better under scrutiny.[3] "Mutually exclusive" means that individual elements can't apply to multiple categories. "Collectively exhaustive" means you didn't miss any categories in the framework or elements in the categories. Barbara Minto developed this concept for consulting, problem-solving, and business analysis. It's pronounced "mees" and rhymes with "peace." Since she invented it, she decides how to pronounce it. The cupcakes in Figure 5.27 illustrate the MECE concept.

Figure 5.27 Mmm, rainbow cupcakes
Source: Generated with AI using Microsoft Copilot

Assume there are seven cupcakes in the rainbow-cupcake universe. In this framework, group 1 contains red, orange, and yellow cupcakes, and group 2 contains yellow, green, and teal cupcakes. The framework is not exclusive because the yellow cupcake is in two groups. The framework is also not exhaustive because no category includes the blue and purple cupcakes.

The new groupings in Figure 5.28 create a MECE cupcake framework. All cupcakes are in a group, and no cupcake is in multiple groups.

Figure 5.28 No debate over who gets the yellow cupcake
Source: Generated with AI using Microsoft Copilot

Make frameworks easy to digest

Reuse the framework. Repeatedly referring to a framework gives the audience multiple chances to understand and remember it. Each repetition can highlight a different aspect or application. We use the same four-box framework to describe an organization's communication challenges and how our offerings address them. The framework categories are the same, but the bullet points are different.

Avoid framework stack. Too many competing frameworks in one presentation can confuse the audience. Minimize confusion by identifying one framework as the central theme. Then, when introducing other frameworks, choose different framework types or colors to give visual clues. Or build a framework of frameworks to show how they interrelate.

Use color coding. Color distinguishes framework components, such as ownership or differences between preexisting and new elements.

Marketing hacks for memorable frameworks

Critical frameworks, like strategic imperatives, key performance indicators, and product features, must live beyond the presentation. In these cases, break out a marketing hack or two to make the framework memorable:

- **Acronyms:** Name and organize the framework categories so they spell a word. The SMART goal-setting model, created by George T. Doran, is a classic business acronym.[4] SMART stands for "specific, measurable, achievable, relevant, and time-bound." Acronyms create a crossword effect. If you haven't memorized all five words, the acronym gives you the first letter as a clue. Acronyms with numbers are a variation on the theme. B2B uses the "2" for "to."

- **Alliteration:** Name each category to start with the same letter or sound—for example, the four P's of marketing framework (product, price, place, and promotion), developed by E. Jerome McCarthy.[5] This approach also benefits from the crossword effect. John used "The Fab Four" to describe his organization's four strategic imperatives. While not as helpful for remembering the components, everyone knew there were four. In addition to the alliteration, this branding benefited from the Beatles reference!

(continued)

- **Rhyming:** Repeat similar sounds in words—for example, "lack of will, skill, or kill," which describes why many people create black hole presentations. "Lack of kill" is not a common phrase like "lack of will," but in this framework, it maintains the rhyme, and its quirkiness gets a laugh, which makes the framework memorable. "Clicks to bricks" describes how businesses use an online presence to drive customers to retail locations. Ensure rhyming words add value. "Winner, winner, chicken dinner" and "easy, peasy, lemon squeezy" rhyme, but they are extra.

- **Portmanteau:** From the French for "traveling bag," a portmanteau combines two words. Portmanteaus are everywhere: email, spork, edutainment, brunch, and even "Bennifer." Unfortunately, portmanteaus can also be dumb. John received an email that combined "smart" and "marketing" to create "smarketing." Shockingly, it hasn't taken off.

- **Wordplay:** Because many words have multiple meanings, use them in ways that create funny or memorable twists. In humor theory, this is known as conceptual bifurcation. John's favorite dad joke, as with most dad jokes, uses wordplay:

    Q: What's brown and sticky?

    A: A stick.

- **Repetition:** Martin Luther King Jr's historic speech repeats "I have a dream" eight times. He followed six lines with a change he wanted to see in the world. The other two times, he said, "I have a dream today," emphasizing the urgency.

We're guessing most of you know most of these examples. That's the point of marketing tricks. You might naturally resist using these techniques because bad actors abuse them. We get it. But if you're influencing for good, why wouldn't you use all the influencing tools? Just ensure the branding isn't too complicated, forced, or cheesy. These tricks also work for nonframework ideas.

Build on the audience's existing knowledge with analogies

Remember the one-big-idea framework? We described a startup as the Uber of food delivery. Note that we've used Uber as an analogy. Let's say you're the founder of DoorDash. If the audience understands Uber, then describing your idea as "the Uber of food delivery" is easier than describing your company as "a mobile platform where any restaurant can post their menu and take carryout orders from customers, and random people with cars sign up on the platform to pick up the food from the restaurant and deliver that food to customers for a fee."

When using analogies, metaphors, and similes, you stand on the shoulders of giants. Quickly convey information with the comparison and then extend the idea on top of the analogy. Notice that we just used an analogy to describe the power of analogies!

But you might be thinking your concept is more complex than that. True, but start with the simple and layer on only the complexity you need the audience to understand to drive the desired action. The full drivers of climate change are complex. However, understanding how a greenhouse traps heat from the sun helps illustrate how carbon dioxide in the atmosphere can act like a greenhouse, warming the planet. Yes, it's more complex than that, but the audience now understands the core concept.

The icons in Figure 5.29 illustrate useful business analogies.

Figure 5.29 Blueprint, roadmap, playbook, dashboard, and Reese's Cup, oh my!

There are countless business analogies; we'll walk through several:

- **Blueprint:** A drawing of a building used by architects to tell the builders what to build. In business, a blueprint can represent anything you want to build. What's great about the blueprint analogy is that there are different overlays. One drawing outlines the walls, while another overlays the electrical wires. We used this analogy as we redesigned call centers. The call center blueprint showed the organization's structure with overlays for call volumes, routing, and overflow rules.

- **Roadmap:** A visualization of how to get from point A to point B. You plan all the stops and how long it takes to get between them. A good roadmap gives options for taking scenic or alternative routes when construction gets in the way. Unfortunately, no roadmap is perfect. Sometimes, you hit a bump in the road.

- **Playbook:** A set of processes or approaches for different situations. Who doesn't love a good sports analogy, other than people who don't follow sports? "Playbook" sounds more exciting than "procedures" or "instruction manual." The playbook analogy highlights different strategic elements. You might compare the sales force to the offense and customer support to the defense. The sports playbook accounts for different approaches when playing different teams. In business, the playbook might include different sales approaches for different industries. In all cases, teamwork is critical to achieving the goal.

- **Dashboard:** A well-organized display of critical metrics. People use this term so often in business that it's easy to forget its origin as an analogy. Truing back to the analogy highlights essential concepts. A plane's cockpit dashboard requires us to pay attention to more metrics than a car's dashboard, but it still must be simple enough for one or two pilots to fly safely. Dashboards mix key metrics (speed) with warnings (low fuel, check engine). The best dashboards give the root causes when something is going wrong. Looking at past data is like looking in the rearview mirror. You can't drive by looking only in the rearview mirror. For that reason, many organizations call them "scorecards." Leveraging real-time data and building accurate forecasts minimizes this problem.

- **Reese's Cup:** A positive synthesis. This analogy highlights how an idea brings together the best of both worlds. This is the essence of the Reese's Cup: "You got peanut butter on my chocolate." We recently learned that a new naturally occurring hybrid combines a polar bear and a grizzly bear. Polar bear paws are fur covered, and grizzly bear paws are hairless. The "pizzly bear" (we didn't make that up!) has partial fur on its paws to walk on ice or ground. The pizzly bear is the Reese's Cup of the animal kingdom!

Use idioms carefully

Idioms are like analogies, but their comparisons are less explicit. Idioms enrich language, making it more colorful and engaging, but they can be challenging for nonnative English speakers or people on the autism spectrum.

To highlight the power of idioms in the business world, let's explore the two idioms illustrated in Figure 5.30.

Figure 5.30 *Canary in the coal mine and ostrich with its head in the sand*
Sources: (left) Generated with AI using Microsoft Copilot / (right) Andrey Kuzmin / Adobe Stock Photos

A coal miner holding a canary in a cage illustrates the idiom "the canary in the coal mine." This idiom comes from coal miners using a canary as a gas detector. If the canary keeled over, the miners knew there were dangerous levels of toxic gas, and they needed to escape. We assumed the canary died, but in researching this practice, we learned the canary just passed out, and as long as a miner remembered to grab the bird when rushing out, the bird could survive. Of course, "mine-gas breather" still isn't a great job for the canary. Or the miner, for that matter. In the business world, a canary in the coal mine is an early warning signal.

The ostrich with its head in the sand illustrates the idiom "bury your head in the sand." This idiom describes someone ignoring negative information willfully. On a side note, ostriches don't bury their heads. They are either looking for food or turning eggs in a nest dug in the dirt, so we owe them an apology!

In a meeting, John discussed a fraud alert that was highly effective in detecting fraud, but by the time employees could act on the alert, the fraudsters had taken all the money in the targeted account. He described the alert as an "*ostrich* in the coal mine," like in

Figure 5.31. We assume the ostrich, unlike the canary, would pass out after the coal miners. He got a laugh, and the audience understood the issue—we needed to act faster or find a new fraud detection method. The analogy also made the concept memorable. Days later, the fraud operations leader passed John in the hall, shook his head, and said, "Ostrich in the coal mine."

Figure 5.31 Ostrich in the coal mine
Source: Collage / Generated with AI using Microsoft Copilot

Idioms are all around us. The animal kingdom and sports are generous idiom suppliers. Pairing idioms with images or icons, like in Figure 5.32, makes them more memorable.

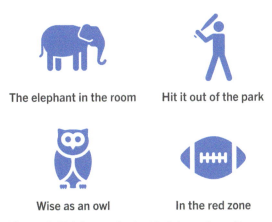

Figure 5.32 Idioms, the inside jokes of a culture
Source: John Polk & Associates

John's mom used the idiom "taking coals to Newcastle." This phrase dates to the 1500s when Newcastle monopolized the British coal trade. So, to take coals to Newcastle is to give someone something they don't need or to pursue something pointless.

Because idiomatic phrases aren't just the sum of their words, learning idioms in a foreign language is challenging. Many idioms are specific to the culture. A cricket fan might not understand "hit a home run," and a soccer fan might not understand "in the red zone." Even within the same language, idioms aren't consistent across countries. The British client who said, "Give me two ticks," didn't want bloodsuckers; she wanted to be excused for a brief time. Figure 5.33 illustrates fun non-English idioms and their English translations. How many did you know? Imagine entire conversations littered with idioms. That's the challenge for nonnative speakers.

Figure 5.33 The shoe is on the other foot, native English speakers!
Source: John Polk & Associates

Some of these came from a great language podcast, *A Way with Words*. Don't be afraid to use idioms from your native language. Regardless of the language, you should explain your idioms if the audience includes nonnative speakers.

Notice the power of images and icons paired with analogies and idioms in this chapter. The visuals bring the concepts to life and illustrate their meanings. Chapter 3, "The Black Hole Trap," discussed how visuals like charts, images, and icons can reduce deck density. They also cut through complexity and give the audience multiple ways to digest ideas.

Caution: When speakers overuse an analogy, idiom, or phrase, it becomes a cliché. Let's retire "think outside the box" and "it is what it is."

Define acronyms and limit jargon

Figure 5.34 shows an email from a client.

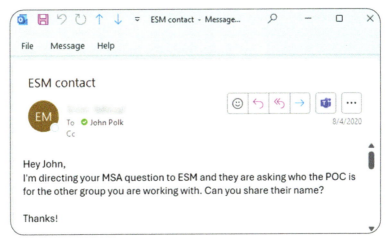

Figure 5.34 Three-letter acronyms (TLAs)
Source: Courtesy of John Polk

Almost 10% of the words are acronyms. In his response, John complimented her on her impressive acronym streak. She responded, "LOL! TTYL." John replied, "ROFL." For the record, MSA means "master services agreement." But it also stands for over 200 other acronyms, according to TheFreeDictionary.com, including "medical savings account" and "Missionary Sisters of Ajmer." ESM is an acronym for an internal department. And POC stands for "point of contact." Even if the audience can figure out what the acronyms mean, the translation effort increases cognitive load if it's not an acronym they use regularly.

Acronyms are an efficient shorthand for those in the know. Unfortunately, they are confusing for everyone who spends mental energy wondering what they mean. The confusion risk increases when someone forwards the deck to someone who wasn't in the meeting. Not only are acronyms and jargon confusing, but they create an us-and-them effect for those who don't "speak the language," making them feel like outsiders.

The fix for this problem is easy. When using acronyms, spell them out the first time, then put the acronym in parentheses. Then, use the acronym for the rest of the presentation. Similarly, define any jargon or technical terms at first mention. Or use language that is accessible to everyone. Put yourself in the audience's nonexpert shoes. If you can say it without jargon, say it without jargon.

Review your work with experts and nonexperts

Another driver of the Expert Trap is reviewing your work only with other experts. Don't get us wrong—other experts make great reviewers. They can double-check the work, test assumptions, and call BS on your ideas if necessary.

But they won't catch undefined acronyms, confusing jargon, or the complex concepts you didn't make clear. For that, you need an "ignorant reviewer"! "Ignorant" has become a loaded term, but it just means being unaware or uninformed about a topic. No one can know everything; therefore, everyone is ignorant about many topics.

To ensure the presentation is understandable to a broader audience, ask someone who isn't an expert to review the deck. Encourage them to be honest about what they find confusing, as some ignorant reviewers may hesitate to admit their uncertainty, assuming it's clear to others.

Key Takeaways

Use analogies, visuals, and frameworks to make complex concepts digestible for nonexperts.

- ✓ If necessary, summarize the background information to ensure everyone has the same foundation.
- ✓ Reverse engineer your expertise so nonexperts can follow it.
- ✓ Distill long bulleted lists, preferably into MECE (mutually exclusive, collectively exhaustive) frameworks.
- ✓ Choose frameworks that illustrate the hierarchies and relationships between components.
- ✓ Apply marketing techniques, like alliteration and rhyming, to make frameworks memorable.
- ✓ Simplify complex concepts with analogies, metaphors, and similes that build upon the audience's knowledge.
- ✓ When using idioms, ensure understanding and avoid clichés.
- ✓ Avoid unnecessary jargon and define necessary jargon. Spell out acronyms the first time they occur.
- ✓ Ask expert reviewers to test key assumptions and recommendations. Ask nonexpert reviewers to highlight confusing concepts and undefined jargon and acronyms.

Figure 6.1 Easel with workshop objectives
Source: KaterynaVS / Adobe Stock Photos

6

The Peice of Cake Trap

Review your work to catch typos, grammar mistakes, and inconsistent formats, which damage credibility.

How many of you noticed — and judged us for — the intentional typo in our chapter title: "peice" instead of "piece"? The pesky "i before e" rule is just too complicated! We ask participants what they want to learn at the beginning of our workshops. When teaching in person, we write their responses on a flip chart or whiteboard, like Figure 6.1.

John returned from lunch during a workshop and noticed he had misspelled a word on the flip chart. He asked the group, "Did anyone notice I misspelled this word?" About half the participants raised their hands. Then he asked, "And what did you think?"

"I thought you were an idiot," said a guy in the back.

Did you notice that "PowerPoint" is misspelled in the illustration? "PowerPint" would be a good name for a pub, but it's an embarrassing typo.

John spent four hours that morning teaching with the confidence of an expert. But with that one handwritten typo, he convinced half the participants that he was an idiot! Of course, judging someone for one minor misspelling is unfair, but that doesn't change the fact that people naturally judge others.

When your deck has typos, some in the audience will judge you negatively. And when they judge, they will reach one of three conclusions: (1) you're an idiot, (2) you're sloppy, or (3) you're both. None are good for your reputation. If the audience concludes you're an idiot, they won't trust your recommendations. If they conclude you're sloppy, they won't trust the data analytics or logic that led to the recommendations. The more typos, grammar mistakes, and inconsistently formatted objects in your deck, the more negatively the audience will judge you. At some point, like the last straw on the camel's back, they will dismiss your ideas and reject your proposed actions.

> ### The real consequences of typos and grammar issues
>
> If you don't think this stuff is important, Figure 6.2 has two headlines that illustrate the real-world consequences of typos and grammar mistakes.
>
> | Oakhurst Dairy settled a lawsuit for $5M over an overtime dispute that hinged on the use of the Oxford comma. | Prospective partners are 14% less likely to message eHarmony users with spelling or punctuation errors in their profiles. |
> |---|---|
> | *The New York Times*, 3/16/17 | *The Telegraph*, 10/17/15 |
>
> **Figure 6.2** Sloppy writing is bad for business and your love life
> Sources: The New York Times / The Telegraph[1]
>
> Presenters fall into the Piece of Cake Trap when they let typos, grammar issues, and unprofessional slides reduce their credibility. A root cause of the Piece of Cake Trap is a belief that you can effectively proofread your material. When reviewing and editing your work, you miss things. You're too close to the work. If you missed a typo the last three times you edited a slide, what makes you think you'll find it on the final pass?
>
> Avoid the Piece of Cake Trap by reviewing for common style issues, using checklists and electronic editors, finding good editors, and helping them help you. But don't let perfectionism distract you from ensuring you create a compelling story.

Write like you speak

Kevin from *The Office* demonstrates the problem with not writing like you speak, or in this case, not speaking like you speak, as shown in Figure 6.3.

Figure 6.3 Kevin, not speaking like you speak
Source: *The Office* (2005–2013) / NBCUniversal Media, LLC

One day, Kevin decides he can save time by cutting out all the unnecessary words in his speech and ignoring grammar rules. His behavior throws off his officemates so much that they assume he must be having a stroke. Because of the formality of business communications, writers often adopt "lawyerspeak." Here are strategies for writing like you speak:

- Don't drop articles ("the," "a," and "an"). This happens often during the quest for shorter text.
- Break up complex sentences into multiple shorter sentences.
- Put verbs near the beginning of the sentence and modifiers next to the word they modify.
- Use pronouns when the doer is clear: "he/she/they," not "the party of the first part."
- Use contractions: "can't," not "cannot."
- Don't forget to not use double negatives.
- Don't abbrev. when you don't have to.
- Avoid lawyerspeak words:
  - Hereby/thereby
  - Herein/therein
  - Heretofore
  - Notwithstanding
  - Shall
  - Whereas
- Avoid jargon and spell out acronyms the first time you use them, as discussed in Chapter 5, "The Expert Trap."

Ensure content has parallel structure

Consider the anonymous, real-world slide in Figure 6.4. Please focus on the content and ignore that this is a plain bullet-point slide we told you to never, never, never create.

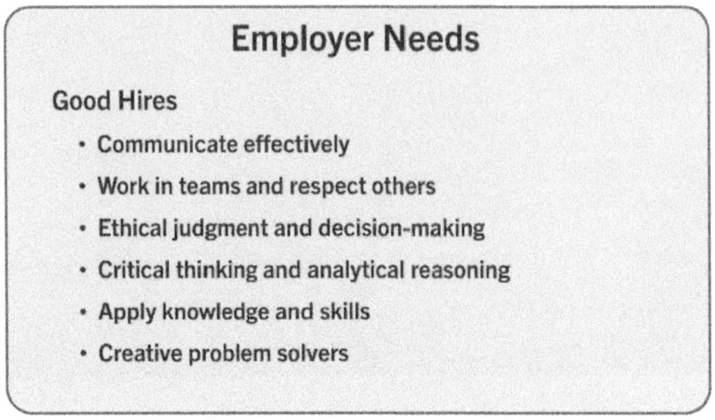

Employer Needs

Good Hires
- Communicate effectively
- Work in teams and respect others
- Ethical judgment and decision-making
- Critical thinking and analytical reasoning
- Apply knowledge and skills
- Creative problem solvers

Figure 6.4 What bullet points made you slow down or stumble?
Source: John Polk & Associates

Notice anything wrong? If not, read it aloud. We'll wait. Now do you notice anything wrong? If you still don't hear anything wrong, reread each bullet point, but repeat the "Good Hires" opening phrase for each.

The first two bullet points read correctly—e.g., "Good hires communicate effectively." But would you ever say, "Good, hires ethical judgment and decision-making"? Of course not, but that's what the slide creator did. And that slide creator made the same error for half the bullet points! Having all bullet points read consistently is called parallel structure. When bullet points are parallel, they must be either all sentences or all phrases, maintaining the same grammatical form, like active voice and present tense.

After having a good proofreader, reading text aloud is the best way to catch parallel structure issues and lawyerspeak issues. If you stumble or sound like a robot, you're not writing like you speak! Read Figure 6.5, the updated slide, with edits to make the bullet points parallel.

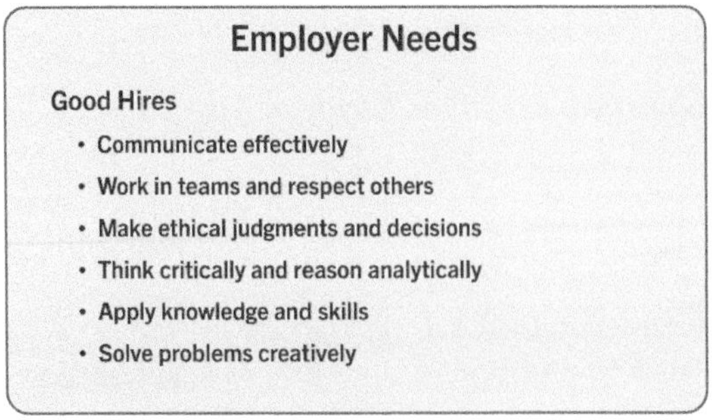

Employer Needs

Good Hires
- Communicate effectively
- Work in teams and respect others
- Make ethical judgments and decisions
- Think critically and reason analytically
- Apply knowledge and skills
- Solve problems creatively

Figure 6.5 Parallel-structure version that rolls off the tongue (still a weak slide)
Source: John Polk & Associates

Notice the resolution to the fourth bullet. If the approach were to fix the bullet points by adding a verb, you might rewrite that sentence as, "Demonstrate critical thinking and analytical reasoning." Instead, look for verbs disguised as nouns, like "thinking" and "reasoning," and turn them back into verbs. That achieves parallel structure without adding words.

The case against periods—"Guilty!"

Your English teacher and the Strunk & White grammar reference taught you to put a period after a sentence. We don't use periods in sentence titles or bullet points in our decks, even when the bullet point is a sentence. The cat pitch in Figure 6.6 demonstrates why we're team "no period." This short deck made the rounds on X (formerly Twitter).

Figure 6.6 "A cat oh yeah yeah"
Source: Reproduced with the permission of Christopher Doyle / X Corp / @chrisdoyle

A young girl created this to convince her parents to buy her a cat. She naturally applied some of our teachings (nice icons, hanging indents, and an engaging cat photo). Unfortunately, her house style includes periods for bullet points. And she made it all the way to the last bullet point before she missed one. Don't worry. This minor omission did not affect her mission. The family adopted a rescue kitten! No word on the hamster.

(continued)

In all our years reviewing decks, only one managed to include periods at the end of sentences without missing at least one. When the house style omits periods, Find and Replace can easily locate and remove them. However, when the house style includes periods, you must rely on proofreading skills to find missing periods.

You may now be screaming, "All sentences must end in a period!" We get it. That's what grammar books teach. But the real purpose is to *separate* two sentences with a period. In a deck, white space and the bullet points do a fine job separating sentences. In our decks, we don't use multiple sentences in bullet points. If you need multiple sentences in one bullet point, separate them with a semicolon or em dash instead of a period. Quotations or mission statements with more than one sentence are an exception to this rule.

Most decks include bulleted lists with sentences and phrases. Should you use periods with all bullet points? It doesn't make sense to use periods with bullet points that aren't complete sentences. When using periods for sentences and not for phrases, the bullet points look inconsistent. And it requires making many decisions on the fly about whether to use a period. As a bonus, consider all the ink saved in printed documents!

We use the question mark for questions so no one thinks that it's a statement. In rare circumstances, we allow an exclamation point. When leading strategy and analysis teams, we told the analysts they could use an exclamation point only if their project added at least $10M in value to the bottom line. And, no, you don't get two exclamation points if you add $20M in value.

We've mellowed our stance on exclamation points. They create emphasis, but don't overuse them or it will read as insincere. There's a great episode of the TV show *Corporate* where a character is almost fired because his exclamation-point key broke, and his coworkers misinterpret all his emails as rude![2]

[Editor's note: Because this is a book, I requested the authors use more periods. After a lengthy discussion of the Platinum Rule and the "book" setting, they agreed to use them for complete-sentence bullet points—mostly because their electronic editor wouldn't stop flagging it.]

Learn the grammar and style rules many presenters get wrong

Teaching grammar rules in our workshops is challenging. The participants who know the rules get bored, and the participants who don't know the rules often think it shouldn't matter. However, there are a few mistakes most presentation designers make, which can create confusion or damage credibility.

Avoid elegant variation. Presenters sometimes use different expressions or synonyms to avoid repeating the same word throughout the deck, worrying it may bore the audience. But that can lead to confusion if the audience thinks the difference was purposeful. During a presentation on "fraud alerts," the presenter interchangeably used the term "fraud warnings." The team spent 15 minutes discussing the difference before concluding that none was intended.

Hyphenate multiword modifiers. Presenters often forget to use a hyphen when two or more words together modify another word. The "man eating chicken" in Figure 6.7 is not the same as a "man-eating chicken"!

Figure 6.7 A single hyphen is the difference between predator and prey
Source: Generated with AI using DALL-E

Use one space after a period. Many presenters missed the memo that there is now only one space after a period (or any punctuation like question marks, exclamation marks, or colons). It's easy to find and replace two spaces for one electronically.

Don't use apostrophes for plural acronyms. Many presenters use an apostrophe for plural acronyms, like "the CEO's conference." If this is a conference of CEOs and not the conference belonging to the CEO, don't use an apostrophe. We think this habit started to ensure audiences don't assume the s is part of the acronym. But making the s lowercase is sufficient to avoid that confusion. The company Mars didn't get the memo when they named their candy-coated chocolate "M&M's." When making a single letter plural, like in the phrase "mind your p's and q's," include the apostrophe for clarity. Technically, CEO is an initialism because you pronounce each letter. NASA and NATO are acronyms because you pronounce them like words. We call them both acronyms from here out.

Learn the grammar and style rules many presenters get wrong   167

Avoid acronym redundancy. The TV guide in Figure 6.8 created acronym redundancy.

Figure 6.8 Baseball squared
Source: TiVo

Since MLB stands for "Major League Baseball," this phrase translates to "Major League Baseball *Baseball*." Other common redundant acronym phrases include "PIN number" and "ATM machine." For the record, "IRA account" is correct. The "A" stands for "Arrangement."

> ### Lies your English teacher told you
>
> Grammar is hard. The rules are complex and keep evolving, and many of the ones your English teacher taught aren't as rigid as they once were. At the start of the chapter, we referred to the "i before e" rule:
>
> > i before e,
> > Except after c,
> > Or when sounded as "a,"
> > As in neighbor and weigh.
> > Chief exceptions are either,
> > Seize, leisure, ceil, neither.[3]
> >
> > Ebenezer Cobham Brewer,
> > Rules for English Spelling
>
> Now that you know the entire rule, you're good to go, right? Not so fast! Even with the long rule, there are two more exceptions. Some names with an "eye" sound, like Heidi and Einstein, have e before i. Also, many words, such as "efficient," have the letters "cien." We guess that's why it's a grammar rule and not a law.
>
> Grammar continues to evolve, and several "rules" taught in school have changed. When in doubt, check in with Grammar Girl at quickanddirtytricks.com. These new rules *allow* you to write more like you speak:
>
> - **Use "they" as a first-person singular noun.** Previously, you had to pick a gendered pronoun or use the dreaded "he/she" in sentences.

(continued)

- **End on a preposition.** Prepositions are words that describe a relationship between two nouns, like "on," "after," and "for." This solves a common write-like-you-speak issue. You used to have to do grammatical gymnastics to avoid it.

- **Split that infinitive.** Infinitives are typically formed by adding the word "to" to a verb. Putting a word between "to" and the verb is called splitting the infinitive. Splitting infinitives is now acceptable unless you're talking to a Latin teacher.

- **Reduce hyphen use in nouns.** Words evolve away from hyphens. It used to be "electronic mail," then "e-mail," and now it's "email."

- **Use "%."** The old rule was to spell out percent in a sentence. Substituting the % sign makes it stand out and saves space.

- **Allow "none" and "a number of" to be plural.** In the past, they had to be singular. For example, "none of the presenters are prepared" is now acceptable.

- **Start a sentence with a conjunction.** As learned from *Schoolhouse Rock!*, conjunctions like "and," "but," and "or" perform the function of "hooking up words and phrases and clauses."[4] When you split a sentence with two long phrases joined by "and" into two sentences, you make it easier to digest. And you increase emphasis on the second phrase.

We're open to new rules but aren't ready to implement these ourselves:

- **Don't use "literally" when you mean "figuratively."** *Merriam-Webster* has given up, and the second definition of "literally" is "in effect: VIRTUALLY—used in an exaggerated way to emphasize a statement or description that is not literally true or possible."[5] Still, we literally won't be using the second definition.

- **Use "who" instead of "whom" (eventually).** Because of the complex rules, "whom" is slowly going out of fashion. Also, Xscape's hit "Who Can I Run To" is catchier than "To Whom Can I Run." We're not there yet, but we realize that some people, to whom this may sound outdated, might be further along the curve.

Caveat: Know thy audience. If the audience feels strongly about the old rules or didn't get the memo, it's not worth debating. The goal isn't to be the smartest person in the room but to influence the audience.

Proofread and edit your work

As leaders, we often heard secondhand, "Why should I spend time making this deck look good if John and Justin are just going to mark it up anyway?" We get it. Iterating on a slide, even to improve it, feels like redoing homework you thought was finished. But having a proofreader doesn't let you off the hook for proofing your work.

The higher the quality of the draft you give a proofreader, the more valuable the feedback they will give you. When reviewing a deck full of typos, grammar mistakes, inconsistent formatting, parallel structure issues, and unaligned boxes, it's hard to give feedback on the content and the story. You can't see the forest if each tree you look at is on fire. Here are tricks for proofreading your work:

Use electronic editors. Just because you've spell-checked doesn't mean all is well. Spell-check won't catch some issues, like homophones. We regularly catch there/their/they're, your/you're, and to/too/two mix-ups in our emails. Sometimes, transposing letters creates a different word. When no one proofs the sign for the "quiet zone," and the maintenance staff hangs it anyway, you get Figure 6.9.

Figure 6.9 That's quite a zone!
Source: Courtesy of Eric Bowers

Justin spell-checked and proofread his Branch Network Analysis and Recommendations deck and asked a peer to review it. The peer noticed the misspelling in the title, "Brach Network Analysis and Recommendations," which didn't have the same punch. It turns out that "Brach" is a place in France. At best, his audience would think that Justin was a little sloppy. At worst, they would ask someone else to validate his analysis.

Spell-checkers won't fix grammar errors. That's where electronic editors (a.k.a. grammar checkers) come in. The best electronic editors also check for style issues, like run-on sentences, passive voice, clichés, repetition, and redundancies.

Time-saving software add-ins, extensions, and online tools

Developers have built add-ins that improve productivity and make it easier to make slides consistent. Not all work with Macs. You might need to lobby the technology department to allow them. This is a small sample of add-ins and their tools, and we can't promise they'll still be available when you read this. If you've ever thought, "There's got to be an easier way," chances are someone has created an add-in for it.

Here are useful PowerPoint add-ins and resources:

- **BrightSlide** has tools to match size, format, and animations across shapes, images, charts, and tables. Functions like Align to First and Distribute to Grid make it easy to lay out objects on a slide. And you can standardize animations with an animation library, quickly building storytelling animations.

- **Build-a-Graphic** provides over 10,000 editable, professional graphics useful for infographics, icons, and presentations. It transforms plain text into polished, visually engaging designs.

- **Diagrammer** is a free tool from Duarte with over 4,000 downloadable diagrams. The customizable diagrams are organized by relationship type, like an idea board that sparks new ways to illustrate complex concepts.

- **Power-user** has dozens of tools, including a pipette that works like an advanced format painter, selectively applying format elements. You can use it to paint an object's background and font color, font size, bullet style, or position, without painting anything you don't want. The pipette can be used across multiple slides—for example, copying title formatting and position to all titles in the deck or applying a bullet style to all bullets.

- **Slidewise** identifies and fixes inconsistent fonts, empty placeholders, and hidden objects. It also detects slide layouts from other templates that infected the standard template and audits images for size and quality.

- **SPICE** has an automated agenda and bumper slide tool. It also automates footnote numbering and creates a bibliography slide summarizing all footnotes. It includes fully customizable maps for the world, continents, and US states.

(continued)

- **Think-cell** has a drag-and-drop interface that makes building charts easier. It automates annotations, like difference arrows and scale breaks. It also includes hard-to-build chart types, like Gantt charts.
- **Thor's Hammer**, part of PPTools, makes it easy to put common elements, like tombstones, in the same location across slides.
- **ToolsToo Pro for PowerPoint** has over 130 tools, including the ability to add (or remove) shapes to (or from) a group without ruining the animation. It also copies formatting for tables and rounded-corner arcs. The ability to extract notes to Microsoft Word is worth the price of admission.

Here are useful Google Slides extensions:

- **Insert Icons for Slides** has over 1,800 icons. Icons come in any color and have transparent backgrounds.
- **SlidesPro** adds a toolbar for quick access to color management, layout, and alignment functions. It also has tools for inserting and customizing icons, images, videos, maps, and graphs.
- **Slides Toolbox** streamlines tasks, including table-of-contents creation, batch text editing, and bulk removal of elements like empty text boxes. It also supports batch alignment and bulk image importing, speeding up repetitive tasks.

Read text aloud. This has three benefits. First, it slows you down, making it easier to catch typos. Second, you notice write-like-you-speak issues, like dropped articles or nonparallel structure. Third, it forces you to review the entire deck. In this review, you'll catch text that you never finished writing or that you included on a reused slide but now isn't related to the current presentation.

Create presentation-review checklists. In 1935, the US Air Force was evaluating aircraft from three manufacturers. In pretest evaluations, the Boeing plane was considered superior to the competition. However, during the test flight, the plane stalled and crashed. The investigation ruled the cause as pilot error. One crew member failed to release the elevator lock before takeoff. Given the new plane's complexity and the consequences of missing a key step, the test pilots developed the first aviation checklist, shown in Figure 6.10. Those checklists enabled pilots to safely fly the Boeing plane, and the military eventually ordered over 12,000 planes, now named the B-17.[6] When lives are at stake, getting it right is everything.

Figure 6.10 Pilot's checklist for the B-17
Source: Boeing and US Air Force / Public Domain

Although most presentations aren't a matter of life and death, use checklists to capture common errors. Sample checklists for planning, story, titles, grammar, and slide design are in Figures 6.11–6.15.

> **Presentation Planning Checklist**
> ❑ Assess the audience, purpose, and setting
> ❑ Mind map and storyboard the presentation
>   ❑ Put the most important slides up front
>   ❑ Have the fewest slides required to tell a clear story in the time allotted
> ❑ Write an executive summary if the deck will be forwarded

Figure 6.11 Before starting
Source: John Polk & Associates

Proofread and edit your work   173

> **Story Checklist**
> ❑ Write a presentation title that describes the scope and purpose
> ❑ Test the story for logic, flow, and clarity
> ❑ Ensure key takeaways are clear
> ❑ Include frameworks to support the story
> ❑ Ensure frameworks are consistent across slides

Figure 6.12 Starting engines
Source: John Polk & Associates

> **Slide Titles Checklist**
> ❑ Write slide titles as complete sentences
> ❑ Ensure titles are concise (1 or 2 lines)
> ❑ Read the titles to test if they tell a clear story (horizontal logic)
> ❑ Verify the titles give the main point of each slide (vertical logic)
> ❑ Review titles to ensure they have only one main point

Figure 6.13 Before takeoff
Source: John Polk & Associates

> **Grammar and Style Checklist**
> ❑ Read text aloud to test for tone and parallel construction
> ❑ Word diet text and eliminate runts
> ❑ Spell out acronyms the first time
> ❑ Resolve tautologies—e.g., "general consensus"
> ❑ Eliminate elegant variation—e.g., using "alert" and "warning"
> ❑ Check homophones—e.g., "there," "their," and "they're"
> ❑ Review "e.g." and "i.e." for correct usage and punctuation
> ❑ Find and replace double spaces
> ❑ Search for inappropriate possessives ('s)
> ❑ Search for and delete periods
> ❑ Run spelling and grammar checkers

Figure 6.14 After takeoff
Source: John Polk & Associates

> **Slide Design Checklist**
> ❑ Ensure slides are consistent with the brand standard
>   ❑ Verify colors match the brand palette and don't clash
>   ❑ Replace inconsistent fonts
> ❑ Remove chart junk—e.g., borders, gridlines, and data markers
> ❑ Scan objects for consistent color, size, font size, and location
>   ❑ Titles
>   ❑ Running heads
>   ❑ Tombstones
>   ❑ Footnotes
>   ❑ Page numbers
> ❑ Align and distribute objects
> ❑ Check printouts for printer errors, missing pages, or color issues

Figure 6.15 Final approach
Source: John Polk & Associates

When reviewing slides, there are two options:

- Review the entire checklist for the first slide before reviewing the second.
- Review the first checklist item across all slides before reviewing the second checklist item on each slide.

Both strategies are useful, but we make the case for the second option. Let's say you want to ensure sentence titles are formatted consistently. Focusing on that one aspect on each slide is faster and more effective. Page down quickly to find inconsistencies. You'll get in the zone when fixing issues. Use Format Painter or Repeat Last Command to fix inconsistencies quickly across all slides. It's more effective because you won't get distracted before you've fixed every issue.

Avoid Polk's First Law of Presentations. Several years ago, John decided to craft a set of presentation laws. We modestly call them "Polk's laws of presentations." Here's the first one:

> *The error in your presentation*
> *will be in the last thing you change.*
> John Polk, Polk's first law of presentations

The typical presentation-design process, shown in Figure 6.16, illustrates Polk's first law of presentations in action.

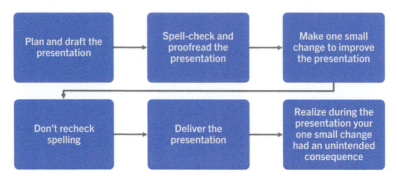

Figure 6.16 The road to hell is paved with good intentions
Source: John Polk & Associates

Polk's First Law of Presentations manifests in many ways:

- Duplicating a slide to preserve the original before a significant change, then forgetting to delete the original version

- Reordering slides for a more effective flow but forgetting to change the agenda, executive summary, or running heads

- Changing a callout box to a less-neon yellow, then forgetting to change every other callout in the deck

- Using the Replace Fonts tool to change the font, then not noticing that the new, slightly bigger font means some text no longer fits in its box

- Grouping objects on a slide to enable aligning and distributing but forgetting that grouping and ungrouping can mess up animation

Have you experienced any of these? We didn't make them up—we've lived through all of them.

The lesson here is to review any last-minute changes manually and spell-check one last time. So, what about the other Polk's Laws? John hasn't written them yet. He needs at least two more to catch Newton!

Find an editor

While working toward his industrial engineering degree, John worked at the Bureau of Engraving and Printing, the government agency that prints currency and stamps. He worked on a project with the production staff to reduce ink usage. As part of training,

John and his boss asked the production staff to complete the following exercise. Please play along at home.

Read this sentence and count how many f's you see. Count them in only one pass—don't go back and recount them.

FINISHED FILES ARE THE RESULT OF YEARS
OF SCIENTIFIC STUDY COMBINED WITH THE
EXPERIENCE OF YEARS.

How many did you count? Many people count only three, but there are six f's. If you counted fewer than six f's, you almost certainly missed the f's in the three instances of the word "of." Because the word "of" is pronounced "ov," your brain may see the f's as v's.

FINISHED FILES ARE THE RESULT OF YEARS
OF SCIENTIFIC STUDY COMBINED WITH THE
EXPERIENCE OF YEARS.

The worst performers on this exercise at the Bureau of Engraving and Printing were the quality inspectors, who checked the finished stamps for printing errors. You'd hope they'd have the best attention to detail! But when John saw them in action, he could see why they were more likely to miss the word "of." When inspecting stamps, the quality inspectors didn't look at individual stamps; they looked at uncut sheets like in Figure 6.17.

Figure 6.17 Curtiss Jenny certified plate proof
Source: Smithsonian / National Postal Museum / CC0 1.0

As the stamps flew past them on a conveyor belt, the inspectors used soft eyes to stare at the pattern created by the moving stamps. When that pattern shifted, they stopped the belt and inspected the sheet at that spot.

You miss the detail when you read the "Finished files" sentence with soft eyes, as most speed-reading courses recommend.

A variation on this theme happens when reviewing your decks. After staring at the slides over days or weeks, you're too close. If you didn't see a typo when creating the draft or revising the content, you're less likely to see it when proofreading because you know what it says. You won't see what's confusing to others because it's not confusing to you. It also doesn't help that it's nine o'clock at night, and you're sick of working on these slides.

We use the term "editor" because good editors do more than proofread. They also contribute in other meaningful ways:

- Giving tough feedback
  - Calling out when dramatic improvements are required
  - Giving feedback on all dimensions, including content and speech
- Paying attention to the details
  - Finding inconsistencies within and across slides
  - Knowing and applying grammar rules
  - Catching typos and double spaces
- Applying their expertise or ignorance, as discussed in Chapter 5, "The Expert Trap"
  - Stress testing the strategy
  - Asking challenging questions
  - Calling out what's unclear to a nonexpert
  - Identifying undefined acronyms and terms

Editors naturally find typos, grammar mistakes, and misaligned boxes. Share the audience, purpose, and setting assessment so they can give content feedback. Share the in-house style guide and preferred external style guide so they can catch design issues.

We do this for a living and don't present or publish anything without John's wife reviewing our material. And she always catches something. She has a unique skill that makes her qualified as a proofreader. She's found hundreds of four-leaf clovers in her lifetime. We call it her "eye for symmetry." Can you see the four-leaf clover in Figure 6.18?

Figure 6.18 How many four-leaf clovers can you find?
Source: Courtesy of Marty Polk

If you found one, did you find the other two? There are three in this photo.

Avoid the Perfectionist Trap by embracing drafts

Wait, are there 11 traps?! There are way more than 10 traps, but that's what sequels are for (working title, *Presentation Pitfalls II: Trap Harder*). The Perfectionist Trap occurs when perfectionism leads to writer's block or wasted time polishing a deck beyond a reasonable return on investment.

> *Trying is the first step toward failure.*[7]
> Homer Simpson, *The Simpsons*

Whether your perfectionist's brain thinks that or not, the desire to be perfect is a roadblock when drafting a deck. Worrying about creating the ideal slide prevents you from even starting.

The mind-mapping and storyboarding techniques from Chapter 2, "The Bury the Lede Trap," mute perfectionism by design. In these exercises, perfection is completing a map and storyboard, not finishing the deck.

Author Tucker Max taught us the "vomit draft" concept: write a first draft quickly to get the ideas out of your head without self-editing.[8] By separating the drafting and the editing stages, editing won't slow down writing.

> *If it's writing time, I write.*
> *I may write garbage, but you can always edit garbage.*
> *You can't edit a blank page.*[9]
> Jodi Picoult, NPR (attributed)

Of course, we don't advise presenting a vomit draft. You must edit. As perfectionists ourselves, it's hard to admit, but there is a point where incremental work to improve a presentation doesn't deliver an incrementally better outcome. A typical presentation-review process follows Figure 6.19.

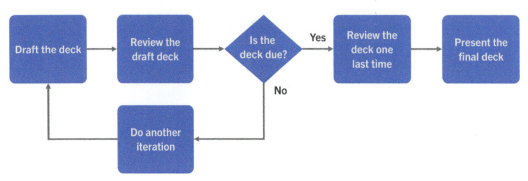

Figure 6.19 The never-ending story
Source: John Polk & Associates

And when you must review a deck with your boss and boss's boss, this iteration process becomes more complex. While iteration is inevitable and valuable, it doesn't have to be endless. Figure 6.20 shows a more rational process.

Figure 6.20 The eventually ending story
Source: John Polk & Associates

The key to knowing when iteration reaches diminishing returns is to refer back to the audience, purpose, and setting assessment. A less stringent review process is sufficient *if* any of these conditions are true:

- The audience knows, trusts, and likes you.
- The purpose is to get feedback on an early-stage idea or project versus a final recommendation or decision meeting.
- The setting is more casual versus an in-person, boardroom presentation.

To silence our inner perfectionist, we turn to two pieces of advice from different executive coaches:

- **"Done is better than perfect."** This clever non sequitur reminds us that we can't change the world until we share our work with it. This phrase motivates us when debating whether to set aside a near-final but potentially imperfect deck, proposal, or email to review later. Usually, it's better to drive action sooner by hitting send than to delay for the sake of perfection.

- **"Get comfortable with soft launches."** We received this advice when agonizing over our website. Yes, a shoddy website will hurt your professional image, but a professional-looking website, even without the sections we eventually want to build, is better than an unlaunched website. Most of our work is electronic except for printed books, so we can continuously improve it after a soft launch.

Typos and other mistakes can be frustrating and embarrassing. Despite our best efforts, typos invariably infect our work. If you catch one while presenting, don't let it throw you. If all else fails, blame the mistake on the guy on the left in Figure 6.21.

Figure 6.21 Titivillus and an error-prone scribe
Source: Jean Hey / Jean Pichore / Master of the Scandalous Chronicle / Wikimedia Commons / Public Domain

Meet Titivillus, a demon who works for Satan to introduce errors into scribes' work. Imagine if you had to create a deck on parchment with a quill pen and ink. Or imagine you're a printer who forgot the "not" in one of the Ten Commandments and wrote:

"Thou shalt commit adultery." This happened in England in 1631, resulting in what is now called the "Sinners' Bible" or the "Wicked Bible."[10] Of course you would want to blame the error on a demon.

Note: Portions of this chapter were first published in the article "Get Behind Me, Titivillus! How to Avoid Mistakes in Your Work" by John Polk in *Nightingale Magazine*, the journal of the Data Visualization Society, June 8, 2022.

Key Takeaways

Review your work to catch typos, grammar mistakes, and inconsistent formats, which damage credibility.

- ✓ Write like you speak, not like a lawyer.
- ✓ Correct common grammar and style mistakes like non-parallel structure, elegant variation, acronym redundancy, and two spaces after a period.
- ✓ Stay current on grammar rules, which evolve.
- ✓ Use electronic editors to check spelling, grammar, and style during writing *and* as the last step.
- ✓ Read text aloud to catch typos, nonparallel structure, and write-like-you-speak issues.
- ✓ Prevent common errors with presentation checklists for planning, story, slide titles, grammar, and slide design.
- ✓ Always find someone else to review and proofread the presentation and tell them not to hold back any feedback.
- ✓ Share the audience, purpose, and setting assessment and relevant style guides with reviewers.
- ✓ Understand the point of diminishing returns to avoid wasting time making slides better than necessary to get the job done.
- ✓ Blame errors on a demon!

Figure 7.1 Digital lipstick on a pig
Source: Laura Anderson / Unsplash

7

The Lipstick on a Pig Trap

Design professional, engaging slides using an elegant format and intentional contrast to let your robust content shine through.

Presenters often tell us, "I want to make my slides look pretty." That's the wrong goal! The right goal is to make the slides more impactful.

> *Most of us know as much of history as a pig does of lipsticks.*[1]
> Charles F. Lummis, Los Angeles Times editorial

> *A hog in armour is still but a hog.*[2]
> Thomas Fuller, Gnomologia

Whether it's pigs or hogs, wearing lipstick or armor, combining them doesn't make them prettier or tougher; it just makes them angry (although the lipsticked pig in Figure 7.1 looks happy).

Presenters fall into the Lipstick on a Pig Trap when they spend significant time creating pretty or overly designed slides for content that isn't robust enough to support the message. Lipstick on a pig hurts both components of the signal-to-noise ratio discussed in Chapter 3, "The Black Hole Trap." You add noise by making design choices solely to make slides pretty. And you reduce the signal when the effort to make slides pretty distracts you from improving the content.

Previous chapters focused on ensuring you have great content. This chapter focuses on ensuring that designs are professional, accessible, and engaging without wasting time on non-value-added formatting choices. That distinction is often hard to make.

Avoid the Lipstick on a Pig Trap by ensuring every design decision serves a purpose and by actively removing visual noise. Boost the signal with effective eye flow, white space, and contrast with a consistent, accessible slide format. Finally, build design principles into the theme and template, supporting slide and content libraries.

Make intentional design decisions not driven by arbitrary preference

Presentation software gives you many options. Like a pig at a buffet, sometimes more isn't always better. The multitude of options forces you to make time-consuming decisions or to stick with weak defaults. Every design decision affects your communication.

Remember the Platinum Rule of Presentations from Chapter 1, "The Frankenstein Trap," shown in Figure 7.2?

Figure 7.2 We're repeating this because it's important
Source: John Polk & Associates

Decisions based on the Platinum Rule add signal. Decisions based on what might look cool add noise. The irony isn't lost on us that we combined several fancy design choices for the Platinum Rule graphic. While we agree this might seem extra, the design draws attention to an important concept.

Sometimes, presenters and designers justify a design decision by saying, "I like it that way." They often copy from existing designs or embrace a design trend. This doesn't mean they are wrong, but it's insufficient justification. At that point, we ask, "Why?" If they can tie the why back to the audience, purpose, or setting, we can evaluate whether it's the best decision to achieve that goal.

Effective design shapes the audience's experience by aligning with the purpose and using the setting thoughtfully. It can be bold, like a full-slide image, or subtle, like a default background color choice. In all cases, good design should be intentional.

Avoid inherently noisy presentation software capabilities

Early in our workshop we ask participants to note their presentation best practices and pet peeves. A typical virtual whiteboard session looks like Figure 7.3, with a zoom-in on pet peeves.

Figure 7.3 Pet peevers gonna peeve
Source: John Polk & Associates

Unsurprisingly, asking 30 workshop participants to write on the screen creates a noisy slide! Often, a pet peeve is simply the opposite of a best practice. But asking for pet peeves lets the haters get it out of their system. The quadrant with design pet peeves always includes the visual noise issues discussed in the following sections.

Presentation software makes it easy to crank up the noise in decks. Noisy design choices are everywhere, and they distract from the content, including in Figure 7.4.

Figure 7.4 Aren't there enough distractions in life?
Source: John Polk & Associates

We advise against these common noise sources in most scenarios:

- **Distraction 1: Clashing colors.** Red text on a blue background is a common corporate combination. However, this combination can create an optical artifact called "color vibration" that makes it hard to focus on the words. Using neon colors or mixing pastels with dark colors also generates noise.

- **Distraction 2: Gradients.** In addition to being noisy, the X gradient has the unintended consequence of subtly crossing out important text.

- **Distraction 3: Shadows.** This effect gives the illusion that objects are hovering slightly above the slide. Do you want the audience to believe the box is hovering slightly over the slide? We make rare exceptions to create depth for physical objects.

- **Distractions 4 and 5: ALL CAPS and *italics*.** These typographic emphasizers are harder to read, and writing in all caps is associated with shouting in texting culture. Writing in all caps is less of an issue for short headers or stylized quotations. Save the italics for emphasizing short words or phrases, foreign words, quotations, or book and movie titles, depending on your style guide.

- **Distraction 6: Word art.** Most word art, by definition, adds visual noise to text. Save it for birthday party invitations.

For most uses, bold is sufficient for emphasis, and font size is sufficient for hierarchy.

Remove the noise from charts

Presentation software has a ton of options for customizing charts. The chart in Figure 7.5 illustrates the common noise found in data visualizations.

We've never seen a chart in the wild with all these issues, but we've seen *all* these issues in the wild. How many can you spot? Edward Tufte, Yale professor emeritus and

Figure 7.5 The noisiest chart ever built?
Source: Adapted from "Communicating Your Analysis" by John Polk, in *Data & Analytics for Instructional Designers* by Megan Torrance, ©ASTD DBA the Association for Talent Development (ATD); 2023 / Reproduced with the permission of John Polk and ATD

author of multiple data visualization books, called this type of visual noise "chartjunk."[3] Remember, anything that isn't signal is noise. The yellow callouts in Figure 7.6 annotate the chart noise.

Figure 7.6 So much wrong

Source: Adapted from "Communicating Your Analysis" by John Polk, in *Data & Analytics for Instructional Designers* by Megan Torrance, ©ASTD DBA the Association for Talent Development (ATD); 2023 / Reproduced with the permission of John Polk and ATD

We'll go through the issues one at a time:

- **Issue 1: Backgrounds.** Filling in the color behind a chart draws attention to the part of the chart with no information. Thankfully, most presentation software no longer has a default background color for charts.

- **Issue 2: Borders.** The x- and y-axes already define the chart area, making borders redundant. It's exaggerated with a thick red border for effect, prompting one workshop participant to say, "That border is literally giving me a headache." For objects, contrasting colors define edges clearly, so borders are unnecessary and burdensome to keep consistent in thickness and color.

- **Issue 3: Crowded axis labels.** The defaults for axis labels typically set major units too frequently. Thin them out to reduce clutter. Medium-gray axes minimize distractions by keeping the focus on the data.

- **Issue 4: Beveled edges (a.k.a. 3D format).** This graphic effect creates a 3D look using properties like light angle and gradients, but it has two issues. It slightly complicates chart interpretation and requires additional effort to ensure consistency. Avoid other graphic effects like glow, soft edges, and patterns—they may work for images but rarely suit charts.

- **Issue 5: Gridlines.** Gridlines are the most common chartjunk. While they help estimate column sizes, they rarely align with column tops, forcing the audience to interpolate. Removing them simplifies the chart and improves clarity.

- **Issue 6: Data tables.** A data table forces the audience to look away from the column tops, making comparisons harder. Data *labels* are more convenient and better convey column heights than gridlines.

- **Issue 7: Legends (a.k.a. keys).** Using a legend forces the audience to bounce between the chart and the key, like watching a tennis match from center court. Instead, add data series labels directly to the chart. Yes, it's more work, but labeling reduces confusion. Place labels on the right for clarity, avoiding clutter near the y-axis.

Looking at the before-and-after charts in Figure 7.7 is like standing on an airport runway without and then with noise-canceling headphones. Blasting the audience with too much visual noise obscures the main point. During workshops, participants breathe an audible sigh of relief when shown the clean chart.

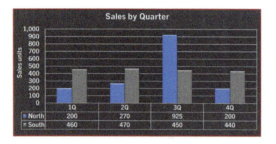 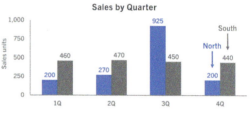

Figure 7.7 Better one or better two?
Source: Adapted from "Communicating Your Analysis" by John Polk, in *Data & Analytics for Instructional Designers* by Megan Torrance, ©ASTD DBA the Association for Talent Development (ATD); 2023 / Reproduced with the permission of John Polk and ATD

Employ eye-flow principles and white space

Your eyes follow a natural flow determined by culture and reading habits. Visually compelling slides follow these rules to leave a lasting impression.

Apply the rule of thirds for visual appeal. John Thomas Smith described this visual design rule of thumb in 1797.[4] Dividing an image into nine identical rectangles creates four intersections, called power points (no relation), like in Figure 7.8.

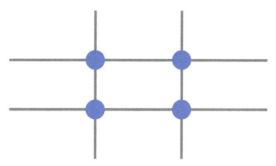

Figure 7.8 Four power points
Source: John Polk & Associates

Essential components should rest on these points. Compare two treatments of the waterfall image in Figures 7.9 and 7.10.

Figure 7.9 Centered waterfall, hogging the spotlight
Source: Courtesy of John Polk

Figure 7.10 Rule-of-thirds waterfall, confident in its brilliance
Source: Courtesy of John Polk

When the waterfall sits in the center, it dominates the image. The waterfall draws your eyes back to it, and it's hard to look at anything else. Nature isn't orderly and centered; it's messy. Doesn't the rule-of-thirds image feel more natural? The waterfall sits along the right power points, which allows it to stand out without taking up the entire image.

Position elements along the Gutenberg (a.k.a. Z) pattern to follow natural attention flow. In Western culture, eyes start at the upper left-hand corner, then proceed to the right before dropping to the next row, as if reading a book, like in Figure 7.11.

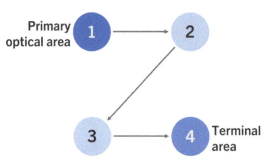

Figure 7.11 Zig-zagging focus
Source: John Polk & Associates

Edmund Arnold named this pattern after Johannes Gutenberg, who invented the movable-type printing press. The overall reading gravity is down and to the right. The workshop agenda in Figure 7.12 assumes participants follow the Z pattern.

Figure 7.12 How do you scan the agenda?
Source: John Polk & Associates

Most participants track from "Tell a clear story" to "Leverage graphics," then to "Reduce noise," and finally to "Present with confidence." Even when including bullet points under each box, participants read the blue boxes before reading the bullet points.

Design text-dense slides with the F pattern to match natural information scanning. Using eye-tracking cameras, Jakob Nielsen discovered that readers use the pattern in Figure 7.13 to consume web pages with text-dense content.[5]

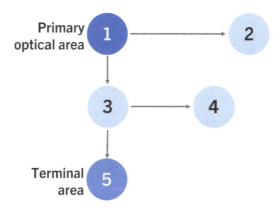

Figure 7.13 Scanning dense information content
Source: John Polk & Associates

Readers start in the upper left and then scan to the right. Their eye flow anchors to the left side and then proceeds downward, scanning to the right occasionally. This is an information-skimming technique. When reading a book, you follow the Z pattern, reading most of the content. When reading web pages or newspapers, you scan headlines to see if you're interested, then read content until you're bored and move on to the next paragraph, bullet point, or headline.

In the upper left of Figure 7.14, you take in the slide title, graphic title, and two blue boxes, reading left to right. Then, you likely scan the benefits listed under "Driving action" but might not read them all. You're more likely to skip the benefits under "Saving time."

Figure 7.14 Did you read the whole thing or scan it?
Source: John Polk & Associates

Employ eye-flow principles and white space   193

Embrace white space (a.k.a. negative space) to declutter and create emphasis. Empty areas between and around objects reduce noise and guide the audience to focus on the signal. More white space signals more importance. Clutter is taxing because it creates competing signals of importance. Apple's advertising elegantly uses negative space in Figure 7.15.

Figure 7.15 White space can be black
Source: Apple Inc.

Consider using white space as a cleaner, modern alternative to bullet points. Bullet points are a subtle visual cue, but they are ubiquitous. Their goal is to separate thoughts cleanly. Figure 7.16 illustrates the same slide with and without bullet points.

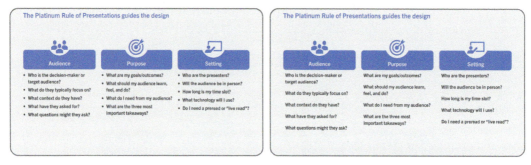

Figure 7.16 Separation is necessary; bullet points are not
Source: John Polk & Associates

When designing without bullet points, increase the line spacing between rows. This creates additional white space, serving the same purpose as bullet points.

Without bullet points, text columns appear closer together. If that leaves too little white space between columns, shrink the column width. As a last resort, add vertical lines to ensure clear separation, like in Figure 7.17.

Figure 7.17 Vertical lines create overt separation; dashed lines create noise
Source: John Polk & Associates

We don't recommend dashed lines. Dashed lines became popular in architectural drawings to show hidden elements. Designers often make lines dashed or dotted to de-emphasize them, but these styles are inherently noisy. Some readers see each dash rather than a line made of dashes. Instead, de-emphasize the lines by making them gray and narrow. However, dotted lines can be used to contrast solid lines—for example, in a line chart that has data representing actual (solid) and forecast (dotted) performance.

We use all these styles but avoid vertical lines if possible. Bullet points are such an easy default that they continue to be popular in business decks, so we want to demonstrate how to use them correctly. Removing bullet points gives a more polished look but requires additional real estate to create effective separation between the text. The no-bullet-point approach works best for marketing materials, all-hands decks, and TED-style presentations. Using separator lines is our least recommended style. It takes time and effort to maintain consistent separator lines. We still use bullet points for internal decision-making decks.

Squinting for clarity

Artists and designers know that squinting at their work gives them a different perspective. It allows the details, words, and lines to fade so they can focus on shapes and colors. It enables them to see the forest without the pesky trees getting in the way.

By squinting, artists and designers evaluate visual harmony through relevant design principles:[6]

- **Balance:** Create symmetrical or asymmetrical arrangements to distribute visual weight.
- **Contrast:** Use opposing properties in color, size, and texture to highlight critical elements.

(continued)

- **Emphasis:** Highlight objects strategically to create clear focal points.
- **Movement:** Generate a sense of motion to guide the audience's eyes.
- **Proportion/scale:** Establish size relationships among objects to signal relative importance.
- **Repetition/rhythm:** Repeat objects throughout a deck to improve navigation and recall.
- **Unity:** Leverage consistency to ensure all objects contribute to the cohesive whole.

Compare the slide and its blurred version that simulates squinting in Figure 7.18.

Figure 7.18 Blurring lets you see objects' locations and proportions clearly
Sources: (screen) vasabii / Adobe Stock Photos / John Polk & Associates

The slides are unified in their message and color consistency, but the blurred version highlights the unbalanced space in the upper left, which fights against the Z pattern. Do your eyes go to the camera or the slide? Also, the screen image is large and imposing compared to the camera and text. Figure 7.19 fixes these issues.

Figure 7.19 Balanced slide following the Z pattern
Sources: (screen) vasabii / Adobe Stock Photos / John Polk & Associates

(continued)

> The updated composition starts with the screen, flows into the text, and ends with the camera as the focal point. We resized the screen and camera for balance.
>
> Squinting at slides in slide sorter view highlights where the deck may be dull or predictable. When slide after slide looks the same, the audience might become bored. Adding contrast, like a full-slide image or a different background color, creates an opportunity to recapture the audience's attention. This is useful lipstick ... if it emphasizes something important!

Establish a consistent design baseline

> *Consistency is one of the most powerful usability principles:*
> *when things always behave the same,*
> *users don't have to worry about what will happen.*[7]
>
> Jakob Nielsen, *Eyetracking Web Usability*

Good design embraces the tension between consistency and contrast. Both are important; however, effective contrast cannot exist without a consistent baseline.

The design baseline acts as a visual language, with standards for size, color, borders, space, and proportion. We include a title at the top of most slides with the same font and brand color. A consistent, clean format ensures content remains the focus. Inconsistent formatting can distract the audience and waste time. A uniform approach tells the audience that similar objects share a relationship or hierarchy.

Because big-box electronics stores are bright and loud, factory TV defaults max out screen brightness and bass to try to stand out. These defaults are unsuitable for a home setting. Similarly, presentation software developers often create defaults with a setting in mind that differs from yours. In addition, presentation software defaults are often designed to showcase flashy features rather than practical ones. Software that is designed with a TED Talk in mind may encourage you to use design elements that are inappropriate for a decision meeting.

Additionally, defaults become dull and uninspiring with repeated use. The phrase "familiarity breeds contempt" applies to design; overused colors like black and white, standard fonts such as Times New Roman and Arial, and common slide elements like bullet points feel increasingly mundane and unprofessional the more you see them.

To impart a high-quality feel to decks, move away from some factory defaults and establish a visual language with intentional design defaults.

We designed our most popular workshop for participants who create slides for internal presentations, prioritizing functionality over flashy aesthetics. Our goal is to demonstrate a simple yet elegant style that slide creators who aren't graphic designers can achieve. Its primary purpose is to support an internal decision meeting, not a TED Talk.

A combination of themes, templates, slide masters, brand kits, and styles control design decisions that apply across slides, depending on your software. A blank deck holds infinite possibilities—and just as many decisions. Leveraging a theme and its cousins reduces those decisions by establishing the colors, fonts, background, and slide layouts. A template includes standardized slides and footer text.

In a perfect world, your brand team provided a simple, elegant presentation template with the company's color palette and preformatted slides. However, brand-standard templates often lack built-in design elements, include unnecessary elements, or are impractical for daily use. Combining slides from mismatched templates guarantees additional formatting work. When you have a good template, you *still* must ensure that all authors start from that template.

In an imperfect world, your brand team slapped a logo on the default theme. In that case, create a clean, elegant template, distribute it to authors, and insist they use it. You still need to review for inconsistencies and glitches when consolidating the deck—a process we call "getting your pigs in a row."

If you need to create a template, check out *Building PowerPoint Templates* by Echo Swinford and Julie Terberg. It's a comprehensive guide to themes and templates.

Choose high-contrast, complementary colors. Before the audience has time to read the slides or look at the images, they notice the colors. Using too many colors is distracting. Choose one dark color from the brand palette for solid objects. Use the eyedropper from your presentation software to look up the exact hex code.

We make an exception for red logos. Red appears in many retail logos because it grabs attention on street corners. That attention-grabbing aspect is too much when used as a background color or for standard shapes. We use light blue for lower-priority solid objects. Arbitrary color choices mean the audience is looking for meaning where there isn't any. Red can mean stop, warning, or bad in most Western cultures. People say "red ink" when a company loses money. So, save the other colors in the brand palette for data visualization or imparting meaning, like red/yellow/green for project status.

You've seen our color palette, in Figure 7.20, throughout the book.

Figure 7.20 John Polk & Associates' color palette
Source: John Polk & Associates

The first significant design choice was selecting a primary brand color, blue. Using dark and light gray gives a softer, less factory-default look than the default black and white. Design decisions can be subtle. Most audience members won't be conscious of the light gray backgrounds and dark gray text, but subconsciously, it creates a more professional impression. For logos with white backgrounds, use a background removal tool. We use medium gray to de-emphasize objects, while our accent colors are shades of blue. The complementary shades of green, yellow, and red indicate status. Quickly select colors and ensure consistency by building them into the theme.

Check the color palette against light and dark backgrounds. This highlights the need to avoid the red-on-blue combination causing vibration.

Pick one font. Pick one font. Just one. Not two. A popular template style uses a serif font for titles and a sans-serif font for everything else. Monsters! Ensuring consistency with two fonts is nearly impossible and usually not worth the effort. Most presentation design software and some add-ins have replace-font tools. Having two fonts thwarts these tools.

> [Avoid] anything silly, jazzy,
> medieval, comic, too small, too large ...
> The font should never shout louder than the work.[8]
>
> Max Porter, quoted in "When Fonts Fight,
> Times New Roman Conquers" by Alison Flood

Choose a font that connotes your business style, unlike the fonts in Figure 7.21.

Jazzy

Comic

Silly

Medieval

Too Small

Too Large

Figure 7.21 Fonts to avoid if your business isn't a Medieval Times restaurant
Source: John Polk & Associates

Rather than defaulting to Arial or Times New Roman, we went with the more modern, although still business appropriate, Trade Gothic New. Here are additional font considerations:

- **Avoid specialty fonts.** Not all fonts are free or included in all software. If you use a specialty font, you may have to embed it in decks.

- **Ensure the font has "built-in" bold and italics.** Otherwise, the software has to generate bold and italics, and you might not like the results.

- **Pay attention to kerning, lining figures, and specialty characters.** Narrow or condensed fonts help label chart elements clearly while keeping text readable. However, overly tight or wide spacing can make words blend, or spaces appear doubled, like in Figure 7.22. Also, avoid fonts with nonlining figures or odd special characters.

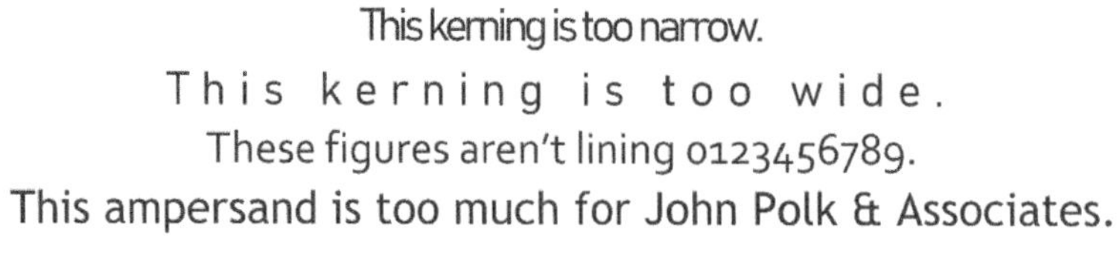

This kerning is too narrow.
This kerning is too wide.
These figures aren't lining 0123456789.
This ampersand is too much for John Polk & Associates.

Figure 7.22 Kerning and lining and ampersands, oh my!
Source: John Polk & Associates

Julie Terberg covers these topics and more in her white paper *Choosing Fonts for PowerPoint Templates*, available on her website, designtopresent.com.[9]

Keep the template simple. Many templates developed by corporate brand groups or external graphic designers are extra. They have more stuff than they need to do the job: fonts, objects, colors, backgrounds, and brand logos or graphics. These objects often encroach on the space required for content, introducing the risk that content and template objects clash.

Build a clean blank slide master. The goal is clear, simple readability. While we don't recommend text-only slides, the slide in Figure 7.23 serves as the theme's foundation, and most slides inherit its structure. Use dark text on a light background selected from your color palette for high contrast.

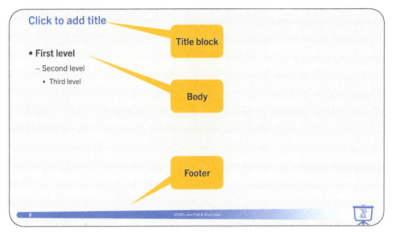

Figure 7.23 Blank slide master with standard components labeled
Source: John Polk & Associates

Let's discuss the three main components:

- **Title:** Draw attention to the title through location, color, and size. Positioned at the top left, it's the first thing the audience reads, whether they follow a Z or F pattern. The bold blue font, our brand's primary color, is 24 pt.—large enough to stand out but compact enough for a precise two-line sentence title. Left and top text alignment prevents shifting during slide transitions and ensures text starts at the same location, whether there are one or two lines of text. Balanced margins, about ½-inch from the left and right slide edges, provide white space.

- **Body:** Use a dark gray font. In corporate templates, it might not be worth fighting the inevitable inconsistency between black and dark gray text. The text placeholder matches the title placeholder in width, with height and placement ensuring healthy white space above and below. For readability, we set line spacing to 1.2 with 6 pt. after, and bullet points alternate between solid circles

Establish a consistent design baseline

and dashes to indicate hierarchy. Differentiate text in the hierarchy; we bold primary text and use unbolded, smaller fonts for de-emphasis. We set hanging indents to ¼-inch for clarity, with second-level dashes aligning under first-level text, grouping items neatly without wasting space, as shown in Figure 7.24.

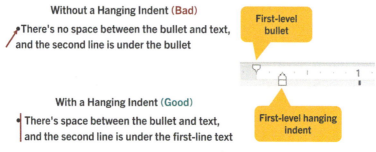

Figure 7.24 Finally getting the hang of it
Source: John Polk & Associates

- **Footer:** The slide footer holds information the audience can find if needed but usually ignores, like slide numbers, copyright, and a logo. Our footer includes a blue gradient stripe, echoing a projector light beam shining on the screen in our logo, adding subtle visual appeal without distraction. The footer contains small-font slide numbers and a copyright statement, set automatically in the slide master—essential for consistency. To the right, our logo rests on the bottom edge, giving the appearance of a projector screen sitting on the slide base.

Having a logo on every slide is a given for most business presentations. The theory is that all communications should support the brand identity. However, Garr Reynolds, author of *Presentation Zen*, has made the case to eliminate logos from slides.[10] For an internal presentation, everyone knows what company they work for. For an external presentation, having a logo on the cover and a "contact information" slide is sufficient for the audience to know your company and its brand.

Even so, we include the John Polk & Associates logo on our slides because they often serve as reference material for coaching and workshop clients. Since our slides are frequently shared without a cover slide, the logo ensures they can be traced back to us. If a logo appears on every slide, keep it small, use a low-key version (such as monochrome), skip the slogan, and place it in the footer.

Audiences rarely focus on the footer, so the logo fades into the background rather than attracting unnecessary attention. A coaching client works for a company with fancy scrollwork incorporated into their brand identity. On cover or section divider slides, it's a cool nod to the brand. On content slides, it's a noisy distraction that eats up precious real estate.

Use a dark background for text-sparse slides. For slides with minimal text, like quotations, use light gray font on a dark background, like Figure 7.25. The font is light gray to contrast with the background. Shifting from a light background to a dark background creates emphasis and reengages the audience's attention. Importantly, we don't recommend using the dark-background slide just for a change of pace.

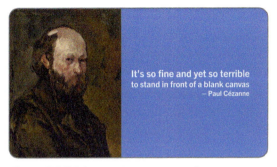

Figure 7.25 Cézanne knows our pain
Source: Paul Cézanne / Wikimedia Commons / Public Domain

Designers often use dark backgrounds for presentations projected on a large screen. This avoids the harsh glare from a white background, but this is a deal with the devil. Dark backgrounds limit color choices for slide objects. And with a blue background, red objects, especially text, might appear to vibrate.

Make it easy to duplicate the most-used objects. We include the slide in Figure 7.26 in our template to round out our visual language. It has the most common objects. Think of this slide as the Swiss Army knife in the presentation tool kit—everything you need

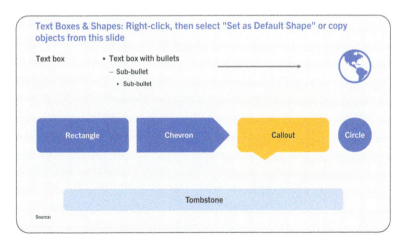

Figure 7.26 A slide-design Swiss Army knife
Source: John Polk & Associates

Establish a consistent design baseline 203

in one place. To maintain format consistency, copy and paste objects from this slide. Copying and pasting tombstones and "source" text boxes from this slide also maintains consistent object location across slides. Some presentation software can save formatted shapes and text boxes as the default. Then, shapes and text boxes always match the standard.

We also create standard slides for tables, charts, and other common layouts.

Set guides to enforce white space. These dotted lines can be visible when building slides but don't show in presentation mode. Use guides, like in Figure 7.27, to maintain margins and ensure consistent slide layout. Setting guides in the slide master or theme makes them appear on all slides using that layout and helps maintain consistency across slides. Setting them in the slide master also prevents users from unintentionally moving the guides. Setting guides outside the slide master supports consistent alignment within a slide.

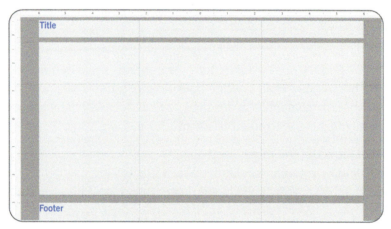

Figure 7.27 Guides set to maintain margins and enable the rule of thirds
Source: John Polk & Associates

The guides show the correct title placement and include a white-space border (highlighted in gray) so objects don't crowd it. They also create a border around the slide so objects don't go to the edges. The remaining guides support using the rule of thirds for slide objects.

Putting space around the slide borders is useful for two reasons. Margins prevent crowding the edges and minimize the risk that a misaligned projector cuts off content. It's embarrassing when slide titles aren't visible during the all-hands presentation because they are too close to the border and get cut off. True story.

Minimize design objects intended to create separation. Solid color blocks behind the slide title or lines below the slide title, like in Figure 7.28, are common but unnecessary design objects.

Figure 7.28 Overused color block and line title "lipstick"
Source: John Polk & Associates

Yes, color blocks and lines can separate a title from the body, but so can white space and a larger or bold font in your brand color.

Templates with a brand design or color block on the right or left side make it prohibitively time-consuming to center or distribute objects evenly in the remaining white space. Compare the slides in Figure 7.29. When centered on the slide, the white space to the left and right of the globe is uneven. But centering the globe within the white space accurately requires adding lines at the edge of the white space, distributing the globe between those lines, and then deleting the lines—way more work than you want to do on every slide.

Figure 7.29 Confusing centering caused by an unnecessary right color block
Source: John Polk & Associates

Establish a consistent design baseline 205

Make the template the default. Does your corporate template automatically appear when creating a new presentation? If not, work with your technology team to add the file to the template folder. This way, no one must search for the template or wonder if it's the latest version. If your technology team won't distribute it, ask everyone to save the template file manually.

> ### A chiropractor for your slides
>
> Aligning and distributing tools are critical to creating professional decks. Like inconsistent formatting, unaligned objects distract the audience from the content and increase the cognitive load to digest it. Less-forgiving audience members might assume you lack the skills to align objects or just don't care. Neither is a good look.
>
> A coworker highlighted this point in the text in Figure 7.30.
>
>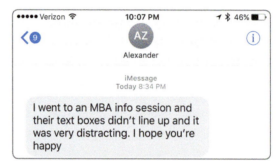
>
> **Figure 7.30** Yes, we are happy
> Source: Courtesy of Alex Zaiken
>
> Here are four strategies for aligning and distributing objects easily while maintaining consistent margins:
>
> - Turn on guides to ensure all objects are within the margins and check object alignment.
> - Use the red auto-align lines that pop up when moving objects.
> - Use the Align and Distribute tools.
> - Add the Align and Distribute tools to a custom toolbar.

We can't stress this enough: a suboptimal template that everyone uses is better than everyone using individually modified templates. Even if the individually modified templates are better, the inconsistency hurts the quality and efficiency of collaborative presentations.

Yes, you should work to improve the organization's template. But go to the source. Influence leaders and the brand team to improve the template for everyone. Influence the technology team to distribute the template. That's what John did despite having no authority over the brand or technology teams.

Take this book to the source. If you need backup, contact us. Good templates are the first line of defense for ensuring consistent formatting.

Reserve contrast for engagement, emphasis, and professional feel

Content is no longer king.
We expect really good content.
Context is king, and contrast is queen.[11]

Mike Parkinson, author of *Do-It-Yourself Billion Dollar Graphics*

Context includes all the Platinum Rule elements described in Chapter 1, "The Frankenstein Trap." There are two broad forms of contrast. The first includes any design element intended to engage the audience and draw their attention to key parts of the slide. This requires establishing a design baseline that improves on the factory defaults. To have contrast, you must first have consistency. Without an established baseline, the deck will look like a hot mess. Once you establish that baseline, introduce contrasting designs to keep the audience engaged. The contrast will grab the audience's attention, and they will assign importance to it just like preattentive attributes from Chapter 4, "The Just the Facts Trap."

The second form of contrast includes design effects that make slides look more professional for more formal presentations, like sales pitches, town halls, and TED Talks. When used with constraint and consistency, design effects make slides stand out from the crowd. Professional-looking slides create a positive halo effect for the work. When the slides look different, people pay attention.

Design decisions made solely for aesthetic diversity create "arbitrary uniqueness." The audience might assume that the change was purposeful and then try to assign meaning to it. At best, this takes cognitive energy away from the true purpose. At worst, the audience assigns unintended meanings.

Figure 7.31 illustrates the natural tension between reducing noise and adding professional design elements. For internal business meetings, keep designs simple but not simplistic. Simplistic decks are boring and look amateurish. For external meetings or important internal meetings, like town halls, include design elements that leverage contrast to increase engagement and demonstrate professional skill. Just ensure all design elements have a reason, or your decks will look extra.

Figure 7.31 Avoid simplistic designs, but don't go overboard
Source: John Polk & Associates

Clients often tell us their bosses will think they have too much time on their hands if they take our design advice. Decide if your designs look overworked or if your boss lacks your design sense or software skill. The last case is an opportunity to raise the bar for the team.

Vary font, color, size, and alignment to create a different voice. An exception to the one-font rule is using a font to illustrate a point. A script font simulates writing on a whiteboard. A serif font, like Times New Roman, simulates text in a newspaper. The dark background, script font, and shadow effect in Figure 7.32 contrast with typical content slides.

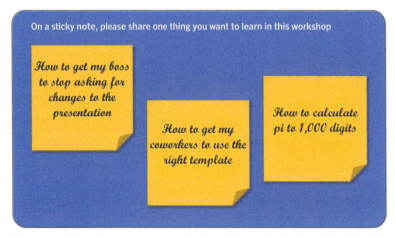

Figure 7.32 It's like someone wrote the sticky notes by hand but legibly
Source: John Polk & Associates

The script font echoes handwritten sticky notes, the shadow effect reinforces the shapes' curled edges, and the lack of alignment mimics sticky notes on a wall. Since the script font is harder to read, make the font larger and keep the notes short.

For quotations and other low-text slides, use a large font. For a polished look, adjust each line's font size to make them left and right justified, like Figure 7.33.

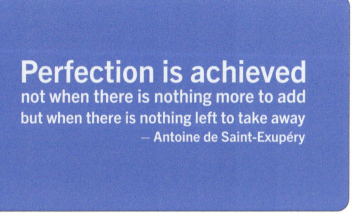

Figure 7.33 Perfect margins
Source: John Polk & Associates

Notice how the quotation lines break at the sentence clauses? This makes it easier for the audience to parse. Avoid breaking up a thought or phrase. Here are rules of thumb for splitting lines:

- Break after commas.
- Break before coordinating conjunctions, like "and," "but," "or," "nor," "for," "so," and "yet."
- Break before subordinating conjunctions, like "although," "because," "since," "unless," and "while."
- Make important phrases span an entire line, like "Perfection is achieved."
- Don't break in the middle of a phrase, like "the quick brown fox."

To test line breaks, read the text aloud and insert a long pause at the end of each line. You're on the right track if the reading feels natural and dramatic.

Use color for emphasis. When presenting several options, use color to accent the recommendation. The black, red, and green colors in Figure 7.34 reinforce the terrible, bad, and good assessments for the quadrants.

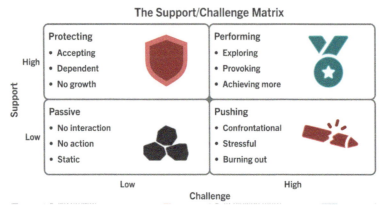

Figure 7.34 Green is good, like high-performing teams
Source: John Polk & Associates

Design in layers and use spotlights to emphasize objects. Because maps are information dense, like in Figure 7.35, they are naturally noisy.

Figure 7.35 Washington, DC, a monument to monuments
Source: Google LLC

210 The Lipstick on a Pig Trap

When used in a talk on presidential monuments and memorials, the map's detail will distract the audience. A spotlight effect solves this problem by making parts of the image stand out. To create a spotlight effect, duplicate and layer the map. Make the map on the bottom layer light gray, then use Crop to Shape to create oval spotlights to direct the audience's attention, like in Figure 7.36. The combined image in Figure 7.37 highlights the presidential monuments and memorials on the map. Animation lets you discuss the spotlights one at a time.

Figure 7.36 Grayscale map and monument measles
Source: Google LLC

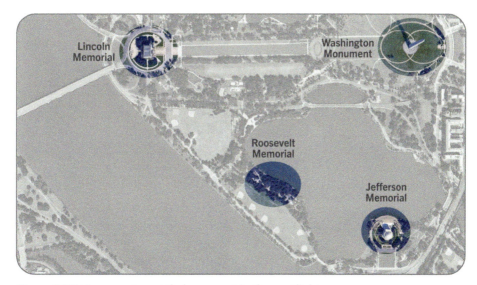

Figure 7.37 Monuments get their moment in the spotlight
Source: Google LLC

Use gradient boxes to make text legible on images. Images are big, bold, and dramatic! One challenge with using full-screen images is that it can be difficult to incorporate

Reserve contrast for engagement, emphasis, and professional feel

text. The text in Figure 7.38 is hard to read where it overlaps with the couch and busy background.

Figure 7.38 Break time for yogis
Source: LIGHTFIELD STUDIOS / Adobe Stock Photos

Use a gradient-filled box that goes from opaque to transparent, like in Figure 7.39, to create contrast with the text and make it readable in Figure 7.40.

Figure 7.39 Gradients as calming as a deep breath
Source: LIGHTFIELD STUDIOS / Adobe Stock Photos

Figure 7.40 The pretzel pose?!
Source: LIGHTFIELD STUDIOS / Adobe Stock Photos

Incorporate accessible design, a.k.a. good design

According to the Centers for Disease Control and Prevention, 1 in 4 adults in the US have at least one disability as of a 2022 study.[12] Design choices that help people with disabilities help everyone in the audience better digest your content. Here are three goals to consider when designing presentations:

Make text easy to read. If the audience has trouble reading the text, they will stop paying attention or miss important information. These tips keep your audience focused:

- **Increase font size.** Font size advice often includes complex calculations based on screen and room size. As a rule of thumb, for virtual presentations or laptops, keep fonts no smaller than 16 pt., except for footers and footnotes. In large rooms or on small screens, use larger fonts.

- **Choose a color palette that accommodates color vision deficiency.** Avoid red/green combinations, as they're hard for those with color vision deficiencies to differentiate. Use high-contrast shades and thicker lines. And avoid relying solely on color for meaning. For status updates, combine colors with text, icons, or arrows, as shown in Figure 7.41.

- **Run an accessibility checker.** These tools check for issues like font size, contrast, color deficiency, and alternate text for images.

Figure 7.41 Status symbols
Source: John Polk & Associates

Reduce audible noise and enable captions. Background noise and unwanted sounds are distracting in virtual settings. These tips will improve your signal-to-noise ratio:

- **Buy a high-quality microphone with background noise reduction.** Low-volume output, dropouts, static, and background noise all increase the audience's cognitive load.

- **Turn on live captioning.** Captioning is widely available in video and presentation software—use it when needed and show the audience how to enable or disable it on their monitors. Avoid using captions unnecessarily, as the screen motion can be distracting.

Ensure ease of access in person and virtually. Creating an inclusive environment ensures everyone can contribute and connect. These tips ensure your audience can participate:

- **Plan adequate space for in-person meetings.** If any audience member uses a wheelchair, ensure sufficient space for them to participate in all activities.

- **Don't require a mouse for navigation.** Choose a virtual meeting platform that participants can navigate without a mouse and use keyboard shortcuts. Give instructions with and without mouse navigation.

- **Increase comprehensibility.** Everyone processes information differently. These tips allow your audience to adapt to their preferences:
    - **Define idioms.** As discussed in Chapter 5, "The Expert Trap," idioms enrich language. However, undefined idioms challenge nonnative speakers and people on the autism spectrum.
    - **Write for a sixth-grade reading level.** The goal isn't to impress the audience with a vast vocabulary. The goal is to communicate clearly.
    - **Share prereads.** Sharing the deck beforehand allows those with reading disabilities to take the necessary time to digest content and allows processors and perfectionists to form opinions and questions. However, not everyone reads the preread, leaving you either repeating content for prereaders or skipping context, confusing those who don't preread.

Invest in slide and content libraries to improve efficiency and effectiveness

There are two types of libraries. The first library type contains slide layouts with no content or only placeholder content. The second library type contains content used across multiple decks, like the company history slide in a sales deck.

Maintain slide libraries without real-world content to reduce the time to build new slides and ensure consistent formatting. Slide libraries also act as an idea board, inspiring deck writers with relevant slide layouts to convey their ideas. Figure 7.42 is a screenshot from the charts section of our slide library.

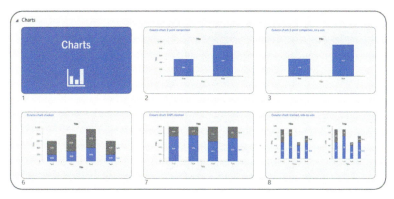

Figure 7.42 Chartapalooza!
Source: John Polk & Associates

Because charts have so many design options, they are harder to build than most slide layouts—and harder to keep visually consistent across multiple authors. That makes charts the most valuable section in the slide library. Here are best practices for building a slide library:

- **Build and stabilize the theme and template first.** Slide libraries quickly become incompatible or require maintenance if the template changes regularly.

- **Thoughtfully consider what you control through a template versus a slide library.** You can add slide layouts to the slide master, but it's easier to design and manage new slide layouts in a slide library. While you can delete slide layouts from the slide master, don't. This ensures there aren't unintended consequences when pasting content from another template.

- **Design for usability.** For text objects in templates, add the word "Text" as a placeholder to ensure correct formatting.

- **Include reference slides.** Provide guidance for consistent slide creation, including brand colors, standard fonts, logos, line spacing, and icons. Include tips on accessibility, confidentiality labeling, and proprietary content. Set design standards as defaults in the template and document them for use outside the template or slide library.

- **Organize slides for easy access.** A 350-slide library (yes, ours has over 350 slides and counting) needs a clear organization system to help users find what they need. Group similar slides, such as covers, agendas, bumpers, frameworks, charts, tables, and image layouts. Use bumper slides and section breaks for navigation. Our slide library has 20 slide groups, as shown in Figure 7.43.

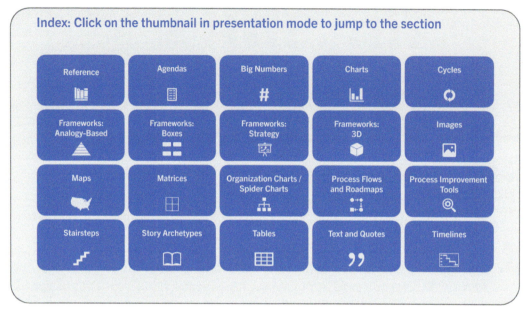

Figure 7.43 Slide library index
Source: John Polk & Associates

- **Apply an organizing framework within each section.** For frameworks, organize by box number and orientation. For charts, alphabetize or order by frequency of use.
- **Label each slide with keywords.** Naming the waterfall chart "waterfall" lets users search for that chart type.

Maintain real-world content in a content library to ensure consistency across decks. We include bio slides in the appendix of any deck sent to prospects, clients, or workshop participants. That way, they know our credentials and how to reach us. We've tweaked that slide regularly over the years. Without a content library, we'd have to remember the last presentation that used that slide; otherwise, we risk pulling an older version. Content libraries are commonly used for sales presentations. Some presentation software allows you to link slides to sync them across decks. Anytime you change the linked slide in one deck, it updates in the linked deck.

Key Takeaways

Design professional, engaging slides using an elegant format and intentional contrast to let the robust content shine through.

- ✓ Make intentional design decisions that align with the audience, purpose, and setting assessment.
- ✓ Ensure readability by minimizing clashing colors, gradients, shadows, *italics*, ALL CAPS, and word art.
- ✓ Reduce noise in charts by eliminating chartjunk, like 3D effects, gridlines, and data tables.
- ✓ Arrange objects using white space and common eye-flow patterns, such as the rule of thirds, Z pattern, and F pattern.
- ✓ Test for harmony and balance by squinting at slides.
- ✓ Establish a consistent slide design baseline, including high-contrast, complementary colors, one font, light and dark background options, and common objects.
- ✓ Build good design into the template or theme and ensure everyone uses it. Include reference slides in the template to help slide creators create consistent slides.
- ✓ Align and distribute objects to ensure a balanced design. Use guides to maintain healthy white space.
- ✓ Reserve contrasting designs, like font changes, gradient effects, or layers, for emphasis and a professional feel.
- ✓ Make designs accessible to improve readability and comprehension for everyone.
- ✓ Create and maintain slide and content libraries to ensure consistent formatting and style and to enable easy access to the most recent version of slides shared across decks.

Figure 8.1 Quite the curtain closer
Source: Aina with AI / Adobe Stock Photos

8

The Under (or Over) Confidence Trap

Boost confidence to boost credibility,
but don't let overconfidence lead to mistakes.

A legendary study reported people fear public speaking more than they fear death, portrayed in Figure 8.1.[1] It made the rounds on all the late-night talk shows.

To clarify, study participants chose public speaking as one of their common fears more than any other fear, including death. However, when participants chose only their top fear, they selected death most often. In a more recent Chapman University study, "public speaking only comes in at 29% ..., just a few percentage points below a fear of sharks."[2]

The fear of public speaking is real regardless of its ranking in the surveys. We hear this fear from workshop participants, coaching clients, and MBA students. Even though we teach on this topic, we're not immune from the fight-or-flight response triggered by an upcoming speech or workshop. The techniques in this chapter will help you manage your stage fright.

The goal isn't to eliminate fear. The goal is to manage fear and harness physical reactions so they enhance performance and show excitement.[3]

> *Most people think they should calm down when they feel anxious. Instead, staying in a high-arousal state and reframing anxiety as excitement is much more effective for performing well on high-pressure performance tasks.*[4]
>
> Professor Alison Wood Brooks, Harvard Business School Profile Page

Presenters fall into the Under (or Over) Confidence Trap when they let their fear of public speaking hurt their credibility or let overconfidence cause mistakes.

Avoid the Under (or Over) Confidence Trap by preparing, practicing, and pumping yourself up to manage your nerves before a stressful presentation. Show up confidently without becoming overconfident by applying leadership presence techniques, effectively reacting to the audience, and building in space for discussion.

Prepare

John doesn't like to brag, but he's a bit of an expert on expertise. [Editor's note: This is sarcastic braggadocio and does not represent the opinion of Justin Hunsaker or John Wiley & Sons, Inc.] He titled his master's thesis "The Effect of Expert Power on Consensus Decision-Making." You've probably read it, so we won't discuss the details. The critical aspect of expertise for our purposes is its effect on confidence. When you prepare, you know your stuff. When you know your stuff, you're less likely to make these mistakes:

- Forget your lines.
- Use filler words, stumble, or restart mid-sentence.
- Worry about someone challenging your ideas.
- Panic when getting a tough question.

When we coach presenters on this point, many say, "But I'm not the expert." The goal isn't to be *the* expert who knows the most about a topic but to be someone with a high degree of knowledge of the topic you're discussing and to have something important to say. Encouraging you to be an expert is supposed to motivate you to prepare, not give you impostor syndrome! As James Whittaker writes, "If you feel like an impostor, you have most of humanity for company. The only ones who don't feel it are frauds."[5] Here are strategies for increasing your expertise:

Know the material. Simple! Just spend 20 years mastering a single topic, earn a PhD in it, and casually quote obscure journals at dinner parties. But since your presentation is next Tuesday, let's talk about some effective short-term strategies:

- **Present only on topics where you have expertise.** This sounds obvious, but it's hard to say no to speaking opportunities outside your expertise.

- **Balance real-world experience with academic theory.** If you learned a best practice through experience, a professor has probably written about it. We knew the effectiveness of sentence titles from experience; however, researching the science behind them made us even more confident in defending their value with presenters who were just being lazy, er, didn't like them.

- **Read books and articles.** This can be annoying when you already know much of the content. But there's strength in numbers and confidence in knowing other experts agree. It lets you bring reinforcements (virtually) when someone questions your ideas. You'll also pick up something you didn't know or learn how to explain a complex concept better.

  If you agree with everything in the book you just read, you're not yet an expert. Keep reading books until you start to identify the things you do *and* don't agree with. Then you're beginning to have your own point of view.

- **Reference the experts when you're not the expert.** One of John's bosses taught him this trick: if you don't know the answer, find the experts and bring back their solutions. Then, in the presentation, you get to say, "I'm not the expert here, but I asked the experts, and here's what they said."

Write speaker notes. We're huge fans of speaker notes. Writing them, *not* reading from them, like the guy in Figure 8.2.

Figure 8.2 Know your stuff, dude!
Source: fauxels / Pexels

Prepare

Writing speaker notes is a form of planning and practice for your speech. There are several categories of speaker notes, each with different pros and cons:

- **Outline:** A speech outline is like a storyboard. In bullet-point form, an outline is like an agenda. In sentence form, it's like an executive summary.
- **Key points:** Remember the "three most important takeaways" question from the Platinum Rule assessment? That's the start of effective speaker notes. Then, flesh it out with other essential points.
- **Script:** For every presentation you deliver, there is a theoretical perfect speech—you never get close by winging it. If you want to get close, write down all the words you want to say, edit, test, and edit again. This is a lot of work, and we don't do this for every presentation.
- **Hybrid:** These approaches aren't mutually exclusive. A great strategy is to organize key points under a high-level outline, then script out the opening, closing, key stories, and any complex concepts.

While overtly reading from speaker notes is bad in most situations, there are benefits to reading from a script. Scripting makes it easier to deliver a concise, logical speech with fewer filler words.

The problem with reading from speaker notes is that, for most speakers, it's obvious that you're reading from notes. When reading from notes, you don't sound natural, authentic, or expert. Compare amateur improv comedy to a well-acted movie. Amateur improv is disjointed and rambling, and much of the humor comes from screwing up. In a movie, professional actors read from a script they've memorized, but they deliver their speech with dynamics, emotion, pacing, and authentic movement. Here are situations where scripting a speech is most appropriate:

- **Newscasts, press conferences, and political speeches.** In these situations, the speakers use teleprompters and read a speech designed to sound natural. For newscasters, even saying, "Back to you, Jane," is scripted on the teleprompter. But it takes practice to deliver a speech this way. We've seen inexperienced public speakers use a teleprompter at conferences, and it's painful.
- **Recorded webinars.** Recorded speech can live forever. So, it's worth the extra effort to capture the benefits of reading a script. When listening to a speech in real time, the audience is more forgiving of rambling sections, wordy phrases, and filler words. When it's recorded, every "um" becomes noticeable.

- **Presentations when you genuinely need the crutch.** If you aren't an expert or didn't practice and know the audience will judge you, you might perform better if you read from a script. This only works in a setting where the audience can't see your notes, like a videoconference. This is the speech equivalent of driving on a spare tire and should be the last option.

If you plan to use a script or speaker notes, ensure the setting accommodates it. Is there a podium for notes? Is there a monitor to show the presenter view? Do you have multiple screens during the virtual meeting? If you thought public speaking was stressful, imagine what it's like if there's a technical glitch and you can't see the speaker notes you were counting on.

Scripts or speaker notes are a valuable step in the practice process but are counterproductive when used as a crutch during the actual presentation. Review and memorize critical points. Glance at your notes before the big presentation. But focus on your audience and delivery when it's showtime.

Predict questions and prepare answers. One driver of public speaking phobia is the worry that you'll get a question you can't answer and will look dumb. No one wants to look dumb, but most people overestimate how judgmental the audience is. Whether presenting to a judgmental audience or not, predicting questions and preparing answers helps you handle questions effectively. Here are strategies for identifying potential questions:

- **Brainstorm questions.** When finishing the slides and prepping for the speech, predict what questions you might get using the checklist in Figure 8.3.

Audience Question Preparation Checklist
- ☐ What does the audience value? Are they people-, results-, options-, or detail-oriented?
- ☐ What assumptions did you have to make to reach the conclusions and what grounding do you have for each assumption?
- ☐ What other options did you consider?
- ☐ What are the pros and cons for the alternatives?
- ☐ What supporting data or stakeholder opinions do you have that you didn't include in the deck?

Figure 8.3 If I knew what they were gonna ask, I'd have put it in the presentation
Source: John Polk & Associates

- **Capture as you go.** As you build slides and speaker notes, you decide what not to include. Sometimes, you cut something an audience member cares about. Whenever you remove a slide, bullet point, or point from the speaker notes, add that topic to your question list. Save cut slides in the appendix to refer to if you get a question on that topic. Just ensure you don't end up with "appendicitis," as discussed in Chapter 3, "The Black Hole Trap."

- **Get expert and nonexpert reviews.** As discussed in Chapter 5, "The Expert Trap," experts and nonexperts give different feedback. They also ask different questions. The socialization process also lets you answer stakeholders' questions *before* the meeting.

- **Meet with detractors.** If you know there are detractors, meet with them before the decision meeting. That way, you'll know their concerns and can address them in the proposal. And you'll be more prepared to handle tough questions.

It's impossible to know the answer to every question, so be prepared for that moment. Have the confidence to say, "I don't know, but I'll find out."

You might be thinking, "But wait—there's an entire chapter on how expertise is a trap." It becomes a trap when that expertise makes it difficult for you to communicate clearly with nonexperts. Build expertise to boost confidence, then use the techniques from Chapter 5, "The Expert Trap," to convey that expertise without overwhelming the audience.

Practice

If you're a professional, you practice. Athletes practice. Actors rehearse. Artists create studies and sketches. Why would it be any different for a presentation? But the number of people who wing it when giving a presentation is astonishing. We assume they think they're just talking, and they talk all the time, so they must be good at it, right? Even when they do practice, they don't give it enough time, or they don't practice effectively.

John's dad had great advice: "Practice like you play." He said this to John on the driving range when John was taking a running swing at the golf ball, like Adam Sandler in the movie *Happy Gilmore*, shown in Figure 8.4.

Even when working on specific parts of the game, like driving or putting, you should approach them with the same mechanics and mindset as you use in a real game.

Plan and memorize key points and stories. Using your speaker notes, identify the key points in your speech, then memorize them. Having the most important points memorized allays the fear that you'll forget something. Word diet your scripted key points so the speech is concise and impactful.

Figure 8.4 Practicing like Happy Gilmore plays
Source: NBCUniversal Media LLC

Fear of forgetting what you want to say is a significant driver of stage fright. While you should memorize key points, the fear of forgetting them is often a bigger worry than it should be. The audience doesn't know what you plan to say, so if you forget a point you want to make, just move on to the next point. If it is a critical point, you'll remember it later and can work it back into the speech. Or an audience member will ask a question that will remind you. Pausing to say, "I forgot what I wanted to say," only draws attention to your mental block and creates an awkward pause. Here's a rhyming mnemonic device to remember this point: don't sweat what you forget.

Rehearse with slides. This is like a practice round in golf or a preseason football game. It doesn't count but pretend it does. The closer you make your practice to the actual presentation, the better. Practice in the location where you'll present. Use a timer to ensure you won't run over. Recruit a surrogate audience. Dress the part. Don't tell your surrogate audience *how* you plan to present; just present. Don't tell them *what* you'd say; say it. Don't stop and restart for every miscue; recover and plow through like you would in a live presentation.

Encourage the surrogate audience to ask questions as they would in a live presentation, but ask them not to interrupt to give feedback. Ask them to take notes to debrief at the end. That's not to say there's no value in stopping at points to try a different approach; it's just that the complete, uninterrupted run-through is a valuable approach that most people skip.

And if you really want to amp up the pain, video record the rehearsal. Remember how painful it is to listen to your voice on a recording? Now, multiply that pain by 10. In addition to hating your voice, you'll also notice poor posture, flailing hand gestures, filler words, and every stumble.

Much of this will be feedback the surrogate audience is too polite to tell you. And that's why you need to record the rehearsal. Maybe you prefer to be blissfully ignorant, but the actual audience will notice these things, and they will judge you. It's better that you see these opportunities and practice to improve them.

Rehearse without slides. In the 2018 Winter Olympics, the cameras showed Mikaela Shiffrin standing at the top of the hill before entering the gate, poles in hand, goggles on, eyes closed. She subtly moved her poles and shifted her position as if she were already racing down the hill.

She visualized the run she was about to make—every gate, every corner, every place she would catch air. Studies have shown that visualization strategies can improve skill acquisition.[6] When preparing for a presentation, practice a form of visualization—rehearsing without slides. Visualize what each slide looks like from memory in order, speaking the main point of each slide, typically a paraphrase of the sentence title, and the critical piece of information that's not on the slide, like the story that illustrates the key point.

We like to do this rehearsal in the car. The person in the next car will assume you're singing along to the radio. Practicing without slides or speaker notes removes the crutch and enables you to memorize the presentation flow and key points. When you achieve unaided recall, the gold standard of knowledge, you can be confident that you'll know your stuff when presenting live.

The checklist in Figure 8.5 tracks preparation and practice steps before a critical presentation.

Presentation Delivery Preparation Checklist
- ☐ Make speaker's notes, but don't read from them when delivering
- ☐ Mentally run through the presentation to review each idea in sequence
- ☐ Give a dry run of the presentation using all visual aids in the setting where you will present
- ☐ Test drive any audience engagement activities—e.g., breakouts, chat, polls, videos, whiteboards
- ☐ Make a list of questions you might get and practice your answers
- ☐ Practice the full presentation again—e.g., videotape yourself, have a friend give feedback
- ☐ Rehearse with the presentation in its final form

Figure 8.5 Prepare to present perfectly
Source: John Polk & Associates

Pump yourself up

> *Stress happens when something*
> *you care about is at stake.*
> *It's not a sign to run away—*
> *it's a sign to step forward.*[7]
>
> Kelly McGonigal, *The Upside of Stress*

In the chapter introduction, we mentioned the fight-or-flight response. Managing that reaction is vital to looking confident in the moment. The audience will know you're not confident if you're visibly nervous (shaky hands, cracking voice, or flop sweat). And that will reduce their confidence in you. In our workshops, we ask participants to share how they pump up or calm down before a presentation using physical or emotional techniques. Figure 8.6 shows the output from one workshop.

Figure 8.6 Shout (or nap) your way to a stress-free presentation!
Source: John Polk & Associates

While we can't endorse "Shout!" if you have coworkers nearby or "Sniff cat" if you have allergies, this list demonstrates many ways to manage nerves. Some strategies are backed by science, and some aren't. But if a placebo reduces stage fright, who cares? Here are our favorite ways to manage nerves.

Practice mindfulness. Meditation, deep breathing, visualization, and appreciation are all mindfulness practices that reduce the body's reaction to stress. Stress creates physical symptoms in the body, including rapid heart rate, quick or shallow breathing, muscle tension, and sweat. Most mindfulness practices include an active approach to managing breathing pace and depth, which slows your heart rate, directly countering the fight-or-flight response.

When you visualize success, you create a positive self-fulfilling prophecy that compels you to take the actions needed to bring that vision to life. Gratitude practices—actively thinking about what's good in life—put the upcoming stressful presentation in perspective.

Give yourself a pep talk. Affirmations boost self-confidence, reinforce positive thinking, and align your mindset with your goals.

> I'm good enough,
> I'm smart enough,
> and doggone it,
> people like me![8]
>
> Stuart Smalley, Saturday Night Live

Stuart was a character on *Saturday Night Live* who hosted a self-help show called *Daily Affirmations with Stuart Smalley*. This quotation was his most common affirmation spoken into a mirror. While cheesy, this simple pep talk mitigates impostor syndrome, reminds you of your expertise, and helps you realize the audience wants you to succeed.

Exercise. Exercise offers numerous benefits, such as disease prevention, increased longevity, and improved mental health, but it also directly enhances your ability to present by increasing confidence, calmness, focus, and energy. Ever since Hans and Franz first said, "We want to pump [clap] you up!" on *Saturday Night Live*, weightlifting has been linked to pumping yourself up.[9] Any exercise produces endorphins, improving your mood so you appear more positive and energized.[10] Also, exercise is an excellent time for creative thinking or rehearsing without slides.

Dress the part. "Dress for success" is another rhyming cliché. Not only do clothes signal credibility and assurance to the audience, but they also boost confidence.[11] This goes beyond the "power suit" effect. Wearing a suit jacket or sports coat improves posture by reminding you to keep your shoulders back. When you shine your shoes, you're controlling the things you can control. That improves your ability to manage unexpected challenges, like a missing projector cable or a tough question from your boss's boss.

Focus on the audience and purpose, not on yourself. Anxiety is all about you. It's a vicious cycle of emotions. When you're stressed, your body responds. Then, your mind notices the changes in your body and gets even more stressed. To tame the anxiety, widen your scope and get out of your head. Focus on the purpose and why you're passionate about it. Focus on the audience and how to help them.[12] Reframe your nerves as positive energy to amp up your presentation.

Play your walk-up song.[13] It's a simple but fun tradition. The batter walks to the plate, and the mediocre stadium sound system blares the Troggs' "Wild Thing," like in the movie *Major League*. If you've ever seen a football game at Virginia Tech's Lane Stadium, you've experienced the full-participation version of the walk-up song. As the team runs out to Metallica's "Enter Sandman," the crowd jumps in rhythm. It registers on the campus seismograph. Here's how music can pump you up or calm you down:

- **Music lowers stress.** Public speaking causes fear, and fear releases cortisol, the stress hormone. And music decreases cortisol levels.

- **Music makes you happier.** Music boosts dopamine. When you're happier, you're more confident and better able to be present.

- **Music enhances physical performance.** Runners who listen to fast or motivational music outperform those who listen to calm or no music.[14] A fast or motivational walk-up song can amp up your energy if your natural speaking patterns are more subdued.

Remember the 3F framework from Chapter 1, "The Frankenstein Trap"? Of course you do! That's the power of mnemonic devices. (In case you forgot, the 3Fs are facts, feelings, and follow-ups.) To summarize the strategies to fight stage fright, we created the 3P framework in Figure 8.7. If only someone would invent a mnemonic device for how to spell "mnemonic." We asked Gemini AI to do just that: "My never-ending memory needs occasional nudging and inspiration, clearly." This sentence uses the first letter of each word to spell out "mnemonic."

Prepare   Practice   Pump Up

Figure 8.7 I see your 3Fs and raise you 3Ps
Source: John Polk & Associates

> ### Embracing the spotlight
>
> When Justin's daughter expressed interest in joining the children's choir, he couldn't help but smile. She was the kid who sang her heart out in the backseat—off-key but enthusiastic.
>
> She loved being part of a group that embraced music and fun, welcoming every child regardless of ability. But as the big recital approached, her excitement turned to nerves. "Dad, I'm really scared to sing in front of all those people," she admitted. Justin encouraged her by saying, "Sometimes doing what we love means stepping onto a bigger stage."
>
> On recital day, she was filled with anxiety. Justin hugged her and said, "You've got this. Remember how much fun you had practicing with your friends." With a deep breath, she stepped into the spotlight. Her voice wasn't perfect, but her courage was undeniable. The audience applauded with delight, and afterward, Justin praised her bravery. She smiled, confessing, "When I signed up for choir, I didn't *realize* I'd have to sing in front of so many people."
>
> Her journey mirrors our careers. We pursue passions out of love or talent, but growth brings bigger challenges. Like her choir director, we need mentors to help us shine on larger stages.
>
> Over time, Justin's daughter improved and joined more choirs, though she never stopped feeling nervous. That's normal. Even seasoned presenters feel jitters before conferences. With guidance and practice, we can grow and succeed, no matter how intimidating the spotlight.
>
> _____
>
> Note: Portions of the sidebar were first published in "Embrace the Spotlight: A Lesson from My Daughter," Justin Hunsaker, John Polk & Associates' blog, December 26, 2023

Display confidence in delivery

After preparing, practicing, and pumping up, present with confidence (the fourth P)! Your confidence is a prerequisite for earning the audience's trust. But if you deliver poorly, the audience will lose trust in you. Notice the speaker in Figure 8.8. His gestures and leaning-in posture convey authority. This chapter discusses how to display confidence with body and voice when presenting in person, while Chapter 9, "The Virtual Fatigue Trap," discusses presenting virtually.

Figure 8.8 Leaning in before it was cool
Source: Stump Speaking (1853–1854) / George Caleb Bingham / Artvee.com / Public Domain

Demonstrate confidence through your pitch, pace, and volume. Monotony undermines your message.

*It's hopeless. We'll never make it. We're done for.
It'll never work. We're doomed.*[15]

Glum, *The Adventures of Gulliver*

Figure 8.9 Glum made Eeyore sound upbeat
Source: Hanna-Barbera

Display confidence in delivery   231

Glum, shown in Figure 8.9, was a character on *The Adventures of Gulliver*, a Saturday-morning cartoon. It isn't a great cartoon, but the Glum character stuck with us. His monotone "we're doomed" comes to mind whenever we encounter someone profoundly negative or with monotonous speech. The negativity from the "Glum" in a meeting sucks the energy out of the room. And monotony is inconsistent with an upbeat message.

Why would you expect the audience to be excited if you're not excited? Many analysts believe data and logic should win all arguments. Unfortunately, people don't work that way. People are emotional creatures, and enthusiasm is contagious.

The opposite of monotone is *dynamic*, characterized by energy or effective action. In physics, it refers to energy or forces that produce motion. In music, it's the variation in loudness between notes or phrases. All these dynamics concepts apply when delivering a presentation. Show energy. Push for effective action. Vary your volume to emphasize key points.

There are three voice elements to consider when presenting: pitch, pace, and volume.

- **Vary pitch.** Using higher and lower pitches at key moments engages the audience. A favorite trick is to introduce the key insight or most important recommendation with the phrase "I'm super excited about this." Thanks to cognitive dissonance (the tension that occurs when trying to hold two contradictory beliefs in your head), your brain won't let you say, "I'm super excited," in a monotone voice. Glum never said, "I'm super excited about this!" Remember the "three most important things you want the audience to remember" from the Platinum Rule assessment? Those three things are good places to use these overt statements of emotion.

- **Manage pace.** A steady pace can be monotonous. Don't change your pace randomly, but speak more slowly during dramatic or emotional sections and more quickly during exciting sections. Many presenters tell us they received feedback that they talk too fast. That might be true, but speech speed usually isn't the real issue. You can listen to most podcasts at twice the speed with no problems. Often, the feedback really means they sound nervous or rambling or don't pause to let others engage in the conversation.

- **Adjust volume (without yelling) so everyone can hear you clearly.** We had a coworker who was typically soft spoken. But when presenting to a senior audience, he spoke so loudly that it was awkward. When asked about this, he realized he instinctively used his "drama" voice from acting in high school plays where he had to project his voice to the back row.

Speak louder than in a one-on-one conversation, but don't blast the audience. Talking louder or softer both convey emphasis. A whisper can be shockingly effective at captivating an audience's attention.

Use a microphone if the back row can't hear you, without blasting the front row. We recommend a lapel (a.k.a. Lavalier) mic. Once set correctly, lapel mics provide consistent volume, which doesn't happen with a handheld mic. Handheld mics also interfere with hand gestures. And a podium mic keeps you stuck in one spot, making you look stiff.

Demonstrate confidence through your eyes, hands, and stance. Body language can project and reinforce confidence or distract from the message. This applies to both presenting and listening. Reinforce your message with eye contact, gestures, posture, and movement.

- **Maintain good eye contact.** Shift attention between three points in the room. Maintain eye contact for one to three seconds, long enough to show connection without being creepy.

- **Use hand gestures.** A study of TED Talks by the Science of People found that the most popular speakers used almost twice as many gestures as the least popular speakers.[16] To get the right level of gesturing, pretend you're having an animated conversation with a friend. When presenting in person, keep hand gestures within "the box." The box is a rectangle from shoulders to waist, like in Figure 8.10. The width of the box depends on your setting, with wider gestures

Figure 8.10 Hello from the gesture box
Source: RDNE Stock Project / Pexels

appropriate for bigger stages. Gestures within the box look more confident and trustworthy. To make gestures more engaging, punctuate your speech with mime-like motions, like the thumb-and-pinky-to-the-ear gesture for a phone.

Palm-up, openhanded gestures signal openness or an offering.[17] They are an effective way to start any presentation, convey emphasis, or invite audience interaction.

On the other hand (see what we did there?), pointing is usually perceived as a negative. It's strongly associated with accusation. If you must point, point with five fingers, like a flight attendant pointing out the exit doors. Figure 8.11 illustrates this subtle difference.

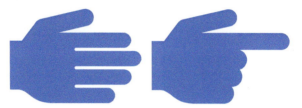

Figure 8.11 It's a thin line between "Please take your seat" and "J'accuse!"

- **Keep posture upright but relaxed.** If you have the choice, stand. Standing has an immediate impact on presence and energy. You look and sound more confident when standing. Standing makes it easier to have good posture and to speak from the diaphragm.

- **Don't shift your weight back and forth.** You don't want to look fidgety. Moving on a stage is appropriate, but don't pace like a caged animal. Instead, use natural breaks in the content to move to a different spot on stage.

Demonstrate leadership presence in presentations

In their book *Leadership Presence*, Kathy Lubar and Belle Linda Halpern outline the PRES model of leadership presence.[18] Here's how each element shows up in a presentation:

- **Presence:** Stay present and flexible to handle the unexpected. If your mind is on the last or next meeting, the current one will suffer. Being present lets you focus on the audience and adapt to their needs rather than sticking rigidly to your plan.

- **Reaching out:** Build relationships through empathy, listening, and authentic connection. Engage with the audience beforehand, check for understanding, actively listen to questions or comments, relate your stories to their experiences, and share credit with coworkers for shared successes.

- **Expressiveness:** Express feelings and emotions using words, voice, body, and face to deliver a congruent message. Maintain high energy. Tell emotional stories. Reinforce your emotions with body language and gestures.

- **Self-knowing:** Accept yourself, be authentic, and reflect your values in decisions and actions. Be willing to say, "I don't know," when you get a tough question.

Speaking. With? Punctuation! (And gestures.)

The power of speaking lies in more than just words—it's in the delivery. Dynamic range, pauses, and gestures add punctuation to spoken language, giving it rhythm and meaning.

Pauses act like commas or periods, letting the audience chunk up and absorb complex ideas. Silence creates verbal white space, emphasizing thoughts and allowing your message to resonate. A rising pitch signals curiosity, turning statements into invitations for dialogue, like a question mark. Exclamation points come alive through energy and volume, expressing excitement and passion without shouting.

Facial expressions and nonverbal cues, like parentheses, enhance your message. Aligned with your words, they emphasize key points, convey emotion, and bring your speech to life. Gestures act as physical punctuation, turning presentations into memorable, engaging narratives.

While excitement can naturally increase pace, pitch, and volume, avoid using a high pitch in business settings—it may seem like nervousness. Reserve pitch changes for questions and use pace and volume to convey enthusiasm effectively.

Read and react to the audience

> *Everyone has a plan until they get punched in the mouth.*[19]
>
> Mike Tyson, quotation from
> "Biggs Has Plans for Tyson"

This wise man said this to a reporter when asked about his plan for an upcoming Evander Holyfield boxing match. All the confidence from your expertise, practice, and nerve management can go out the window when the boss doesn't like your recommendation or you get a tough question from a critic. And bored or confused participants don't always speak up to tell you they are bored or confused.

Learning to read and react to the audience without abandoning the plan is the key to staying confident throughout a presentation. Figure 8.12 lists subtle and not-so-subtle audience clues and potential ways to react to them.

Read	React
When you move to the next slide, the decision-maker makes a face or doesn't turn the slide	• Pause • Ask if the decision-maker has questions
The decision-maker flips ahead to a later slide	• Pick up the pace • Get to the punch line • Ask if the decision-maker has questions
The audience looks bored	• Increase enthusiasm • Tell a story • Take a break
A stakeholder on the phone hasn't spoken	• Ask the stakeholder to give input • Share the stakeholder's input from your premeeting conversation
Two participants in the back of the room tilt their heads and look confused	• Speak up • Ask if there are any questions
A critic asks a question that is inconsistent with the story flow	• Say you'll cover that in x slides • Jump to the answer in the appendix • Use the "parking lot" to cover it offline

Figure 8.12 Don't stick with the plan if the plan ain't working
Source: John Polk & Associates

Early in his career, Justin briefed the organization's VP weekly on critical metrics. Although important, these metrics often made for boring updates. Justin's boss, Gus, suggested closely observing the VP's body language during the next update. The VP was disinterested, leafing through the deck and not asking questions. Afterward, Justin proposed eliminating the metrics from the weekly briefings. However, Gus pointed out that doing so would miss an opportunity to drive the strategy. In the following meeting,

Justin shared the usual metrics and presented broader trends with a lineup of upcoming programs that would influence these metrics. That meeting ran long due to the interactive and insightful discussion!

Create space for discussion

As with all presentation design decisions, how you manage discussion depends on the audience, purpose, and setting. In conference presentations and town hall meetings, presenters often hold discussion until the end. In a decision meeting, you want an interactive session where the audience can raise questions and share comments throughout. Here are strategies for encouraging interaction:

- **State up front that you want the session to be interactive.** If the audience doesn't know the session is interactive, they'll be less likely to jump in. Be clear about when and how you want interaction.
- **Prime the pump with a short, interactive activity.** We kick off each in-person workshop with a sticky note exercise.
- **Pause after each slide.** Because the audience doesn't want to interrupt you, they naturally hold their questions until you finish covering a slide. A brief pause signals you're finished. Don't ask, "Any questions?" after every slide.
- **Ask for questions at major topic shifts.** "Before we shift topics, what questions do you have?" Note the subtle difference in phrasing. "What questions do you have?" implies there should be questions, and it's time to bring them up.

You don't need all these steps in every interaction, but you need more of them when presenting virtually.

Beware the overconfidence trap

Most of this chapter focused on underconfidence because it's the more common trap (impostor syndrome, anyone?). This observation surely has selection bias—overconfident presenters don't seek out presentation coaches.

But overconfidence is a trap, too. It often shows up when presenting material you've presented before. Overconfidence leads you to conclude that you don't need to modify or practice delivering the material. While you don't need to start from scratch, take the time to reassess the audience, purpose, and setting and adjust the material. Then, practice your delivery focused on what's new. This chapter's strategies will improve your performance even when you feel confident.

Critically assess your performance

One way to check your overconfidence is to record and review your presentation critically. Every "um," every stumble, every awkward gesture jumps off the screen. The camera finds issues you didn't know you had and motivates you to improve. This process is painful but critical to improving. For each area of self-criticism, ask the following:

1. **What is valid about this criticism?** I stumbled when describing my central idea.

2. **What could you do differently?** I could script and practice that section.

3. **Did you meet the goal?** I got the decision I needed, but it took longer than necessary.

4. **What valuable feedback did you get?** After the meeting, my boss suggested an analogy to explain my central idea.

Key Takeaways

Boost confidence to boost credibility, but don't let overconfidence lead to mistakes.

- ✓ Show up as expert by knowing the material, writing speaker notes, and preparing for questions.
- ✓ Rehearse with *and* without slides, focusing on the key points and anecdotes. Time yourself to ensure you have the right amount of content.
- ✓ Manage nerves through a combination of mindfulness, exercise, pep talks, and music.
- ✓ Display confidence through voice, posture, eye contact, and gestures.
- ✓ Speak with punctuation! Vary pace, pitch, and volume to show enthusiasm. Use pauses and gestures for emphasis.
- ✓ Exhibit leadership presence with the PRES (presence, reaching out, expressiveness, and self-knowing) model.
- ✓ Read and react to the audience during the presentation to track engagement and understanding.
- ✓ Consciously build in space for interaction.
- ✓ Don't be overconfident just because you've given the presentation before.
- ✓ Record the presentation and critically assess your performance.

Figure 9.1 John taking extreme precautions while teaching
Source: Courtesy of John Polk

9

The Virtual Fatigue Trap

Reimagine what works well in person for the virtual world, leveraging its advantages while minimizing virtual fatigue.

In mid-March 2020, John taught two full-day sessions of our Presentations That Drive Action workshop in Cleveland for a corporate client. On day one, there was a lot of talk about a novel coronavirus named COVID-19. On day two, the world shut down.

The client shut down corporate travel, but John made it home safely. Every client postponed their upcoming workshops "for a couple of weeks."

After multiple couple-of-weeks delays, clients eventually conceded that we would need to shift to virtual.

The pandemic presented new challenges for most businesses. We *love* teaching in person. We feed off our audience's energy, so we weren't excited about the shift to virtual. How would we know if the audience liked our jokes if everyone in the audience was muted?

John's Data Visualization MBA course was the first to go virtual. Through research, consulting with peers, and experimentation, he retooled everything we teach for the virtual world, like in Figure 9.1.

Presenters fall into the Virtual Fatigue Trap when they don't adapt their presentations to the virtual world effectively. A root cause is the incorrect assumption that everything you do in person will work if you simply share your screen and talk. Remember, the third component of the Platinum Rule of Presentations is "setting." The virtual setting magnifies the challenges of in-person presenting.

Avoid the Virtual Fatigue Trap by setting up an effective home studio, restructuring your presentation, engaging participants, adjusting your delivery for the virtual world, and mastering the technology.

Understand virtual fatigue and its impacts

*We are stuck with technology
when what we really want is just stuff that works.[1]*
Douglas Adams, *The Salmon of Doubt*

Meeting over videoconferencing software drains us physically and mentally. Here are the reasons:

- **Drain 1: It's unnatural to look at yourself while speaking.** Unless you practice with a mirror, you're not used to looking at yourself while speaking. Anything unnatural can cause stress. And then the self-critic kicks in. "I'm having a bad hair day. Is my complexion really that red? Is that how my nose looks?"

- **Drain 2: Eye contact is often all or nothing.** It's also unnatural to look directly into someone's eyes for extended periods. Among the many phrases the TV show *Seinfeld* invented is the "close talker," someone who invades your personal space while speaking.[2] Everyone is a close talker on video because we sit close to the camera. People reserve consistent, close eye contact for close relationships, so experiencing this in a virtual meeting causes stress.[3]

    People naturally look at the person they're talking to. In the virtual world, people look at the face on the screen, not the camera. If the video panel isn't near the camera, the person on the other end thinks you're looking away from them. Compare the difference in Figure 9.2. If you've ever told your kids, "Look at me while I'm talking to you," you know the stress this causes.

- **Drain 3: It's harder to send and receive nonverbal clues.** Because it's impossible to tell where someone is looking, you must exaggerate head nods and hand gestures to ensure they're seen. Reading the audience's nonverbal clues requires scanning multiple tiny video faces.

Figure 9.2 Close Talker and Distracted Dude
Source: Courtesy of Justin Hunsaker

- **Drain 4: Voice over Internet Protocol (VoIP) compression can cause "robot voice."** VoIP technology compresses the digital data that makes up your voice to optimize bandwidth. Unfortunately, this compression can make the sound on the other end tinny or robot-like. In addition, low-fidelity microphones and speakers on cheap laptops or earbuds further degrade sound quality.

- **Drain 5: Technical challenges frustrate us and waste time.** Speaking while on mute, like in Figure 9.3, is probably the number one virtual meeting glitch.

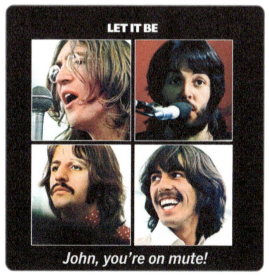

Figure 9.3 Mic check
Source: Apple Corps

Understand virtual fatigue and its impacts   243

Dropped calls, frozen videos, microphone static, and breakout rooms where the computer video is in one room and the phone audio is in another are irritating when someone else experiences them. And they're embarrassing when you experience them.

- **Drain 6: You speak louder on video calls.** You unconsciously compensate for all the potential technical challenges between your microphones and your listeners' speakers. But speaking loudly takes more physical effort, tiring you out more quickly.

- **Drain 7: You assume participants with their video off are disengaged.** If the audience is on mute and off video, you have no clue if they're engaged, casually paying attention, or playing solitaire. And you can't feed off their energy. A 2022 survey by Vyopta, a software company, found that 93% of executives say employees who turn their cameras off are less engaged in their work.[4] There's tension between your need as the speaker to see engagement and the audience's need to take a break from being on camera all day.

- **Drain 8: Home offices have distractions that "office" offices don't.** During the COVID era, when most people with desk jobs shifted from office buildings to home offices, the chance to work out on the back deck under blue skies seemed appealing, like in Figure 9.4.

Figure 9.4 A work-from-home dream
Source: vlntn / Adobe Stock Photos

But what you experienced was barking dogs and screaming babies, like in Figure 9.5. And if that wasn't happening in your house, you saw and heard the chaos in your coworkers' videos.

Figure 9.5 A work-from-home nightmare
Sources: (baby) Pro Hi-Res / (dog) Caio / (background) vlntn / Adobe Stock Photos

Dogs barking, babies screaming, delivery people ringing the doorbell, or housemates walking on camera or talking loudly are all distractions that don't happen during in-person presentations.

Improve your home studio

We use the term "home studio" purposefully. When presenting virtually, you're broadcasting. Before recent technological advances, setting up a home studio might look something like Figure 9.6.

Figure 9.6 Justin's home studio
Source: New Old Stock / Public Domain

Today, laptops, smartphones, and tablets have cameras, microphones, speakers, and software to enable you to broadcast. Problem solved, right?

Most laptops have lower-quality components than if you bought them separately. And spare bedrooms, dens, basements, and garages certainly weren't designed to optimize lighting, sound, and background views. We've discussed the importance of reducing visual noise in decks. Here are tips for improving your setup to minimize visual and auditory noise in your broadcast:

Invest in high-quality equipment. It's easy to upgrade your home studio without breaking the bank. This improves broadcast quality, creates redundancy when a component fails, and enables a more ergonomic environment. Worthwhile investments include the following:

- **Camera:** An external HD camera improves video quality and allows flexible positioning by clipping onto a laptop screen or a second monitor.
- **Wired microphone:** The wire eliminates any Bluetooth issues, like static and dropouts. We prefer this over the typical earphone-microphone headset because it can be off-screen, avoiding the podcaster vibe. Add a pop filter to soften the impact of strong p sounds.
- **Headset:** We use gray, wireless earbuds for mobility and subtlety, avoiding the bulk of over-ear headphones and the "headphone bedhead" look. For noisy environments, noise-canceling over-ear headphones may be worth the tradeoff.
- **Monitor:** A large external monitor improves productivity—Justin uses two for extra efficiency! When building decks, the large monitor accommodates the slide sorter view, menus, and a full slide at over 100% scale. When presenting, display shared content on the secondary monitor, which prevents pop-up messages from appearing to the audience.
- **External keyboard and mouse:** This lets you raise the camera to the correct height while keeping the keyboard and mouse in an ergonomic position.
- **Docking station:** With all this extra equipment, you'll need a docking station to connect everything to the laptop.
- **Standing desk:** For virtual presentations, we always recommend standing if you're able. Use an adjustable stand-up desk to switch between sitting and standing. Since you'll be standing more, invest in a standing-desk floor pad to minimize foot and knee pain.
- **Internet:** Test internet speed using a speed-test website. If internet speed lags, upgrade the modem, or choose a service plan with higher speeds. Direct-connecting the modem and laptop removes Wi-Fi from the equation.

Optimize your studio. This is where we've done the most MacGyvering. We didn't invest in creating a soundproof studio with professional lighting. We used things we already had around our houses to create an effective setup:

- **Lighting:** Where possible, use natural light or choose lighting that mimics natural sunlight. Position lighting in front of you. Strong backlighting creates a witness-protection-program effect, where your face is in shadow! Lighting from the side makes you look like one of the Beatles in Figure 9.7. Use curtains or sheers to soften bright natural light. While not an attractive decor choice, we've used sheets and blankets to control natural light when it's too bright.

    Ring lights are convenient and effective, unless you wear glasses. With glasses, ring lights reflect in both lenses. To minimize glare in glasses, spring for the antiglare lens coating, use indirect lighting, turn down monitor brightness, and turn the second monitor on an angle. Turning on the computer's night light (a.k.a. night shift) mode reduces glare, because it reduces the blue, purple, and green colors that reflect the most off glasses.

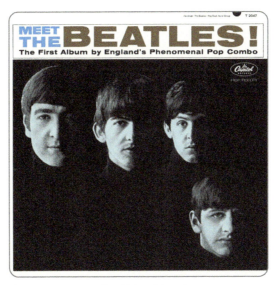

Figure 9.7 Get a ring light, Ringo!
Source: Capital Records

- **Background:** Set up a nondistracting background. If you have shelves, remove clutter, but keep some personality. Background objects become conversation pieces when meeting new people virtually. Turn off your ceiling fan—motion is the biggest distractor.

    Fake backgrounds are not ideal. Because the technology is imperfect, hands or hair often fade in and out of the background. Fake backgrounds can create webbed fingers or bald heads that don't exist in person. If a fake or blurry background is necessary, position yourself in front of a plain wall or green screen. Dr. Carmen Simon, a cognitive scientist, performed neurological studies of different backgrounds during sales presentations and concluded that fake backgrounds make the audience less attentive.[5]

- **Sound:** Any sound other than your voice or audio you intend to broadcast is noise. If possible, choose a home office space with a door. If you have a noisy roommate or neighbor, use blankets to muffle sound. Mute phone and computer alerts. In a great podcast about the *Get Back* documentary, the hosts griped about the beep tones in many of the songs used to sync the start of a new film reel. Ironically, a podcast guest had their audible phone notifications on.

- **Camera setup:** Set the camera at eye height so the camera isn't looking up or down at you. No one wants to look up your nose! Use a laptop stand or stack of books to raise the camera to the right height. Connect to a docking station with an external camera, keyboard, and mouse. When your head is too low in the frame, you don't look confident. If the camera cuts off the top or bottom of your head, you look incompetent. The Beatles didn't get this memo in Figure 9.8.

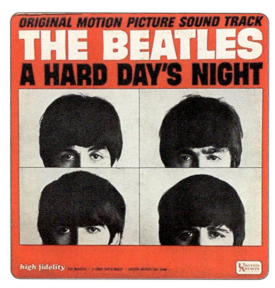

Figure 9.8 Adjust your cameras, boys!
Source: United Artists

Adjust the camera position until your head is in the "newscaster's framing," like in Figure 9.9. Your eyes should be two-thirds up the screen with headroom between the top of the screen and your head. Watch any talking head on a news program, and they'll be in this framing. We're amazed at how many people don't take this simple step.

Figure 9.9 "Professional" newscasters, Colin Jost and Michael Che
Source: Saturday Night Live / NBCUniversal Media LLC

- **Video pane location:** There are two ways to maintain virtual eye contact: train yourself to present to the camera or organize your monitor so the audience video is directly under your camera. In large meetings, pin the decision-maker or a friendly face under the camera.

  If your video software doesn't allow you to customize where the video pane is, try the hacks in Figure 9.10. The smiley-face sticky note lets you present to a friendly "face." Or, if you happen to own a life-size Keanu Reeves cardboard cutout, present to him.

Figure 9.10 Smiley and Keanu, enthralled by our presentation
Sources: (left) Courtesy of John Polk / (right) Governo do Estado de São Paulo / Wikimedia Commons / CC BY 2.0

Improve your home studio 249

It's not expensive to create an effective home studio, like in Figure 9.11. John spent a couple of hundred dollars on the stand-up desk, floor mat, earbuds, microphone, pop filter, and camera. John already had a docking station and repurposed the monitor, keyboard, and mouse from an old desktop.

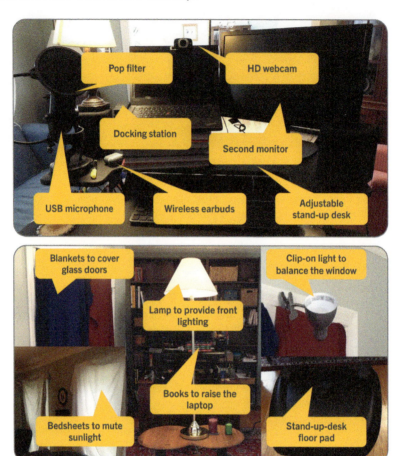

Figure 9.11 MacGyvered home studio
Source: John Polk & Associates

John's wife would like to point out that she has since replaced the blankets and sheets with proper window coverings, but we still need to add a sheet when the sun is at its brightest.

250 The Virtual Fatigue Trap

Plan for technology challenges. A killer presentation loses its edge if the technology fails. But glitches are a fact of life. Minimize issues and confidently adapt when they happen by practicing and creating backup plans:

- **Practice.** To learn the video software, you must practice. Memorize the location of necessary functionality. Understand how the software manages video panels. Some platforms make it impossible to put multiple audience members under the camera. Clients who insist on using their video software fill us with dread! Using unfamiliar software can lead to three bad things:

    - Your presentation is less smooth as you struggle to find the share, mute, or chat buttons.

    - The software doesn't support your engagement activities.

    - Your host's IT department disables certain tools for security purposes. For a workshop, we failed to uncover that a client's IT department disabled video in the breakout rooms. So, we had to punt on an exercise that required it.

- **Do a dry run.** In addition to practice, a dry run can reveal the potential pitfalls of using an unfamiliar video platform. Remember John's dad's wisdom from Chapter 8, "The Under (or Over) Confidence Trap"—practice like you play. Make dry-run conditions as close to the real world as possible.

    Schedule the dry run using the same link as the meeting. Include the host, cohost, administrative support, or tech support if you have them. If you don't have audio/visual tech support, recruit a friend. Run through every planned engagement activity. Ask dry-run participants to chat, complete the poll, and annotate. Send participants to the breakout room, send them a message, join them in the room, and ensure they can turn on video or share screens if necessary. Practice muting participants and changing between speaker view and gallery view. Often, the web version isn't as capable as the desktop application. So, find out if all participants can use the desktop application or test the planned activities through the web version.

- **Build in redundancy.** Good thing you invested in an external camera, a microphone, and earbuds because you now have redundancy when something breaks. Practice how to switch out equipment. The ultimate failure is when your laptop goes down or software force-updates right before your big presentation. Have a backup laptop or ensure access to the video platform from a phone or tablet. Store essential files in the cloud synced to your laptop, or use a thumb drive.

Ask for and give candid feedback on video setups. Because the seismic shift to virtual work during the COVID pandemic was abrupt, everyone was forgiving of home studio glitches. And that made sense for the first few months. While you can't always prevent barking dogs and screaming babies, you can minimize your contribution to virtual fatigue by replacing your grainy camera, staticky microphones, and noisy background. Ask someone you trust to give you feedback on the quality of your "broadcast." And when you notice those problems for others, discreetly let them know. It's like telling a coworker they have spinach in their teeth. It's awkward in the moment, but wouldn't everyone rather know?

Structure presentations to minimize fatigue

Presenting virtually creates both challenges and opportunities for engagement. In person, there are dynamic real-time questions, natural group interactions, fewer distractions, and no hiding off camera. The virtual setting blows that all up. Use these best practices to convert to a virtual-friendly presentation:

- Shrink the session time. Anything more than 90 minutes requires a break.

- Chunk up longer topics into multiple sessions separated by hours or days. Adjust content so it focuses on a key topic or theme.

- Design slides for the small screen.

- Double down on meeting best practices: having clear scope, purpose, agenda, summary, action items, and next steps.

- Convert in-person exercises to virtual engagement activities. Move questions to chat. Convert flip charts to annotate and group exercises to breakout rooms.

- Shorten lecture segments and add more engagement activities. Each module should look like the example in Figure 9.12.

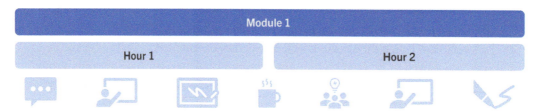

Figure 9.12 Bite-sized segments of engaging and life-changing content
Source: John Polk & Associates

Engage, engage, engage

Because it's easier for the audience to "hide" in a virtual environment, it's critical to up your engagement game. We tried learning tap dancing, but the virtual audience couldn't see our feet!

Set ground rules. Most people are rule followers, especially when their boss is in the room. Setting clear ground rules, like in Figure 9.13, improves engagement and minimizes virtual fatigue.

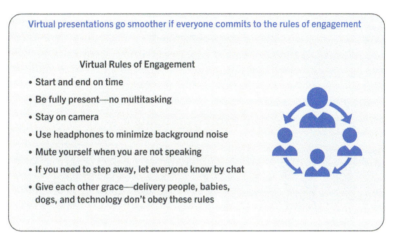

Figure 9.13 Everyone pinky swear
Source: John Polk & Associates

Notice the third bullet point: Stay on camera. But wait, we wrote that having your camera on drives virtual fatigue?! It does. And we have clients with cameras-off (or optional) policies for that reason. There is genuine tension here.

To solve that tension, set different camera policies by meeting type. You may insist everyone be on camera for decision meetings but off camera for daily stand-ups. We'd rather see organizations minimize virtual fatigue by having fewer meetings, so the meetings they do have are high engagement. Another best practice is to join the meeting with the camera on to establish your presence, then turn the camera off except when speaking.

Enable discussion. In the virtual world, speaking up is more challenging for the audience. By the time you think of a question, decide that it's not a dumb question, find the unmute button, and wait for the presenter to pause—the presenter has moved on to another topic. The audio delay in virtual meetings makes it harder to know when it's safe to jump into a conversation.[6] Nonverbal communication is harder to read, so you don't know if the presenter or the leaders in the room want participation. And when two people talk simultaneously, it's even more awkward virtually.

As a presenter, you must pause longer to clearly signal when and how you want questions or discussion. As work-from-home and hybrid policies reduce the time spent in an office, there are fewer opportunities to get to know the audience as people. For many, especially introverts, that ramps up the stress of speaking up in a meeting. For less formal meetings or meetings that rely on interaction, build in time for a get-to-know-me activity.

A simple exercise starts by asking everyone to turn off their camera. Then, ask questions like "Who has been at the company for less than two years?" or "Who has traveled in the last month?" If the answer is yes, participants turn their cameras back on. Then, ask camera-on people where they went on vacation.

Use virtual engagement tools. In addition to generating audience engagement, the virtual tools in Figure 9.14 help democratize presentations.

Figure 9.14 Stop lecturing me!
Source: Zoom Communications, Inc.

In many company cultures, the presenter shares an idea, and then everyone waits for the most senior person in the room to react. With virtual tools, everyone can share ideas simultaneously, enabling the best ideas to win. Most video meeting platforms have these five engagement tools:

- **Annotate:** Draw diagrams, illustrate concepts, or highlight important info on the shared screen. Ask the audience to write their ideas on-screen. Coordinate brainstorming and idea voting.

- **Breakout rooms:** Host small-group discussions or divide tasks by designing breakout sessions that mimic real-life interactions. Virtual happy hours during the COVID-19 pandemic fell flat because one person talked to everyone, unlike in-person events where small, rotating groups mingle. Instead, recreate that dynamic by using breakout rooms and allowing participants to move between them for more natural, small-group conversations.

- **Chat:** Encourage group discussion, feedback, and questions. Share reference links and repeat discussion questions in the chat for clarity. Use chat for real-time reactions. When teaching software tricks in person, we often get gasps (like when double-clicking Format Painter to apply changes to multiple objects). Now, we ask participants to share their gasps in the chat!

- **Polls and quizzes:** Gauge audience understanding or interest with polls or chats. Let participants vote on ideas. Use them early to signal interactivity and encourage engagement, but avoid overusing polls—keep questions relevant and valuable to the discussion.

- **Whiteboards:** Encourage participants to contribute ideas and design collaboratively. Whiteboards are similar to the Annotate tool but with more real estate, virtual sticky notes, and templates.

Have a cohost. A formal cohost can monitor the chat and manage intense engagement activities. Having someone other than you speak is also a natural engagement booster. Build a "production script" for complicated sessions to keep you and your cohost in sync through transitions. Here is a sample cohost job description for a workshop:

- Kick off the workshop and introduce the presenter.
- Explain why presentation skills are essential to the organization.
- Set expectations for engagement during the workshop and politely nag slackers.
- Review audience questions and decide which ones to ask the instructor.
- Connect the workshop material to the culture and practices of the company and department.
- Monitor technical issues and troubleshoot.

For more tips on how to make virtual meetings engaging, check out *Engaging Virtual Meetings* by John Chen.

Adjust your performance

All the techniques described in Chapter 8, "The Under (or Over) Confidence Trap," apply in the virtual world with the slight modifications in Figure 9.15.

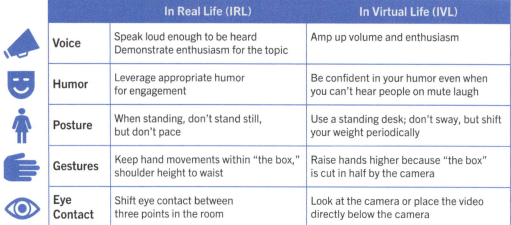

Presentation Performance Strategies

	In Real Life (IRL)	In Virtual Life (IVL)
Voice	Speak loud enough to be heard Demonstrate enthusiasm for the topic	Amp up volume and enthusiasm
Humor	Leverage appropriate humor for engagement	Be confident in your humor even when you can't hear people on mute laugh
Posture	When standing, don't stand still, but don't pace	Use a standing desk; don't sway, but shift your weight periodically
Gestures	Keep hand movements within "the box," shoulder height to waist	Raise hands higher because "the box" is cut in half by the camera
Eye Contact	Shift eye contact between three points in the room	Look at the camera or place the video directly below the camera

Figure 9.15 Whether in person or in pixels, you got this
Source: John Polk & Associates

Dress for virtual success

Chapter 8, "The Under (or Over) Confidence Trap," discussed how clothes signal and boost confidence. All that applies, with these additional considerations:

- **Business dress is more casual in virtual meetings.** In person, we wear sports coats when teaching. For virtual workshops, that felt too formal. Who wears a sports coat at home? But we still wear collared dress shirts. Be careful of the "virtual mullet" approach: business on top, party on the bottom. The internet has many videos of virtual meeting participants who thought their gym shorts (or worse) would stay off camera.

- **Video creates new challenges.** Make sure your clothing stands out clearly against your background and lighting—avoid colors that are too light or too dark, as they may blend into the background. A solid, medium-toned color usually works well. The classic blue shirt or solid jewel-toned blouse may be clichés, but they are effective for a reason. Shiny fabrics can create glare.

Patterns can create visual noise or digital noise. The moiré effect, seen in Figure 9.16, is a digital artifact caused by the interlaced scanning in monitors. The moiré effect often happens with houndstooth, tight stripes, or checks.

Figure 9.16 The wrong shirt causing a distracting moiré effect
Source: Courtesy of John Polk

Digital facelifts and other tips

We've compiled our favorite virtual technology tips. Your virtual software might not have all this functionality, or it might give them a different name. There are two broad categories:

- **Functionality:** Knowing how to use these video software tools can mitigate fatigue for you and the audience:
  - Turn off the self-view after you've ensured the lighting and framing are good. If you prefer to see yourself on video, mirror it because it looks more natural to see yourself reflected that way.
  - Try the Touch Up My Appearance tool. Digital facelifts are free! Figure 9.17 compares the video before and after using this feature.

(continued)

Before  **After**

Figure 9.17 The miracle of the Touch Up My Appearance tool
Sources: (before) Courtesy of Marty Polk / (after) White House / Pete Souza / Wikimedia Commons / Public Domain

- Hide nonvideo participants. Looking at a gallery of black boxes is depressing because it signals disengagement.

- Know where the Mute All button is in case there's a noisy participant you can't identify.

- If you're on mute to block background noise, hold down the space bar to unmute temporarily.

• **Security:** If uninvited guests sometimes crash your meeting or add graffiti to your slides, know how to use these common security settings:

   - Limit screen sharing to the host.

   - Set up a waiting room to prevent meeting crashers or keep your next meeting attendees from joining early.

   - Turn on Allow Host to Put Attendee on Hold so you can kick out meeting crashers.

   - Turn off Annotation to protect against unauthorized graffiti and know how to erase someone else's annotation.

Do all this and more for a hybrid presentation

Hybrid presentations, with some participants in the room and some on video, are the worst of both worlds. With a poor setup, video participants can't see or hear in-room participants. And if you ask in-room participants to log in to the video software from their laptops, they'll wonder why they bothered to show up in person. The key to a successful hybrid presentation is to assess the setup from remote and in-person participants' perspectives and then test the setup with each group.

Focus on these three areas:

- **Audio:** Meet in a room with multiple high-quality mics, if possible.

- **Video:** Set up a gallery view of in-person and remote participants. Use extra cameras to share flip charts or whiteboards, or use a digital whiteboard to develop engaging activities for all participants. Test new technologies to make sure they increase engagement and not distraction.

- **Facilitation:** Actively pull remote participants into the conversation and assign them in-room "buddies" with a direct communication line (IM, text, chat). Buddies can submit in-room "votes" or let the group know if there is an audio problem. While separating remote and in-person participants for breakouts is convenient, it may not always provide the best participant mix.

In the hybrid setting, the people on the phone or video are disadvantaged. They might not be able to hear parts of the conversation. And they have a more challenging time contributing to the discussion. So, they are more likely to tune out and check email. To keep remote participants engaged, make a point to ask for their input at critical points in the presentation.

To avoid embarrassment if they tuned out—call their name, then restate the current topic within the question to give them a chance to catch up. If you know someone won't be in person, socialize your ideas before the meeting. Then, in the meeting, say, "Sally, when we spoke earlier, you raised a concern about the impact on our call center. Does this new rollout plan address your concerns?"

Key Takeaways

Reimagine what works well in person for the virtual world, leveraging its advantages while minimizing virtual fatigue.

- ✓ Invest in your home studio, focusing on noise reduction, lighting, and background. Create redundancy in case of equipment failure.
- ✓ Adjust the camera height so your eyes are two-thirds up the screen.
- ✓ Amp up your enthusiasm, adjust gestures, and create virtual eye contact by tucking the video pane under the camera.
- ✓ Find a partner and give feedback on each other's virtual setup.
- ✓ Chunk up long presentations and use multiple interaction activities to maintain engagement.
- ✓ Set video rules of engagement with coworkers to maximize participation and minimize virtual fatigue.
- ✓ Engage the audience with virtual interaction tools—like annotation, breakout rooms, chat, polls, and whiteboards.
- ✓ Don't dress too formally or sloppily, and avoid distracting clothing patterns.
- ✓ In hybrid sessions, ensure everyone can hear, and actively engage those not in the room.

Figure 10.1 You get no respect when you make a poor first impression
Source: Wall of Celebrities

10

The First and Last Impression Trap

Start strong while avoiding widespread speech clichés, then finish strong to cement your key messages.

Imagine you're attending a conference, listening to a presenter who looks as nervous as Rodney Dangerfield in Figure 10.1.

Poor presenter: So, um, ah, (*clears throat*) hi, hello. Can you hear me OK? How's everybody doing today?

Audience: (*tepid applause*)

Poor presenter: C'mon, you can do better than that. HOW'S EVERYBODY DOING TODAY?

Audience: (*forced enthusiastic applause and whoops*)

Poor presenter: That's better. I've never presented to an audience this big before. I didn't have much time to prepare. Let me start by telling you a little about myself. For those of you who don't know me, I'm Justin. I'm an expert in presentation design. Why are we here? Oh, yeah. I'm sorry for starting late. I had to fly in from Cleveland, and boy are my arms tired. (*pause for laughter*)

Audience: (*silence*)

Poor presenter: We have a lot of slides to get through. (*click*) You probably can't read this slide in the back. You know what? I don't need these slides. Without further ado …

How many times have you heard one or more of those lines or seen a nervous presenter like Rodney Dangerfield? From our experience, it's close to 100%. How many presentations have you started with one of those lines? You don't have to answer that.

Presenters fall into the First and Last Impression Trap when they lose their audience with a poor opening or fail to make concepts memorable with a botched finish. You know it's important to make a good first impression when meeting someone. When presenting, the opening makes the first impression on the audience, whether speaking to one or thousands.

Avoid the First and Last Impression Trap by speaking clearly and articulately, introducing yourself humbly, stating the purpose clearly, emphasizing key points with slides, leaving time for discussion, and ending on time.

So, like, reduce, um, filler words, you know

"Ums" and their cousins in Figure 10.2 are the scourge of the public speaker. We've heard seasoned speakers average almost two "ums" per sentence! It makes it impossible to pay attention to the message. Filler words, also called disfluencies, are endemic to speaking, appearing in almost every language, so how do you manage them?[1]

Understand your filler words and their purpose. Filler words serve a real purpose in communication. Otherwise, people wouldn't have started using them in the first place. Here are typical purposes for filler words:

- **Thinking:** "Please don't interrupt me while I'm thinking." Pausing in conversation can signal an opportunity for others to speak. Saying "um" or "uh" serves as a verbal placeholder, keeping control of the conversation while searching for the right words.

Figure 10.2 Well, I mean, that speech bubble is filled with filler words or something
Source: John Polk & Associates

- **Precision:** "I need a moment to choose my words carefully." This is not about crafting the idea but about delivering it carefully. Whether disagreeing, giving bad news, or refining a point, a brief pause allows for careful phrasing. Stretching out an "ahhh" lets the audience know you're being deliberate.

- **Dibs:** "Excuse me, I'd like to speak next." In fast-moving discussions, overlapping voices are common. Leading with "so" or "well" acts like a verbal hand-raise—it's better to be talked over at the start of a sentence than in the middle of an idea.

- **Clarification or comparison:** "Let me say that more clearly." The phrases "I mean," "I think," and "to be honest" refine statements or indicate confidence levels. Words such as "like" and "kind of" introduce comparisons.

- **Rapport building:** "Do you agree with me?" Softening phrases like "right?" and "you know?" encourage agreement and check for alignment.

Clients often say, "I don't even notice I'm doing this." Filler words often begin as helpful and end as reflexes. While filler words serve a purpose, they become distractions when they appear in every sentence. The first step to reducing them is awareness. You may notice that you use filler words more in big meetings. That's because your mind subconsciously realizes you must coordinate speaking with other people and amps up the level of filler words to communicate intent.

But the presenter already has everyone's attention. When presenting, you don't need filler words to let the audience know you're going to speak next. And you don't need filler words to let them know you're thinking; they can tell by your expression.

Understand the impact filler words have on the audience. Understanding how much you're annoying the audience can motivate you to improve. Audience members can form negative opinions due to your filler words:

- **Um or ah:** Since these classic filler words are associated with thinking about what to say next, the audience might assume you haven't thought through your ideas or proposals. Or they might assume you're nervous. This might make the audience nervous for you. Now everyone is nervous!

- **And:** Many speakers connect all sentences with "and." This sounds better than "um," but it can make your speech sound like one run-on sentence.

- **Like, kind of, or sort of:** We call these "power zappers" because they make you sound less confident. If you say, "We should, like, cut costs," the audience might interpret that as, "We should do something less powerful than cut costs." We used to call them "power sappers," but a client misheard the phrase, and a better phrase was born!

- **I mean, I think, or well:** When these are overused, the audience might interpret the constant need for clarification as an inability to express yourself or a weak position. But it should go without saying that the things you say are things you think or mean!

- **You know:** In its filler-word form, "you know" comes across as insincere. This is especially true if you don't pause to check for understanding or when presenting to a large audience where it's impractical to check for understanding. In those cases, the audience can assume you don't care if they understand or not.

- **Actually, basically, seriously, totally, or literally:** These are useful for emphasis, but overuse might make you sound like a know-it-all. And in the case of "literally," you literally meant "figuratively."

Slow down and insert a short pause instead. As much as there is a trick to reducing filler words, this is it. A fundamental habit-breaking principle is to substitute a good habit for a bad one.[2] People trying to quit smoking might try chewing gum. So, to break an "um" habit, practice inserting a pause instead.

> *The right word may be effective,*
> *but no word was ever as effective as*
> *a rightly timed pause.[3]*
>
> Mark Twain, *Writings of Mark Twain*

Think of the pause as a thing you actively insert into speech rather than the absence of words. Pauses don't seem as long to the audience as they do to you. And they make speech more dynamic.

Know your stuff. Since many filler words occur when thinking about what to say next, knowing the key points reduces that thinking time. Know the intro well enough that you don't use filler words. Write it out. Memorize it. Then, practice saying it with an authentic speech that doesn't sound like you memorized it. Many presenters are so worried about sounding scripted that they sound unprepared. We're guessing many of you watch movies or TV shows—we hear Netflix is popular. We hate to burst the illusion, but those people on the screen are actors who've memorized a script, as discussed in Chapter 8, "The Over (or Under) Confidence Trap."

Practice in a safe space. Filler words are a powerful habit to break. It takes concentrated practice. But practicing during a high-stakes presentation, say your first meeting with the CEO, is a recipe for disaster. When you notice filler words, you self-criticize—then you get in your head, and your speech begins to falter. Instead, find a low-stakes setting where you're confident, in or out of the workplace.

Interviewing job candidates is one safe space. Since the candidates are more nervous than you are, they won't notice any stumbles or awkward pauses as you work to reduce filler words. Practice in low-stress meetings, host a lunch and learn, or practice with a friend, like in Figure 10.3.

Figure 10.3 Safe presentation practice in the cone of silence
Source: Get Smart (1965) / NBCUniversal Media LLC / Wikimedia Commons

Record yourself or find a peer, mentor, or coach to observe, count, and give feedback.

What gets measured gets managed.

Peter Drucker, attributed but likely
paraphrased from Lord Kelvin[4]

Counting filler words on a recorded video or having a friend count them provides data on how bad your filler word "infection" is and whether it's improving over time. Hearing the number can be shocking, and that shock will create motivation to improve. In Toastmasters, there is a role for a filler-word counter. In some exercises, the counter rings a bell for each filler word—a slightly less painful form of shock treatment!

Don't insult the audience

It's not the audience's job to show enthusiasm. It's your job to make the audience enthusiastic! Paul McCartney never says, "You can do better than that!" He just launches into "A Hard Day's Night," and the crowd goes wild.

Unlike Paul, you didn't write "A Hard Day's Night." However, you can give engaging, high-energy presentations that audiences respond to. And asking 100 people how they're doing is a little disingenuous. What would you do if one person responded, "Terrible!"?

Instead of disrespecting the audience, kick off with an engaging story. Chapter 4, "The Just the Facts Trap," discussed the power of storytelling. Surely, you remember the elements of the SUCCESs framework for memorable stories! Here are some more tips for an engaging kickoff:

- Keep it short. A rambling story might illustrate your point, but it also signals a lack of structure.

- Deliver it with high energy.

- Use humor, but make sure the audience gets the joke. And keep it clean!

Introduce yourself efficiently

There's something about a microphone, like in Figure 10.4, that makes people act funny, and we're not talking about off-key karaoke. The mic triggers nerves, which leads to meandering introductions. Why do so many presenters open with, "Let me start by telling you a little about myself"? Would you ever say that to someone you just met?

Figure 10.4 The microphone awaits
Source: Courtesy of John Polk

Neither would we. Just introduce yourself like a normal person—briefly, naturally, and with a purpose.

Whether speaking with a microphone or not, the personal introduction should answer these audience questions: Who are you, and why should I believe you? It makes our skin crawl when speakers say, "For those of you who don't know me, I'm Justin." Guess what? He's also Justin for those of you who do know him. That extra phrase is a small waste of time right when the audience is deciding whether they want to pay attention to you. "Without further ado" is another small waste of time. And because "ado" means a fuss about something unimportant, you've just declared the introduction was a waste of time. While you want the audience to trust your expertise, don't spend time up front reciting every credential. Don't call yourself an expert or guru. The audience won't be convinced until you demonstrate it.

For a better introduction, hit these marks:

- Smile.[5]
- Just say, "I'm Justin."
- Make an open-palm gesture.[6]
- Say what you do, then let your presentation demonstrate your expertise.
- Alternatively, ask someone reputable to introduce you. Although not appropriate in every circumstance, this is an elegant way to highlight your credentials. Coach the introducer not to read your bio bullet points. Instead, ask them to

describe your greatness authentically. David Martin, author of *Free the Genius*, notes that if the audience trusts the introducer, that trust will transfer to you.[7]

- Build expertise proof points into your stories rather than listing them like a résumé. For example, Justin mentions the Monarch Innovation Award while sharing a story about using Agile and design thinking. It's not a humble-brag—your stories reflect the experiences that built your expertise.

- Deliver value early. Many webinars waste time with platform instructions, lengthy intros, mic checks, and tech glitches. Instead, start with a practical tip within five minutes to showcase your expertise and value quickly.

State the purpose up front

The goal of sharing the purpose is to answer these natural audience questions: Why are we here, why should I care, and what's my role?

State the clear purpose at every step. Start with a clear purpose in the meeting invite. Repeat that purpose on the cover slide. Speak to that purpose as you kick off the presentation. Finally, check to ensure you achieved the purpose at the end of the meeting.

Be clear about the WIIFM (what's in it for me). This is central to getting and keeping the audience's attention. The audience must care about the topic before investing energy to focus on the content. If the purpose is at odds with the audience's purpose, no one will achieve their goal.

Be clear about what role you want the audience to play and how they can engage. Is this meeting interactive, or should participants wait until the question and answer (Q&A) section? Do you want them to speak their comments or put them in the chat window?

Don't say you're sorry

Saying "I'm sorry," "I've never presented in front of such a large audience," or "I didn't have much time to prepare" puts you in a weak position. That's not the position you want to be in when starting a speech. And apologizing for starting late delays the start even more. More importantly, don't exhibit behavior requiring apologies. Prepare and manage contingencies so you start on time. Test the technology before speaking. If something genuinely goes wrong, like a 10-minute delay, say "I apologize"—the more powerful cousin of "I'm sorry."

Leaders often use self-deprecation to show that they are just like everyone else. A little self-deprecation goes a long way. With too much self-deprecation, people start to believe you. Often, when we hear self-deprecation from senior leaders, we don't believe they believe it. It's not authentic if you don't mean it.

Toasting, it's not just for weddings anymore

Justin has been the best man at five weddings. Once, he was chosen because he was the only relative, and the groom didn't want to choose between his friends. Another time, he was chosen because he was the only friend, and the groom didn't want to choose between his brothers. Being the best man is an honor, but it's stressful because you must deliver a toast.

Matt Abrahams, lecturer at the Stanford University Graduate School of Business, developed the WHAT framework in Figure 10.5 for these occasions.

Figure 10.5 Cheers!
Source: Adapted from *Think Fast Talk Smart: The Podcast* / Matthew Abrahams LLC / Reproduced with permission of Matthew Abrahams LLC

Think of a toast as a script with stage directions. The audience needs cues when it's their turn to participate. When discussing the newlyweds, look at them so the audience will. When telling a funny story, smile or laugh so the audience will, too. And when it's time for the toast, raise a glass and loudly say, "Raise your glass with me," so the audience knows it's time to start drinking!

For leaders, this framework works in team meetings, project kickoffs, or any time someone asks you to "say a few words."

Use slides to reinforce key points

The bigger the stage, the more important it is to follow the Platinum Rule of Presentations. When you say, "We have a lot of slides to get through" or "You probably can't read this slide in the back," you've already failed. These phrases are red flags that you repurposed a deck created for a longer meeting and different setting.

Occasionally, we work with presenters who don't want to use slides for their presentations. When we ask them why, they say, "I'm a talker. I don't need slides." Yes, we shouldn't assume that every speech requires supporting slides, but sometimes, the "no slides" preference indicates one or more issues. Let's explore each issue and how supporting visuals can make the talker more effective:

- **Issue 1: The presenter is skilled at talking but not skilled at creating supporting visuals.** Just because you're a good speaker doesn't mean that visuals aren't incrementally valuable. Adding great visuals to a great speech makes it even more engaging and memorable. Most TED Talks include presentation slides. Are you such a great talker that you're better than TED?

> *A large body of research indicates that visual cues help us to better retrieve and remember information. ... Our brain is mainly an image processor, ... not a word processor. In fact, the part of the brain used to process words is quite small in comparison to the part that processes visual images.*[8]
>
> Haig Kouyoumdjian, "Learning Through Visuals"

- **Issue 2: The presenter rambles and can't create a clear, logical story.** Even experts struggle to create clear, logical stories about their topic on the fly. Slide creation forces you to organize your thoughts. And clear, logical stories are easier for the audience to digest. Even in cases where visuals aren't appropriate, writing the speech or creating speaker notes helps you be clear and concise. Storyboarding, covered in Chapter 2, "The Bury the Lede Trap," is a fantastic way to organize your thoughts, with or without visuals.

- **Issue 3: Someone else created the deck and didn't understand the nuances of the presenter's style.** Chapter 1, "The Frankenstein Trap," discussed the Platinum (Plus) Rule of Presentations, shown in Figure 10.6.

Figure 10.6 Let's skip this figure—someone else created it
Source: John Polk & Associates

When building a deck for someone else to deliver, consider the presenter's style. Marketing groups, designers, and other centralized presentation writers often miss the mark because they don't understand what happens in a sales meeting, or they design for only one presenter type. These problems compound when salespeople have different presentation styles. When the standard presentation doesn't work for the salesperson, the talkers don't use it; they just talk.

- **Issue 4: The presenter is a BSer and doesn't want to put the BS in writing.** (Forgive us for not spelling out "BS" the first time!) This is probably the most cynical paragraph in the book, but we're convinced some presenters don't want to put anything in writing because they don't want to be held accountable for what they said. Everyone benefits from putting thoughts in writing, because it forces you to structure ideas logically, choose words for maximum impact, and word diet thoughts for conciseness.

In any presentation, there's a real risk that the audience forgets the message soon after it's delivered. People are forgetful and constantly bombarded with information. Memorable stories are one way to combat this problem. The other way is to create and use compelling slides. Not only do slides help the audience digest the message, but if you distribute slides or handouts, the audience can refer to them later.

Slide-free and fabulous

As you've probably guessed, we're fans of using decks for effective communication. But that doesn't mean you always need slides. Here are situations when you might skip the slides:

- **Informal settings:** Breaking out presentation software signals a level of formality and preparation that may not be suitable for some settings, like your first introduction to a new team.
- **Telling a personal story:** In this situation, the focus should be on you and the power of your voice and emotions. If you want to include slides, stick to simple, evocative images.
- **Communicating one-on-one:** Phone, email, instant message, and face-to-face channels are more casual. However, you might need a one-slide visual or short presentation to socialize a complex idea.

(continued)

> People who consider themselves good talkers often forgo slides and miss the opportunity to organize their thoughts and help the audience digest and remember key points. Of course, talkers probably aren't reading this book unless a boss or mentor encouraged them to. If you're reading this book, you probably work with some talkers. Now you have the arguments necessary to convince them to let you help create their decks.

Put it all together to create a great first impression

Here's a solid introduction to a presentation about the impact of communication skills on your career that addresses the common mistakes:

Presenter: Hi, I'm Justin. I want to make you a great presenter so you can engage, influence, and drive action.

Audience: (OK, we're listening)

Presenter: In my former career as a strategy and analysis leader, I sat through over 150 cross-calibration conversations. Cross-calibration is a way for companies to ensure you get a fair performance rating rather than just letting your boss decide.

Audience: (you have some credibility)

Presenter: While I'm a fan of ensuring associates get a fair performance assessment, cross-calibrations can be painful! Over the years, I've experienced full-day calibrations, dot exercises, and forced distributions. If you've never experienced these, trust me, they're painful.

Audience: (we feel your pain)

Presenter: When discussing promotions, I noticed a pattern in the feedback for associates. Rarely did the debate focus on technical skills, subject-matter expertise, or even results—by the time an associate is up for promotion, they've demonstrated those things. The competency gaps that typically held associates back were communication, influence, or the mystical "leadership presence."

Audience: (that's insightful)

Presenter: You show all these competencies through effective presentations. Being a better presenter will change your life, whether getting that promotion or influencing others to make the world a better place.

Audience: (sold!)

Stick the landing to avoid a poor last impression

John's father got kicked out of navy flight school. On his first training flight off an aircraft carrier, like the model in Figure 10.7, he landed hard, bounced, and took off again. On his second landing, he overcompensated and flopped on the deck. Turns out he had a depth perception problem that would have disqualified him from flying.

No one remembers a perfect takeoff and flight when you botch the landing. In flight school, gymnastics, and presentations, you must stick the landing. To stick the presentation landing, summarize key points and next steps, end on time, and eliminate cheesy or unnecessary ending slides.

Figure 10.7 Better stick the landing
Source: Stephen W. Henninger / Smithsonian / CC0 1.0

Leave time for discussion, summary, call to action, and next steps

Outside of TED Talks, town halls, and keynotes—the audience expects discussion. The audience will feel frustrated and unheard if you don't leave time for that discussion. You also need discussion to gather feedback on your ideas and advice on managing the proposed change.

> In the first part I tell 'em what I am going to tell 'em;
> in the second part—well, I tell 'em;
> in the third part I tell 'em what I've told 'em.[9]
>
> Unidentified preacher, as reported by
> J. H. Jowett in "Three Parts of a Sermon"

Summarizing is critical for ensuring the audience remembers key points. A presentation is like a sandwich—it needs a solid introduction, strong content, and a clear summary. Without time to summarize, the sandwich is missing the bottom slice of bread. What a mess! As you summarize, ensure the call to action is clear.

Finally, capturing the next steps is critical for establishing commitments and driving action. Without agreement on the next steps, all the good work devolves into a fog of "I thought someone else was going to do that."

End on time

Overtime is only exciting in sports. In a presentation, you're forcing the audience to choose between being late for their next meeting or missing something important in your presentation. Even if they aren't late for their next meeting, overtime eats into productive work time, lunch, or a coffee break. The *only* way to guarantee everyone appreciates some aspect of the presentation is to end early! Ending a presentation early or on time requires planning, flexibility, and willpower:

- **Planning:** Negotiate for enough time to meet your purpose, then design your content to fit. Allow for a late start and questions, then cover the most critical points early.

- **Flexibility:** Identify skippable content in advance. While ending early is often a win, prepare extra material to cover if applicable. Adjust content during breaks by hiding, unhiding, or rearranging content to stay on track with timing.

- **Willpower:** It's tough but worth it. Ending on time may mean skipping slides, cutting discussions, or leaving questions unanswered. Send skipped content afterward, take discussions offline, or schedule a follow-up. If needed, negotiate with stakeholders: "Can we take 10 extra minutes to resolve this, or should we schedule another meeting?" Most prefer 10 minutes now over a longer meeting later.

We lost count of how often a 30-minute meeting with an executive got cut to 15 minutes. Planning, flexibility, and focus come from preparation. Speeding through a 30-minute presentation in half the time won't impress anyone.

Don't end on an insincere slide

Ever seen a closing slide like Figure 10.8? We see them all the time, although they often include exclamation points and noisy graphics.

Figure 10.8 No thank you
Source: John Polk & Associates

Even if the "Thank you" slide has a simple, modern font with a serene blue background befitting the brand, don't use it. Here are the reasons:

- These thank-you slides are typically part of a corporate template and are included in every deck. That makes the thank-you slide insincere by definition.
- It looks like you needed a reminder to show the audience appreciation.
- Because they make you look insincere, they work against your goal of showing genuine appreciation.

The "Questions?" slide, like in Figure 10.9, is the next most popular ending slide.

Figure 10.9 Is that a question?
Source: John Polk & Associates

We don't like ending on a questions slide, with a few exceptions. Here are the reasons:

- For most meetings, assuming you'll present the entire deck and then take questions only at the end is a terrible design. Instead, build an interactive presentation and pause for questions at critical points.

- Like the thank-you slide, you don't need a questions slide to take questions at the end of the presentation.

- Ending a presentation by taking questions creates a risk that you will run out of time while answering an awkward or low-value question. Manage the Q&A to end with enough time to deliver a stick-the-landing summary and conclusion.

There are two exceptions to the no-questions-slide recommendation:

- **Town hall meetings:** It's common to put a Q&A session on the agenda. If you want a slide to signal that it's time for audience participation, you could repeat the agenda with the Q&A line highlighted.

- **Long virtual events:** Given the challenges we discussed in Chapter 9, "The Virtual Fatigue Trap," a questions slide creates more space for participants to engage. A slide like Figure 10.10 creates space for questions. These slides signal a big topic shift, giving participants time to ask questions.

Figure 10.10 Way too many questions
Source: 9parusnikov / Adobe Stock Photos

How should a deck end? The answer is simple: repeat the cover slide. It signals that the presentation is done. It's not content heavy, so it avoids distraction while answering any final questions. It can also act as a bumper slide before the appendix. For a sales presentation, include contact information on the repeated cover slide, like in Figure 10.11, or repeat a call to action.

Figure 10.11 Cover slides aren't just for covers anymore
Sources: (background) vasabii / Adobe Stock Photos / John Polk & Associates

Yes, those are our actual LinkedIn profile links. If you made it this far in the book, you're someone we'd like to connect with. Sign up for our erratically published newsletter at johnpolkandassociates.com.

How can you thank your audience without a thank-you slide? How about a sincere, from the heart, verbal "thank you." Appreciate their time, engagement, ideas, support, questions, and comments.

If you keep clicking when you reach the end of a presentation, some software drops you into a black abyss, and if you click again, you fall out of presentation mode into editing mode, like in Figure 10.12. The black screen is jarring for the audience. Transitioning to editing mode is like the scene in *The Wizard of Oz* when the curtain falls and Dorothy and friends see the Wizard is just a small man. Other software keeps you on the last slide in presentation mode, making the presenter wonder if the clicker broke. A copy of the cover slide at the end of the presentation acts like a guardrail, preventing embarrassing additional clicks.

Figure 10.12 PowerPoint's black abyss and editing mode
Sources: Microsoft PowerPoint / (right background) vasabii / Adobe Stock Photos

Don't end on an insincere slide   279

Key Takeaways

Start strong while avoiding widespread speech clichés, then finish strong to cement your key messages.

- ✓ Don't insult the audience, rattle off credentials, apologize, or use phrases like "for those of you who don't know me."
- ✓ Reduce filler words by practicing intentional pauses instead.
- ✓ Open with a short, engaging story that illustrates a key theme. Memorize key points, then deliver them authentically.
- ✓ Prepare, start on time, and manage the technology.
- ✓ Build expertise proof points into stories.
- ✓ Articulate the purpose clearly and show the audience what's in it for them.
- ✓ Don't forgo visuals because you're a good talker. Don't force visuals because you're a good designer.
- ✓ Reserve time for discussion, summary, call to action, and next steps.
- ✓ Respect the audience by ending the presentation on time through planning, flexibility, and willpower.
- ✓ Repeat the cover slide to create a soft landing for the presentation.

Figure 11.1 Justin and son's riding lessons
Sources: *Wheels and Wheeling—The Smithsonian Cycle Collection* (1974) / US Government Publishing Office / Public Domain

Conclusion

Combine the tools, techniques, and tricks from previous chapters to create synergy to engage, influence, and drive action.

Justin's daughter learned to ride a bike the traditional (and traumatic) way—with wobbles, crashes, and cries of "Daddy, don't let go!" After a monthlong break to regain confidence, she succeeded.

When it was his son's turn, Justin was determined to spare him the same struggle. Justin signed him up for a "How to Ride a Bike for Kids" class. Handwritten on the advertisement were the words "One Class! No Falls!"

They arrived at the empty parking lot with their bikes, very *unlike* Figure 11.1. The instructor removed training wheels, pedals, and kickstands, transforming the parking lot into a training ground with a few cones.

"We're going to take this one step at a time," the instructor announced, demonstrating how to lift and lay down a bike safely. "Don't get on your bikes yet. Just pick them off the ground and lay them down gently." The parents led by example while the kids practiced. Watching his son struggle to stand his bike upright, Justin questioned how far they would progress that morning.

But each attempt was smoother than the last. Then the instructor showed the kids how to mount and dismount their bikes. As awkwardness gave way to ease, he added steps—lifting the bike, settling onto the seat, taking one step while seated without pedals, then stopping and dismounting.

By the end, Justin's son slowly pedaled while weaving between cones, growing confident without a single fall. On the drive home, Justin's son was already planning the small steps to learn how to ride with "no hands!"

Throughout this book, we've demonstrated the steps to create presentations that engage, influence, and drive action. If it feels overwhelming, practice one skill at a time. After mastering one skill, add more to your repertoire. Soon, you'll be teaching the skills to others as they marvel at how effortlessly you avoid presentation pitfalls.

Put it all together

Any of the tools, techniques, or tricks in this book will improve your presentations. It's when they come together that the magic happens. Let's demonstrate the strategies using a slide summarizing the monthly business review (MBR) tips from Chapter 3, "The Black Hole Trap." No problem if you haven't memorized those tips! For this exercise, we focus on developing one slide. For a complete deck, repeat this process for the rest of the slides after mapping them out with a storyboard.

Tell a clear story. Approaching a presentation like a story marries logical flow and emotional impact. Here are the key story strategies:

- **Assess the audience, purpose, and setting to determine design.** The audience includes business leaders frustrated by the time-consuming, inefficient process of assessing business health. They want a more action-oriented approach. Analysts who coordinate the MBR share frustrations over the time spent building the deck and managing follow-up actions. All are results driven, with the knowledge and interest to dive deep into the topic.

  The purpose is to explain the benefits of using business intelligence software to improve all MBR aspects. The "facts" include common MBR challenges and solutions that employ business intelligence software, including dashboards. The "feelings" include shared frustration with the current process and confidence that the ideas will improve effectiveness and efficiency. The key "follow-up" is to agree to implement the recommendations.

  The setting is an in-person discussion with a small stakeholder group. The slide will also serve as a checklist for action after the meeting.

  The design must balance the tension between being comprehensive and digestible. It should leverage a memorable framework to chunk up the content and be animated to present it in a logical order. It also needs a word diet to ensure there isn't unnecessary content. These steps will help the audience digest the relatively dense slide.

- **Create a compelling story.** The slide is part of a short business case leveraging the "issue, action, impact" story architecture. Ultimately, it'll focus on the issue and action elements, but it starts with a simple recommendation, "We should improve the MBR by applying best practices." The first step is to put initial thoughts on the slide, creating a simple mind map, like in Figure 11.2.

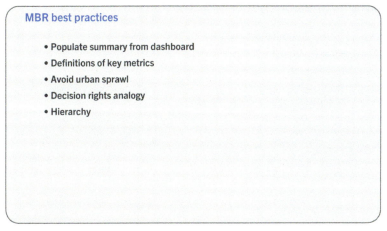

Figure 11.2 Is that all you can think of?
Source: John Polk & Associates

At this first stage, we only wrote a subject title. Note the lack of parallel structure—perfect phrasing isn't a goal yet. The focus is just getting ideas on the slide. This early in the process, the slide is useless without a presenter. People who consider themselves good talkers or take the "less is more" philosophy to an extreme often stop here.

- **Put important things first.** Now that we've captured key content, we can write a sentence title, like in Figure 11.3. The title isn't perfect, but it's better than the

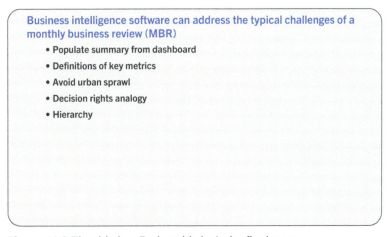

Figure 11.3 The title is a B-, but this isn't the final exam
Source: John Polk & Associates

Put it all together   285

subject title. Writing a sentence title narrowed the scope to focus on how business intelligence software can improve the MBR.

Leverage graphics. Visual slides engage the audience and make complex concepts easy to understand and memorize. These are the primary visualization strategies:

- **Support the story with data and charts.** Now that the sentence title gives a clear "so what," we can blow out the content, like in Figure 11.4.

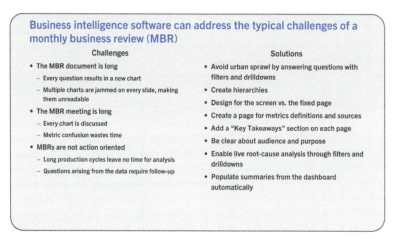

Figure 11.4 Boom! And that's how you get a wall of text
Source: John Polk & Associates

To motivate change, we gathered qualitative data from peers' feedback on MBR challenges. In the complete deck, we used charts to illustrate problems like the growing slide count. We organized the content into a framework with columns for MBR challenges and solutions. We built a hierarchy for the challenges but left the second column unordered for now. At this point, the slide is still a wall of text. If you don't want to read it, we understand.

- **Use frameworks, images, and icons to convey ideas.** The first graphicalization step creates a classic three-boxer, like in Figure 11.5. For real estate efficiency, we swapped the rows and columns. The slide is dense, and the lower section has a separate section title. We added the horizontal line to ensure a clear separation between the challenges and solutions. Usually, white space is sufficient.

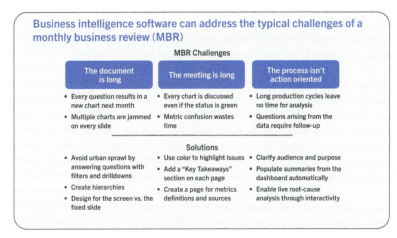

Figure 11.5 Boxes, they're not just for pizza anymore!
Source: John Polk & Associates

Since the column-header boxes represent challenges, we changed them and the "MBR Challenges" text in Figure 11.6 to red to signify a warning. We then changed the "Solutions" text to green.

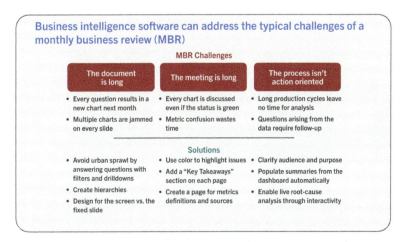

Figure 11.6 Slide design for bulls if they could actually see red[1]
Source: John Polk & Associates

Icons, added in Figure 11.7, let the audience quickly interpret the key challenges and make the slide more engaging. We might not always add icons when the slide is dense, but we left them to illustrate the tactic.

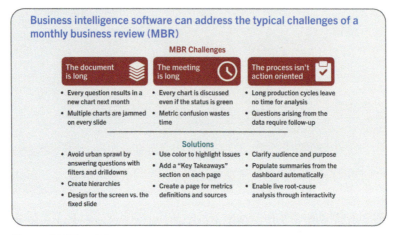

Figure 11.7 Iconic!
Source: John Polk & Associates

Reduce noise. Cluttered, dense slides make it harder for your audience to get your message. Here are strategies for reducing noise and boosting signal:

- **Use a standard template with a simple, elegant design.** Have we mentioned John Polk & Associates' template and slide library? Starting with these tools instead of the default blank deck or an existing deck saves time and ensures consistency across slides.

- **Write professionally.** After organizing the draft text into a framework, we edited for clarity and conciseness at every step. We shortened the phrase "Multiple charts are jammed on every slide, making them unreadable" to "Multiple charts are jammed on every slide." After swapping rows and columns, this bullet point became three rows long, triggering a word diet.

  We also solved the parallel structure problem from the original mind map. In the finished product, all the red boxes and the bullet points are sentences.

  Because the slide is dense, we animated the content. In Figure 11.8, the numbered white boxes show the order in which the content appears.

  The slide opens with the three red boxes on the screen to show the audience the high-level framework. Then, the text boxes below the red boxes come in, one at a time. Then, the divider line, the solutions title, and the bottom-left text box come in. Finally, the remaining two bottom text boxes come in, one at a time. We could animate the text boxes by columns instead of rows, depending on how we want to present the framework.

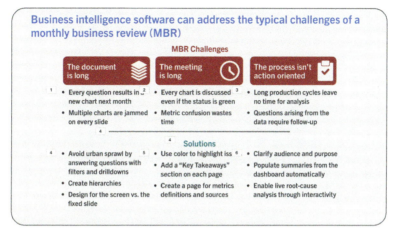

Figure 11.8 Only Harry Potter has animation on a printed page
Source: John Polk & Associates

We realized the slide margins were unnecessarily large, so we widened the columns to take advantage of the extra horizontal space in widescreen in Figure 11.9. This lets the slide breathe and gets the remaining three-line bullet point to two lines.

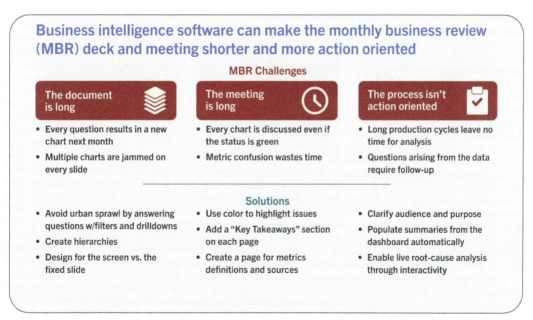

Figure 11.9 Why didn't we use all the white space from the beginning?
Source: John Polk & Associates

Put it all together   289

Obviously, we'd skip this step if we used the entire slide real estate from the start. After finalizing the slide body, we made the sentence title more precise.

- **Use the fewest words required.** We've been word dieting along the way. Reading the slide aloud will help find opportunities to trim text and catch other issues.

> ### Worth it!
>
> We often get the question "Is this worth all the effort?" when teaching slide formatting, grammar and style, or word dieting. You may have dismissed some of the finer points in this book as "no big deal." "If my audience can understand my ideas, the format shouldn't matter." It's true. Format *shouldn't* matter.
>
> But for the hundreds of people who contributed data to the "pet peeves" exercise, format does matter. Calling them "pet peeves" makes them sound insignificant. The French term for pet peeve is *bête noire*, literally "black beast." That's a better mental image for the effects of format, grammar, and style issues on the audience. When you've added these best practices to your design repertoire, you'll create polished and professional decks, allowing the message to shine through.
>
> Chapter 6, "The Piece of Cake Trap," touched on this point, but it bears repeating. For every deck, you must judge when the slides are "good enough" and polishing has reached diminishing returns. This depends on the audience, purpose, and setting. Practice the tools, techniques, and tricks so they become second nature. While it might slow you down now, once they become second nature, you'll design professional decks in less time than it takes to create less-polished decks today. When the process has good design practices built in, it's not extra work to create professional slides.

Present with confidence. Projecting confidence boosts the audience's confidence in your ideas. To project confidence, focus on the following:

- **Prepare and practice.** It's not enough to create great slides. We need to build out the talking points and practice the speech. A relevant story or metaphor is always effective for tying points together. In this case, we compare the current MBR to a black hole that has become so dense that the audience tunes out and no information can escape! Business intelligence software dashboards are the rocket boosters that will alter the course and prevent the MBR from being crushed under the weight of its information density.

- **Show confidence with voice and body.** A steady pace and a moderate volume project confidence. Then, vary pace, pitch, and volume to show emphasis or encourage interaction. Tone and volume will naturally reinforce the message by stating in the intro, "I'm excited about the opportunity to make the MBR more actionable while saving time." Remember to stand tall with your shoulders back and maintain good eye contact.

- **Read the audience as you present.** Are they paying attention? Nodding along? Recognizing the MBR might be boring for some, pay attention to distraction cues. Assess the root cause of the audience's behavior and then react by soliciting questions, amping enthusiasm, or encouraging discussion.

Go forth and present!

When John left the corporate world to start John Polk & Associates, his executive coach encouraged him to ask the corporate leaders he worked with to describe his value proposition. Since these leaders were the target market, this uncovered customer-back language to describe our services and value. When John asked one leader this question, she didn't miss a beat.

> *You make people look like they've got their s#!t together.*[2]
> Sharon McGinty, conversation

This perfectly captures the power of a logical story, told through engaging, noise-free visuals and presented with confidence.

Now that you have these presentation tools at your disposal, it's time to shift from the scissor kick to the Fosbury flop, like in Figure 11.10. Imagine the awe on people's faces as you effortlessly soar above presentation pitfalls, displaying the finesse and confidence of a true expert.

When someone asks for the secret to your promotion, please share this book. Presentation skills aren't the only secret to success, but they are vital. By applying these concepts, you've armed yourself with techniques to transform your career. Improving communication skills will set you apart and propel you to new heights.

Thank you! We sincerely appreciate the time you invested in reading and applying these concepts. We know they'll lead to success. Let us know when you get that promotion!

Figure 11.10 Flopping his way to success!
Source: High jumper Dick Fosbury clearing the bar during 1968 Olympic trials at Los Angeles Memorial Coliseum / Los Angeles Times / Wikimedia Commons / CC BY 4.0

Notes

Introduction

1 "Writing about Music Is Like Dancing About Architecture," Wikipedia, last modified August 5, 2024, https://en.wikipedia.org/wiki/Writing_about_music_is_like_dancing_about_architecture.

Chapter 1

1 Joel R. DeLuca, *Political Savvy: Systematic Approaches to Leadership Behind the Scenes* (Berwyn, PA: Evergreen Business Group, 1999), 128.

2 William Hollingsworth Whyte, "Is Anybody Listening?," *Fortune*, September 1950, 174.

3 Zig Ziglar, *See You at the Top* (Gretna, LA: Pelican Publishing, 2000), 317.

Chapter 2

1 Richard Rodgers and Oscar Hammerstein II, "Do-Re-Mi," from *The Sound of Music*, 1959.

2 *Information Management: Records Management: Preparing and Managing Correspondence*, Army Regulation 25–50, US Department of the Army (Washington, DC: Headquarters, Department of the Army, May 17, 2013).

3 *MythBusters*, season 3, episode 14, "Jet Pack," hosted by Jamie Hyneman and Adam Savage, aired June 9, 2005, on Discovery Channel.

4 "The Egyptian Scarab Beetle and Its Meaning," Jakada Tours Egypt, last accessed January 28, 2025, https://jakadatoursegypt.com/the-egyptian-scarab-beetle-and-its-meaning/.

5 Team Sequoia, "Writing a Business Plan," Sequoia Capital, last accessed January 17, 2025, https://articles.sequoiacap.com/writing-a-business-plan.

6 Garson O'Toole, "Quote Origin: My Customers Would Have Asked for a Faster Horse," *Quote Investigator*, July 28, 2011, https://quoteinvestigator.com/2011/07/28/ford-faster-horse/.

7 George E. P. Box, "Science and Statistics," *Journal of the American Statistical Association* 71, no. 356 (1976): 791–799, https://doi.org/10.1080/01621459.1976.10480949.

8. Simon Sharwood, "AWS Hits $100B Revenue Run Rate, Expands Margins, Delivers Most of Amazon's Profit," *The Register*, May 1, 2024, https://www.theregister.com/2024/05/01/amazon_q1_2024/.

9. Neil A. Bradbury, "Attention Span During Lectures: 8 Seconds, 10 Minutes, or More?," *Advances in Physiology Education* 40, no. 4 (2016): 509–513, https://doi.org/10.1152/advan.00109.2016.

10. Michael Alley, Madeline Schreiber, Katrina Ramsdell, and John Muffo, "How the Design of Headlines in Presentation Slides Affects Audience Retention," *Technical Communication* 53, no. 2 (May 2006): 225–234.

11. Jane Austen, *Emma* (Project Gutenberg, August 1994), https://www.gutenberg.org/files/158/158-h/158-h.htm.

Chapter 3

1. Garson O'Toole, "Quote Origin: If I Had More Time, I Would Have Written a Shorter Letter," Quote Investigator, April 28, 2012, https://quoteinvestigator.com/2012/04/28/shorter-letter/.

2. James C. Abbott, *The Executive Guide to Low Cost Call Centers* (Greenville, SC: Robert Houston Smith Publishers, 2025), 15.

3. Arthur Thomas Quiller-Couch, *On the Art of Writing* (Raleigh, NC: Lulu Press, 2008), 172.

4. Arthur Brisbane, "Debt Carries You for a While But—Groaning and Sweating, You Carry Debt in the End," *New Orleans Item*, July 26, 1915, 6.

5. Garr Reynolds, *Presentation Zen: Simple Ideas on Presentation Design and Delivery* (Berkeley, CA: New Riders, 2008), 68–72.

Chapter 4

1. David Mikkelson, "Dragnet: 'Just the Facts, Ma'am,'" Snopes, March 29, 2002, https://www.snopes.com/fact-check/just-the-facts/.

2. Jim Camp, "Decisions Are Largely Emotional, Not Logical: The Neuroscience Behind Decision-Making," *Big Think*, June 11, 2012, https://bigthink.com/personal-growth/decisions-are-emotional-not-logical-the-neuroscience-behind-decision-making/; Peter Noel Murray, "How Emotions Influence What We Buy," *Psychology Today*, February 26, 2013, https://www.psychologytoday.com/us/blog/inside-the-consumer-mind/201302/how-emotions-influence-what-we-buy.

3. Daniel Smith et al., "Cooperation and the Evolution of Hunter-Gatherer Storytelling," *Nature Communications* 8, no. 1853 (2017), https://doi.org/10.1038/s41467-017-02036-8.

4. Tannia Suárez, "Use the STARC Method for Behavioral Job Interview Questions," LinkedIn, August 31, 2022, https://www.linkedin.com/pulse/use-starc-method-behavioral-job-interview-questions-tannia-su%C3%A1rez; Development Dimensions International, "STAR Method," DDI World, last accessed January 25, 2025, https://www.ddiworld.com/solutions/behavioral-interviewing/star-method.

5 Carmen Simon, *Impossible to Ignore: Creating Memorable Content to Influence Decisions* (New York: McGraw-Hill, 2016), 73.

6 Ilia Gurliand, "Reminiscences of A. P. Chekhov," *Teatr i iskusstvo*, no. 28 (July 11, 1904): 521.

7 Daniel Kahneman, *Thinking, Fast and Slow* (New York: Farrar, Straus and Giroux, 2011), 87.

8 Walt Hickey, "The Worst Chart in the World," *Business Insider*, June 17, 2013, https://www.businessinsider.com/pie-charts-are-the-worst-2013-6.

9 Robert Kosara, "A Pair of Pie Chart Papers," *EagerEyes* (blog), 2016, https://eagereyes.org/blog/2016/a-pair-of-pie-chart-papers.

10 Joe Raposo, Jon Stone, and Bruce Hart, "One of These Things (Is Not Like the Others)," Sesame Workshop, 1969.

Chapter 5

1 Benjamin Franklin, "To Samuel Cooper, 4 August 1772," Founders Online, National Archives, https://founders.archives.gov/documents/Franklin/01-19-02-0200.

2 Garson O'Toole, "Everything Should Be Made as Simple as Possible, but Not Simpler," Quote Investigator, May 13, 2011, https://quoteinvestigator.com/2011/05/13/einstein-simple/.

3 Barbara Minto, *The Pyramid Principle: Logic in Writing and Thinking* (London: Pearson Education, 2009), 82.

4 G. T. Doran, "There's a S.M.A.R.T. Way to Write Management's Goals and Objectives," *Management Review* 70, no. 11 (1981): 35–36.

5 E. J. McCarthy, *Basic Marketing: A Managerial Approach* (Homewood, IL: Irwin, 1960), 205.

Chapter 6

1 Daniel Victor, "Oxford Comma Dispute Is Settled as Maine Drivers Get $5 Million," *The New York Times*, March 16, 2017, https://www.nytimes.com/2017/03/16/us/oxford-comma-lawsuit.html; Jonathan Wells, "Does Bad Grammar Stand in the Way of True Love?," *The Telegraph*, October 17, 2015, https://www.telegraph.co.uk/men/relationships/11916674/Does-bad-grammar-stand-in-the-way-of-true-love.html.

2 *Corporate*, season 2, episode 4, "Thanks!," directed by Pat Bishop, written by Matt Ingebretson, Jake Weisman, and Pat Bishop, aired February 5, 2019, on Comedy Central.

3 Ebenezer Cobham Brewer, Rule 37, *Rules for English Spelling* (London: Jerrold and Sons, 1880), 48.

4 Bob Dorough, "Conjunction Junction," performed by Jack Sheldon, animation by Kimmelman and Associates, *Schoolhouse Rock!*, ABC, 1973.

5 *Merriam-Webster.com Dictionary*, s.v. "literally," accessed May 9, 2025, https://www.merriam-webster.com/dictionary/literally.

6 John Schamel, "How the Pilot's Checklist Came About," Air Traffic Control History, December 9, 2018, https://www.atchistory.org/how-the-pilots-checklist-came-about/.

7   *The Simpsons*, season 9, episode 9, "Reality Bites," directed by Mark Kirkland, written by Dan Greaney, aired December 7, 1997, on Fox.

8   Tucker Max, "How to Write Your First Draft (Scribe and Vomit Draft Method)," Scribe Media, last accessed January 12, 2025, https://scribemedia.com/scribe-vomit-draft-method/.

9   Melody Joy Kramer and Marc Silver, "Jodie Picoult: You Can't Edit a Blank Page," NPR, November 22, 2006, https://www.npr.org/2006/11/22/6524058/jodi-picoult-you-cant-edit-a-blank-page.

10 Samuel Osborne, "Rare 'Sinners' Bible' Containing Unfortunate Typo in the Ten Commandments Up for Sale," *The Independent*, October 21, 2015, https://www.independent.co.uk/news/uk/home-news/rare-sinners-bible-containing-unfortunate-typo-in-the-ten-commandments-up-for-sale-a6702156.html.

Chapter 7

1   Charles F. Lummis, editorial, *Los Angeles Times*, 1926.

2   Thomas Fuller, *Gnomologia: Adages and Proverbs, Wise Sentences, and Witty Sayings, Ancient and Modern, Foreign and British* (London, 1732).

3   Edward R. Tufte, *The Visual Display of Quantitative Information* (Cheshire, CT: Graphics Press, 1983), 107.

4   John Thomas Smith, *Remarks on Rural Scenery* (London: Nathaniel Smith, 1797), 16.

5   Jakob Nielsen and Kara Pernice, *Eyetracking Web Usability* (Berkeley, CA: New Riders, 2010).

6   "The Basic Principles of Design—and How to Apply Them," *Paperform* (blog), December 10, 2023, https://paperform.co/blog/principles-of-design/.

7   Jakob Nielsen, "Top 10 Mistakes in Web Design," Nielsen Norman Group, January 1, 2011, https://www.nngroup.com/articles/top-10-mistakes-web-design/.

8   Alison Flood, "When Fonts Fight, Times New Roman Conquers," *The Guardian*, January 29, 2020, https://www.theguardian.com/books/2020/jan/29/when-fonts-fight-times-new-roman-conquers.

9   Julie Terberg, "Choosing Fonts for PowerPoint Templates," Design to Present, June 2024, last accessed April 12, 2025, https://designtopresent.com/2024/06/20/choosing-fonts-for-powerpoint-templates/.

10 Garr Reynolds, "Who Says We Need Our Logo on Every Slide?," Presentation Zen, accessed January 17, 2025, https://www.presentationzen.com/presentationzen/2007/05/the_source_of_a.html.

11 Mike Parkinson, in conversation with John Polk, January 10, 2025.

12 Centers for Disease Control and Prevention, "CDC Data Shows Over 70 Million U.S. Adults Reported Having a Disability," CDC Newsroom, July 16, 2024, https://www.cdc.gov/media/releases/2024/s0716-Adult-disability.html.

Chapter 8

1. Karen Kangas Dwyer and Marlina M. Davidson, "Is Public Speaking Really More Feared Than Death?," ResearchGate, April 2012, https://www.researchgate.net/publication/271993200_Is_Public_Speaking_Really_More_Feared_Than_Death.

2. "What Scares You, America?," Chapman University, October 1, 2024, https://news.chapman.edu/2024/10/01/what-scares-you/.

3. Allison Shapira, "The Upside of Your Public Speaking Jitters," *Harvard Business Review*, November 6, 2020, https://hbr.org/2020/11/the-upside-of-your-public-speaking-jitters.

4. Alison Wood Brooks, "Profile Page," Harvard Business School, last accessed January 17, 2025, https://www.hbs.edu/faculty/Pages/profile.aspx?facId=684820&view=research-summary.

5. James Whittaker, "A Few Thoughts on Imposter Syndrome," *Medium*, June 12, 2023, https://medium.com/@docjamesw/a-few-thoughts-on-imposter-syndrome-9b0e2c214d8c.

6. Célia Ruffino et al., "Acquisition and Consolidation Processes Following Motor Imagery Practice," *Scientific Reports* 11 (2021): Article 2295, https://doi.org/10.1038/s41598-021-81994-y.

7. Kelly McGonigal, *The Upside of Stress: Why Stress Is Good for You, and How to Get Good at It* (New York: Avery, 2015).

8. *Saturday Night Live*, "Daily Affirmations with Stuart Smalley," season 16, episode 13, aired February 9, 1991, on NBC.

9. *Saturday Night Live*, "Pumping Up with Hans & Franz," season 13, episode 1, aired October 17, 1987, on NBC.

10. "Exercising to Relax," Harvard Health Publishing, July 7, 2020, https://www.health.harvard.edu/staying-healthy/exercising-to-relax.

11. Wendy L. Patrick, "Power Role Play: Dressing for Success Makes You Successful," *Psychology Today*, September 9, 2017, https://www.psychologytoday.com/us/blog/why-bad-looks-good/201709/power-role-play-dressing-success-makes-you-successful.

12. Matt Abrahams, *Think Faster, Talk Smarter* (New York: Simon Element, 2023), 61–62.

13. John Polk, "Find Your Walk-Up Song: How Music Can Boost Your Confidence," *John Polk & Associates* (blog), September 15, 2019, https://johnpolkandassociates.com/2019/09/15/whats-your-walk-up-song/.

14. Michelle Millis Chappel, "15 Benefits of Listening to Music (Backed by Science)," Lifehack, June 28, 2023, https://www.lifehack.org/317747/scientists-find-15-amazing-benefits-listening-music.

15. *The Adventures of Gulliver*, Hanna-Barbera Productions, originally aired 1968–1969.

16. Vanessa Van Edwards, "60 Hand Gestures You Should Be Using and Their Meaning," Science of People, June 13, 2024, https://www.scienceofpeople.com/hand-gestures/.

17 John Tierney, "The Language of the Hands," *The New York Times*, August 27, 2007, https://archive.nytimes.com/tierneylab.blogs.nytimes.com/2007/08/27/the-language-of-the-hands/.

18 Belle Linda Halpern and Kathy Lubar, *Leadership Presence: Dramatic Techniques to Reach Out, Motivate, and Inspire* (New York: Gotham Books, 2004), 9.

19 Associated Press, "Biggs Has Plans for Tyson," *Oroville Mercury-Register*, August 19, 1987, 1B, col. 2, accessed via Newspapers.com.

Chapter 9

1 Douglas Adams, *The Salmon of Doubt: Hitchhiking the Galaxy One Last Time* (New York: Ballantine Books, 2002), 115.

2 *Seinfeld*, season 5, episode 16, "The Raincoats," directed by Tom Cherones, written by Tom Gammill and Max Pross, aired April 28, 1994, on NBC.

3 Jeremy Bailenson, "Nonverbal Overload: A Theoretical Argument for the Causes of Zoom Fatigue," *Technology, Mind, & Behavior* 2, no. 1 (February 23, 2021), https://tmb.apaopen.org/pub/nonverbal-overload/release/2.

4 "Vyopta Survey Reveals 92% of Execs Don't See Long-Term Future for Off-Camera Employees," Vyopta, April 12, 2022, https://www.vyopta.com/blog/releases/vyopta-hybrid-work-survey-2022/.

5 Carmen Simon, "Research Brief: Do Zoom Backgrounds Help or Hinder Sales Presentations?," B2B Decision Labs, accessed January 17, 2025, https://win.corporatevisions.com/rs/413-YED-439/images/Research-Brief-Zoom-Backgrounds.pdf.

6 Julie E. Boland, Pedro Fonseca, Ilana Mermelstein, and Myles Williamson, "Zoom Disrupts the Rhythm of Conversation," *Journal of Experimental Psychology: General* 151, no. 6 (2022): 1272–1281, https://doi.org/10.1037/xge0001150.

Chapter 10

1 Lorenzo García-Amaya, "Why Do We, Like, Hesitate When We, Um, Speak?," TED-Ed video, 5:14, February 2021, https://www.ted.com/talks/lorenzo_garcia_amaya_why_do_we_like_hesitate_when_we_um_speak.

2 Charles Duhigg, "The Golden Rule of Habit Change," chap. 3 in *The Power of Habit: Why We Do What We Do in Life and Business* (New York: Random House, 2012).

3 Mark Twain, *Mark Twain's Speeches*, Stormfield Edition of the *Writings of Mark Twain* (New York: Harper, 1923), xv.

4 Al Bredenberg, "Who Said, 'What Gets Measured Gets Managed'?," *A Thinking Person* (blog), December 2, 2012, https://athinkingperson.com/2012/12/02/who-said-what-gets-measured-gets-managed/.

5 Gemma Gladstone and Gordon Parker, "When You're Smiling, Does the Whole World Smile for You?," *Australasian Psychiatry* 10, no. 2 (2002): 144–146, https://doi.org/10.1046/j.1440-1665.2002.00423.x.

6 Allan Pease, "Palm Gestures," chap. 6 in *Body Language: How to Read Others' Thoughts by Their Gestures* (London: Sheldon Press, 1981).

7 David Martin, in conversation with John Polk, March 2025.

8 Haig Kouyoumdjian, "Learning Through Visuals," *Psychology Today*, July 20, 2012, https://www.psychologytoday.com/us/blog/get-psyched/201207/learning-through-visuals.

9 "Three Parts of a Sermon," *Northern Daily Mail* (Hartlepool Northern Daily Mail), August 13, 1908, 3, col. 4 (Durham, England).

Conclusion

1 Ripley's Believe It or Not!, "Seeing Red: Turns Out Bulls Really Don't Care About Red at All," Ripley's, March 20, 2024, https://www.ripleys.com/stories/bulls-seeing-red.

2 Sharon McGinty, in conversation with John Polk, July 2017.

Further Reading

This section offers a curated collection of additional resources for readers who want to go deeper. We've included influential books and podcasts on presentation design, storytelling, and delivery. We've also included practical guides on presentation tools and works from adjacent fields that shape how we communicate. Each source was selected for its relevance, insight, and ability to help you strengthen your communication and leadership skills in both strategy and execution.

Presentation Design

Altman, Rick. *Why Most PowerPoint Presentations Suck and How You Can Make Them Better.* Pleasanton, CA: Harvest Books, 2012.

Duarte, Nancy. *Slide:ology: The Art and Science of Creating Great Presentations.* Sebastopol, CA: O'Reilly Media, 2008.

Malamed, Connie. *Visual Design Solutions: Principles and Creative Inspiration for Learning Professionals.* Hoboken, NJ: Wiley, 2015.

Minto, Barbara. *The Minto Pyramid Principle: Logic in Writing, Thinking, and Problem Solving.* London: Minto International, 1996.

Reynolds, Garr. *Presentation Zen: Simple Ideas on Presentation Design and Delivery.* Berkeley, CA: New Riders, 2008.

Simon, Carmen. *Impossible to Ignore: Creating Memorable Content to Influence Decisions.* New York: McGraw-Hill, 2016.

Simon, Carmen. *Made You Look: How to Use Brain Science to Attract Attention and Persuade Others.* New York: Random House, 2020.

Storytelling and Presentation Delivery

Abrahams, Matt. *Think Faster, Talk Smarter: How to Speak Successfully When You're Put on the Spot.* New York: Simon Element, 2023.

Chen, John. *Engaging Virtual Meetings: Openers, Games, and Activities for Communication, Morale, and Trust.* Hoboken, NJ: Wiley, 2020.

Duarte, Nancy, and Patti Sanchez. *Illuminate: Ignite Change Through Speeches, Stories, Ceremonies, and Symbols.* New York: Portfolio, 2016.

Gibson, Glenn. *Before the Mic: How to Compose Meaningful, Memorable, and Motivational Presentations.* Victoria, BC: Self-published, 2019.

Halpern, Belle Linda, and Kathy Lubar. *Leadership Presence: Dramatic Techniques to Reach Out, Motivate, and Inspire.* New York: Gotham Books, 2004.

Heath, Chip, and Dan Heath. *Made to Stick: Why Some Ideas Survive and Others Die.* New York: Random House, 2007.

Pollard, Tim. *The Compelling Communicator: Mastering the Art and Science of Exceptional Presentation Design.* Lafayette, CO: Oratium, 2016.

Whittaker, James. *The Storyteller's Spellbook: How to Make Your Ideas More Compelling and Your Career More Magical.* Self-published, 2017. Kindle edition.

Zimney, Sally. *Speaking Story: Using the Magic of Storytelling to Make Your Mark, Pitch Your Ideas, and Ignite Meaningful Change.* Minneapolis, MN: Two Harbors Press, 2017.

Data Visualization

Berinato, Scott. *Good Charts: The HBR Guide to Making Smarter, More Persuasive Data Visualizations.* Boston: Harvard Business Review Press, 2016.

Duarte, Nancy. *DataStory: Explain Data and Inspire Action Through Story.* Sebastopol, CA: O'Reilly Media, 2019.

Evergreen, Stephanie D. H. *Effective Data Visualization: The Right Chart for the Right Data.* Thousand Oaks, CA: SAGE Publications, 2016.

Few, Stephen. *Show Me the Numbers: Designing Tables and Graphs to Enlighten.* Burlingame, CA: Analytics Press, 2012.

Knaflic, Cole Nussbaumer. *Storytelling with Data: A Data Visualization Guide for Business Professionals.* Hoboken, NJ: Wiley, 2015.

Tufte, Edward R. *Beautiful Evidence.* Cheshire, CT: Graphics Press, 2006.

Tufte, Edward R. *The Visual Display of Quantitative Information.* Cheshire, CT: Graphics Press, 1983.

Wong, Dona. *The Wall Street Journal Guide to Information Graphics: The Dos and Don'ts of Presenting Data, Facts, and Figures.* New York: W. W. Norton & Company, 2010.

Zelazny, Gene. *Say It with Charts: The Executive's Guide to Visual Communication.* New York: McGraw-Hill, 2001.

Tool Usage

Bossé, Chantal. *Microsoft PowerPoint Best Practices, Tips, and Techniques: An Indispensable Guide to Mastering PowerPoint's Advanced Tools to Create Engaging Presentations*. Birmingham, UK: Packt Publishing, 2023.

Hogan, Stephy. *The Reluctant Designer's Field Guide to PowerPoint*. Self-published, 2022.

Parkinson, Mike. *A Trainer's Guide to PowerPoint: Best Practices for Master Presenters*. Alexandria, VA: ATD Press, 2018.

Terberg, Julie, and Echo Swinford. *Building PowerPoint Templates v2*. Self-published, 2021.

Communication Adjacent

The Arbinger Institute. *Leadership and Self-Deception: Getting Out of the Box*. San Francisco: Berrett-Koehler, 2000.

Covey, Stephen M. R. *The Speed of Trust: The One Thing That Changes Everything*. New York: Free Press, 2006.

Duhigg, Charles. *The Power of Habit: Why We Do What We Do in Life and Business*. New York: Random House, 2012.

Kahneman, Daniel. *Thinking, Fast and Slow*. New York: Farrar, Straus and Giroux, 2011.

Martin, David. *Free the Genius: How the Very Best Grow Their Meaning, Mission, and Contribution*. Ignite Press: 2019.

Norman, Don A. *The Design of Everyday Things*. New York: Basic Books, 2013.

Podcasts

Abrahams, Matt. *Think Fast, Talk Smart*. Stanford Business School. https://www.gsb.stanford.edu/business-podcasts/think-fast-talk-smart-podcast.

Chollar, Troy, Nolan Haims, and Sandy Johnson. *The Presentation Podcast*. https://thepresentationpodcast.com.

GhostRanch Communications. *Presentation Thinking*. https://www.ghostranch.com/podcast.

Knaflic, Cole Nussbaumer. *Storytelling with Data Podcast*. https://www.storytellingwithdata.com/podcast.

LaCroix, Darren, and Mark Brown. *Unforgettable Presentations*. https://deliverunforgettablepresentations.com/podcast/.

Marshall, Lisa B. *The Public Speaker*. https://www.quickanddirtytips.com/the-public-speaker.

Pica, Lea. *The Present Beyond Measure Show*. https://leapica.com/podcast.

Pierce, Matt. *The Visual Lounge*. https://the-visual-lounge.captivate.fm/.

Port, Michael. *Steal the Show*. https://stealtheshow.com/podcast/.

Staneart, Doug. *Fearless Presentations*. https://www.fearlesspresentations.com/podcasts/.

Index

A

Abbott, James, 73
abbreviations, 33
Abrahams, Matthew, 271
accessibility, designing for, 213–214
acronyms, 150, 157, 167–168
action, driving, 5, 7, 27, 54, 99, 106, 284
Adams, Douglas, 242
add-ins, software, 171
affirmations, 228
agendas, 65–66, 88
Agile methodology, 56, 108, 270
alignment tools, 206, 208
ALL CAPS, 188
alliteration, 150
analogies, 152–153
anecdotes, 104, 271
animations, 27, 28, 94–96
annotated tables, 76–77
annotation tools, 254
answering questions, 223–224, 278–279
anxiety, 219–220, 227–229
apologies, 270–271
appearance, 228, 256–258
appendixes, 93–94
arbitrary uniqueness, 207
Arnold, Edmund, 192
Association for Talent Development (ATD), 8
atom model, 140
attention spans, 58, 150–151

attire. See dressing for success
audible noise, reducing, 213
audience
    assessment of, fig. 1.6
    attention spans, 58, 273
    Audience, Purpose, and Setting Rule,
        13–15, 25–26, 284
    comprehension, 133–135, 158
    Conditions of Satisfaction Checklist,
        fig. 1.8, 19
    connecting with, 234–235, 290
    editing decks for new, 29
    educating your, 17, 134
    engaging the, 104, 106, 137, 253–255, 270
    first/last impressions on, 263–264
    focusing on, 229
    impact of filler words on, 265
    insulting the, 268
    key takeaways for, 22–23
    logical flow for, 65
    nonverbal cues, 242
    off-camera, 244
    reading and reacting to, 235–236, 291
    rehearsals with, 225
    sentence titles for clarity for, 58
    thanking the, 279
    3F framework for reaching, 21–22
    understanding/catering to, 15–21
availability bias, 130
A Way with Words, 156

B

background, delivering necessary, 134–135
backgrounds, visual
    home studio setup, 247
    slide backgrounds, 189
bar charts, 74, 110–111, 126
Barnette, Martha, 270
Barrett, Grant, 270
baseline design, 197–207
the Beatles, 47–49, 76, 121, 136, 137, 139, 140, 141, 247, 248
before-and-after framework, 148
behavioral job interviews, 106
benchmarks, 61
beveled slide edges, 189
biases, 129–130
big-number (shocking statistic) slides, 120–122
black, use of the color, 210
The Black Hole Trap, 7, 71–100, 156, 185
blueprint analogy, 152
BLUF (bottom line up front), 46
body language, 233–234, 235, 242, 291
borders, 189, 204
Box, George E. P., 55
brain dumps, 39–40, 57
breadcrumbs. See running heads
breaking the ice, 254
breakout rooms, 254
Brewer, Ebenezer Cobham, 168
Brisbane, Arthur, 78
Brooks, Professor Alison Wood, 220
bubble charts, 74
Building PowerPoint Templates (Swinford and Terberg), 198
bulleted lists, 88–90, 148, 194–195
bullseye diagrams. See target diagram
bumper slides, 57, 66–67
The Bury the Lede Trap, 7, 37–69, 105, 148, 179
Busick, Don, x

C

camel case, 32
camel decks, 31
camera equipment, 246, 248, 259
captioning, 213
causation, correlation and, 114, 130
cause-and-effect framework, 148
Chapman University, 219
chapter breaks. See bumper slides
chartjunk, 189
charts
    data visualization mistakes, 110–125
    data visualization via, 73–74
    libraries for, 214
    noise in, 188–190
    preattentive attributes in, 126–129
    supporting story with, 286
chat, 255
checklists
    Audience Question Preparation, fig. 8.3, 223
    Conditions of Satisfaction Checklist, fig. 1.8, 19
    Decision Meeting Checklist (a.k.a. "Don Slide"), fig. 1.9, 20
    Grammar and Style, fig. 6.14, 174
    Presentation Delivery Preparation, fig. 8.5, 226
    Presentation Planning, fig. 6.11, 173
    Slide Design, fig. 6.15, 175
    Slide Titles, fig. 6.13, 174
    Story, fig. 6.12, 174
Chekhov's gun, 109
Chen, John, 255
chevrons, 140, 148
"Choosing Fonts for PowerPoint Templates" (Terberg), 200
Christie, Agatha, 36
chunking, 135, 148
clichés, 156
close talkers, 242
clothing. See dressing for success

cognitive load, 72, 78, 137, 157, 206, 213
cohosts, 255
collaboration
    alternate presenters, 272–273
    software tools for, 31
collages, photo, 82
color
    baseline palette, 198–199
    clothing, 256–257
    color vibration, 187
    contrast and, 208–209
    emphasis via, 210
    preattentive attribute of, 126, 127
    vision deficiency, 213
    visual frameworks and, 150
column charts, 74, 110, 111–112, 126
combination tables, 76
"Communicating Your Analysis" (Polk), 8
Communication
    concise, 90–93
    first impressions, 268–270, 274
    illusion of, 17
    jargon, 157
    signal-to-noise ratio, 71, 72–73
    up-front, 37–38, 46
competency, 2, 274
competition, assessing the, 55
complex slides
    animation of, 94–96
    chunking, 135
comprehension, 214
Conditions of Satisfaction Checklist,
    fig. 1.8, 19
confidence
    body language and, 233–234
    delivery with, 230–234
    expertise and, 220
    managing nerves, 219–220, 227–229
    overconfidence, 237
    practicing to improve, 226
    preparation for, 220–224
    presenting with, 4, 61, 290–291
    visible lack of, 227

confirmation bias, 129–130
confounding variables, 130
conn, the, 31
consistency vs. contrast, 197, 207
content
    clear, 60
    libraries, 214–216
    preparation on, 221
context, 207
contrast vs. consistency, 197, 207
controlling ideas. See key points
core concepts, education in, 134–135
Corporate, 166
correlation, causation and, 114, 130
cover slides, 62, 66, 202, 270, 278, 289
Covey, Stephen R., 190
credibility, 107, 109, 129, 274
crisscrossing line charts. See spaghetti
    charts
cropping images, 83, 211
cross-calibration for promotions, 1, 274
cues, visual, 272
cultural sensitivity, 156
customers
    clarifying needs of, 19
    Conditions of Satisfaction Checklist, 19
    support from, 22
    understanding/catering to, 16
    value propositions for, 52–54
cycle framework, 144–145

D

Daily Affirmations with Stuart Smalley, 228
Dangerfield, Rodney, 188, 262, 263, 264
dashboard analogy, 153
dashed lines, 195
Data & Analytics for Instructional Designers
    (Torrance), 8, 189, 190
data manipulation, 129–130
data tables, 190
data visualization, 73–77, 98, 110–125,
    126, 189, 286
Death on the Nile (Christie), 36

decision-makers
  emotions and, 103–104
  stakeholders vs., 16
  successful meetings with, fig. 1.9, 20
decision meetings
  business presentations for, 27
  checklist (a.k.a. Don slide), fig. 1.9, 20
  defined, 25
  takeaways, 23
deck conductors, 31
decks
  camel decks, 31
  collaboration on, 28–29
  defined, 14
  formatting, 31–33
  pitch deck, 23, 51–56
  reusing, 11–12
  storyboarding, 43–44
deductive reasoning, 48, 49
default templates, 206
delivery. See speech
DeLuca, Joel, 16
Design = Audience, Purpose, Setting, 13–15, 25–26, 186
design principles
  checklist for, 175
  consistent baseline, 197–207
  content and design, 185
  contrast in, 207–212
  creating voice with font, 208
  data visualization, 73–77, 110–125
  for executive summaries, 65
  eye flow, 190–195
  image-based slides, 80–86
  leveraging graphics, 4, 61, 286–288
  overview of, fig. 2.26, fig. 0.2
  Platinum Rule of, 13, 15
  presenting with confidence, 4, 61, 290–291
  reducing the noise, 4, 61, 187–190, 208, 288–289
  slide libraries, 214–216
  telling a clear story, 4, 61, 284–286

desks, 246
disabilities, accounting for, 213–214
discussion, 237, 253–254, 275–276
disfluencies. See filler words
distractions, 187
distributing tools, 206
"Don slide" (Decision Meeting Checklist), fig. 1.9, 20
donut charts, 122–125
Doran, George T., 150
drafts, 179–181
Dragnet, 103
dressing for success, 228, 256–257
driver trees, 146
Drucker, Peter, 268
dual-axis charts, 116–119
dynamic speaking, 231–233, 235

E
editing
  checklists for, 172–175
  drafts/iterations, 179–181
  electronic editors, 162, 166, 170
  grammar/typos, 162
  human editors, 176–179
  word diets, 90–93, 288
Effective Data Visualization (Evergreen), 74
Einstein, Albert, 148
electronic editors, 162, 166, 170
elegant variation, 167
"Embrace the Spotlight: A Lesson from My Daughter" (Hunsaker), 230
emotions
  contagious, 232
  decision-making, 103–104
  stories and, 107, 109
endings, 276–279
engaging the audience, 104, 106, 137, 253–255, 268, 270
Engaging Virtual Meetings (Chen), 255
entrepreneurial stories, 105
equal ideas framework, 139
Evergreen, Stephanie, 74

excitement, 220, 232, 235, 291
exclamation marks, 166
executive summaries, 64–65, 88
exercise/movement, 228
expertise
    background information for, 134–135
    confidence and, 220
    editing and, 178
    filler words vs., 267
    introductions of, 270
    preparation for, 220–224
    reverse engineering, 135
    reviews and, 158
    teaching vs., 133–134
The Expert Trap, 133–159, 224
expressiveness, 235
extensions, 171–172
eye contact, 233, 242, 249, 291
eye flow, 186, 190–195

F

facelifts, digital, 257–258
facial expression, 235
fatigue, virtual, 242–245, 252
fear of public speaking, 219–220
features tables, 74–75
feedback, 178, 238, 252, 268
Few, Stephen, 126
fidgeting, 234
fight-or-flight response, 219, 227
filler words, 264–268
The First and Last Impression Trap, 7, 263–280
flaring and focusing, 39
Flood, Alison, 199
focusing
    flaring and, 39
    imagery for, 84
    on key points, 62, 78
    preattentive attributes for, 126–129
    storytelling for, 103, 104, 106, 130, 131
    white space for, 194–195
fonts
    choosing single, 199–200
    contrast and, 208–209
    dull/uninspired, 197
    noise and, 188
    size of, 27
footers, 202
forcefield framework, 145–146
Ford, Henry, 55
formatting
    importance of, 290
    slide libraries for, 214
    style and, 31–33
    3D formatting, 189
    value-adding, 186
Fosbury, Dick, 2, 292
F pattern, 192–193
frameworks, visual
    atom model, 140
    cognitive load and, 137
    creating effective, 136
    cycles, 144–145
    element sequencing (chevrons), 140
    equal ideas, 139
    forcefield, 145–146
    framework stack, 150
    Ginsu, 138
    interrelated lists, 148
    inverted pyramids, 144
    MECE (mutually exclusive and collectively exhaustive), 149
    memorable, 150–151
    one-big-idea, 138
    pros/cons, 147
    pyramids, 143
    slide libraries, 216
    slider bars, 146–147
    stairsteps, 145
    strategic pillars, 147
    supporting story with, 286
    target diagrams, 142–143
    tips for effective, 148–150
    two-by-two matrixes, 141
    umbrella, 139–140
    Venn diagrams, 142

framing yourself, 248
Frankenstein, 10, 11
The Frankenstein Trap, 7, 11–34, 106, 186, 207, 272
Freberg, Stan, 103
Free the Genius (Martin), 270
Friday, Sgt. Joe, 102
funnels, 144

G

Gartner, 141
gesturing, 233, 235, 269, 291
"Get Behind Me, Titivillus! How to Avoid Mistakes in Your Work" (Polk), 182
Ginsu framework, 138
giraffe charts, 122
Glum, 231
goals, declaring clear, 38
Golden Rule of Presentations, 13
Google Slides extensions, 172
gradients, 188, 211–212
grammar
    changes to, 168–169
    checklist, 174
    consequences of poor, 161–162
    electronic editors, 170
    learning common mistakes, 166–168
    setting standards for, 31–32
grammar checkers. See electronic editors
Grammar Girl, 168
graphicalizing slides
    avoiding overwhelm via, 71, 100
    bulleted lists and, 88, 89
    data visualization, 73–77, 286
    data visualization mistakes, 110–125
    leveraging graphics, 4, 61, 286–288
    logos for, 90
    noise and, 187–190
graphs. See charts
gratitude, 227–228
green, use of the color, 210
gridlines, 190

guides, 204, 206
Gutenberg (a.k.a. Z) pattern, 192, 196

H

Haims, Nolan, 130
hallway encounters, 24
Halpern, Belle Linda, 234
hand gestures, 233, 235, 269, 291
headsets, 246
Heath, Chip and Dan, 106
heat maps, 75–76
hierarchical frameworks, 148
history lessons, 45–46, 110
home offices, 244
home studio setup, 245–252
homophones, 170
horizontal bar charts, 110–111
horizontal relationships, 47, 48
Hunsaker, Justin, 30, 45, 220, 230, 236, 243, 271
hybrid environments, 25, 254, 259

I

icons, 86–88, 286
idea generation, 39–40, 45
idioms, 154–156
ignorant reviewers, 158
images, relevant, 78–86, 286
imposter syndrome, 220
indents, 202
inductive reasoning, 49
initialisms, 167
innovation, 42
insincere slides, 277–279
internet connectivity, 246
interrelated list framework, 148
introductions, 47–48, 268–270
inverted pyramids. See funnels
"Is Anybody Listening?" (Whyte), 17
italics, 188
"It depends!" principle, 26–27
iteration, slide, 179–181

J

jargon, 157
job skills, 3
John Polk & Associates, 202, 291
John Wiley & Sons, 220
The Just the Facts Trap, 7, 74, 103–131, 207, 268

K

Kahneman, Daniel, 109
kerning, 200
key. See legends
key points
    agendas for, 65–66
    executive summaries, 64
    forgetting, 225
    help remembering, 57
    highlighting, 62, 232
    for MBR meetings, 99
    memorizing, 224
    slides to reinforce, 271–273
    speaker notes for, 221–223
    stories to illustrate, 104–106
King Jr., Dr. Martin Luther, 151
Knaflic, Cole, 122, 126
Kouyoumdjian, Haig, 272
Kurstedt, Dr. Harold, 13

L

landing, sticking the, 275
lapel mics, 233
last impressions, 275
latticing ideas, 135
Lavaliers. See lapel mics
lawyerspeak, 163, 164
layers/spotlights, 210–211
leadership
    leadership presence, 1, 220, 234–235, 239, 274
    presentations to/for, 3
    presenting with, 234–235
legends, 190
legible text, 211, 213
length of presentations, 25, 252
leveraging graphics, 4, 61, 286–288
libraries, slide and content, 214–216
lighting, 247
line charts, 74, 110
line splits, 209
linked slides, 216
The Lipstick on a Pig Trap, 7, 185–217
logic chains
    executive summaries with, 64
    Pyramid Principle and, 46–50
    stories with, 110
    testing, 44
logos, 90, 198, 202
Lubar, Kathy, 234

M

magic quadrants, 141
main points. See key points
Made to Stick (Heath, Chip and Dan), 106
market assessments, 54
marketing hacks, 150–151
Martin, David, 270
Max, Tucker, 179
MBR (monthly business review), 97–99, 284–289
McCarthy, E. Jerome, 150
McCartney, Paul, 76, 268
McGinty, Sharon, 291
McGonigal, Kelly, 227
MECE (mutually exclusive and collectively exhaustive) frameworks, 149
memorable stories, 106–109
memorization, 224
mentors, 268
Merriam-Webster, 169
microphones, 233, 246, 268–269
mindfulness, 227–228
mind maps, 39–43, 45, 135, 148, 179, 288
minimalism, 26
Minto, Barbara, 46, 47, 49, 149

The Minto Pyramid Principle (Minto), 46, 47
mistakes, 181, 220
moiré effect, 257
Mona Lisa, 83, 134
monitoring plans, 56
monochrome heat maps, 76
monotone speaking, 231
morph transitions, 96
movement/exercise, 228
Mull, Martin, 6
multiword modifiers, 167

N

negative space. See white space
nerves, 219–220, 225, 227–230
newscaster's framing, 248
newscasts, 222
Nielsen, Jakob, 192, 197
noise
    audible, 213
    charts with, 188–190
    dashed lines and, 195
    pie charts with, 122–125
    presentation software and, 187–188, 197
    "pretty" slides and, 185
    reducing, 4, 61, 187–190, 208, 288–289
    signal-to-noise ratio, 71, 72, 182, 186, 213
nonexpert reviews, 158
nonparallel structure. See parallel structure
nonverbal cues, 242

O

off-camera audience, 244, 253
offices, home, 244
one-big-idea framework, 138, 152
one-on-one communication, 273–274
organization
    appendix, 94
    communication challenges for, fig. 7.14, 194
    of ideas, 42
    storyboarding, 43–45
Osterwalder, Dr. Alexander, 52–53
outlines, 222
overconfidence, 237
overplanning, 24

P

P&L (profit-and-loss) spreadsheets, 74, 76–77
pacing, 231–233
parallel structure, 164–165, 288
Pareto charts, 74, 124–125
Parkinson, Mike, 207
Pascal, Blaise, 72
pauses, 266–267
peer feedback, 268
pep talks, 228
perfectionism, 179–180
periods and exclamation marks, 165–166
pet peeves, 187, 290
photographs/images, 78–86
phrasing, 209
Picoult, Jodi, 179
pictures, 78–86
pie charts, 74, 122–125
The Piece of Cake Trap, 7, 161–183, 290
piggybacking ideas, 40
pitch and pacing, 231–233, 235
pitch decks, 23, 51–56
pitfalls. See presentation pitfalls
planning
    mind maps for, 39–43
    overmuch, 24
    Presentation Planning Checklist, 173
    speaker notes, 221–223
    storyboarding, 43–45
Platinum (Plus) Rule of Presentations, 28, 272
Platinum Rule of Presentations
    appendices and, 93–94
    assessment of, fig. 1.4
    context and, 207
    Design = Audience, Purpose, Setting, 13–15, 186, 284

"It depends!" principle, 26
Platinum (Plus) Rule, 28, 272
playbook analogy, 153
Political Savvy: Systematic Approaches to Leadership Behind the Scenes (DeLuca), 16
Polk, John, 4, 8, 175, 182, 220, 241
Polk, Marty, 136, 179, 258
Polk's First Law of Presentations, 175–176
polls/quizzes, 255
Porter, Max, 199
portmanteaus, 93, 151
posture, 234
PowerPoint, 171–172, 198, 200, 279
power-zapper words, 266
practicing
    filler word minimization via, 267
    importance of, 224–226, 290
    new skills, 134
    technology challenges and, 251
preattentive attributes, 125–129
preparation
    checklist for, fig. 8.5, 226
    expertise via, 220–224
    of questions and answers, 223–224
    rest and, 145
    success via, 24, 290
prereads, 214
PRES (presence, reaching out, expressiveness, self-knowledge) model, 234–235
presentation design principles. See design principles
presentation pitfalls
    avoiding, 6–7
    The Black Hole Trap, 7, 71–100
    The Bury the Lede Trap, 7, 37–69
    data visualization mistakes, 110–125
    The Expert Trap, 7, 133–159
    The First and Last Impression Trap, 7, 263–280
    The Frankenstein Trap, 7, 11–34
    The Just the Facts Trap, 7, 74, 103–131
    The Lipstick on a Pig Trap, 7, 185–217
    The Piece of Cake Trap, 7, 161–183
    The Under (or Over) Confidence Trap, 7, 219–238
    The Virtual Fatigue Trap, 7, 241–260
Presentation Pitfalls usage tips, 8
Presentation Planning Checklist, fig. 6.11, 173
presentations
    communication of work via, 4–5
    competency demonstrated via, 1–3
    defined, 14
    effective/efficient, 5, 98, 136
    Platinum Rule of. see Platinum Rule of Presentations
    promotions via, 291
    virtual fatigue and, 242–245, 252
presentation skills
    lack of, 73
    practicing, 6, 134
    promotion via, 2–3
    systematic improvement of, 4
    team learning of, 30
Presentations That Drive Action workshops, 95, 135, 241
presentation titles, 38–39
Presentation Zen (Reynolds), 202
presenters, 28–29, 272
presenting with confidence, 4, 61, 290–291
press conferences, 222
priority highlighting, 147
PROD (people, results, options, details) framework, fig. 1.7, 18–19, 106
product managers, 105
product roadmaps, 23
project phase storylines, fig. 2.17, 50
promotions, 1–3, 274, 291
proofreading, 164, 169, 178
pros/cons framework, 147
public speaking, 219–220
pumping yourself up, 228, 229
punctuation, 32, 165–166, 235

Index   313

purpose of presentations
   clarifying the, 21–23
     Design = Audience, Purpose, Setting, 13–15, 25–26, 284
     editing decks for new, 29
     focusing on, 229
     up-front statement of, 270
Pyramid Principle, 46–50, 105
pyramid visual framework, 143

Q

questions
   discussion, 237
   preparation for common, fig. 1.9, fig. 8.3, 20, 223–224
   sentence titles as, 63–64
   slides for, 277–278
Quiller-Couch, Arthur, 73

R

reading disabilities, 214
reading from notes, 222
reading/reacting to audience, fig. 8.12, 235–236, 291
red, use of the color, 198
red herrings, 37
reducing noise, 4, 61, 187–190, 208, 288–289
redundancy, 91, 251
Reese's Cup analogy, 153
reference slides, 215
rehearsals, 225–226, 251
relationship visualization, 148
repetition, 23, 151
rest/sleep, 145
reuse
   deck, 11–12
   slide, 29–33
reverse engineering expertise, 135
review
   checklists for, 172–175
   critical assessments, 238
   expert and nonexpert, 158

Reynolds, Garr, 93, 202
rhyming, 151
roadmap analogy, 153
robot voice, 243
rule of thirds, 190–191
running heads, 57, 67–68

S

safe space practice, 267
de Saint-Exupéry, Antoine, 90, 209
Saturday Night Live, 228
sausage-making (behind-the-scenes work), 109–110
scatter plot charts, 74, 114
"Science and Statistics" (Box), 55
scorecards, 153
screenshots, 85–86
scripts, 221–223
section breaks. See bumper slides
security, virtual, 258
self-deprecation, 271
self-knowing, 235
self-view, hiding, 242, 257
sensitivity analysis, 55
sentence titles, 56–68
sequencing elements, 140
Sequoia Capital, 51
setting of presentations
   adjusting for challenges in, 24–25
   Design = Audience, Purpose, Setting, 13–15, 284
   design based on, 25–26
   editing decks for new, 29
   speaker notes and, 223
   virtual, 242
shadows, 188
Shark Tank, 15–16, 19
shatter transitions, 96
Shelley, Mary, 11
Shiffrin, Mikaela, 226
Show Me the Numbers (Few), 126
signal-to-noise ratio, 71, 72, 185, 186, 213
Simon, Carmen, 109

simplicity, 201, 205, 208
Simpson, Homer, 179
Sinner's Bible, 182
situational interviews. See behavioral job interviews
slide jockeys, 31
slide master, 201
slider bar framework, 146–147
slides
    animations, 27, 94–96
    baseline design, 197–207
    checklist for editing, 172–175
    common elements on, 57, 201–202
    concluding, 275, 277–279
    cutting noncritical, 27, 93
    deck of. see decks
    defined, 14
    formatting, 31–33
    insincere, 277–278
    key points reinforced by, 271–273
    minimalist, 26
    preattentive attributes for, 126–129
    professional, 290
    rehearsing with/without, 225–226
    reusing, 11–12, 29–33
    slide libraries, 214–216
    slide master, 201
    titles for, 56–59, 64, 174
    tools to edit, 171–172
    transitions, 96
    when to omit, 273–274
slideument, 93
slopegraph charts, 74, 115
Smalley, Stuart, 228
SMART (specific, measurable, achievable, relevant, and time-bound) model, 150
Smith, John Thomas, 190
soft launches, 181
software capabilities
    alignment, 206
    noise and, 187–188, 197
    templates, 198
software engineers, 105

"sorry," never saying, 270–271
sound, 248
spaghetti charts, 115
speaker notes, 221–223, 272
speech
    confident, 291
    defined, 14
    developing presenter, 28–29
    dynamic, 230–234, 235
    filler words, 264–268
    idioms in, 154–156
    public speaking, 219–220
    sentence titles for clear, 58
    speaker notes, 221–223
    supporting visuals, 272
    varied, 231–233
    virtual adjustments to, 256
    virtual challenges, 244
    writing like you speak, 162–163, 168, 172
speedboats. See chevrons
spellcheck, 170
spotlights/layers, 210–211
Springsteen, Bruce, 92
spurious correlations, 114
squinting for clarity, 195–197
stacked column charts, 74, 111–112
stage fright, 219–220, 225, 227–229, 230
stairstep framework, 145
stakeholders
    decision-makers vs., 16
    researching key, 20
standing vs. sitting, 234
STAR (situation, trouble, action, result), 106
STARC (situation, trouble, action, results, connection) method, 106
statistics, burying shocking, 120–122
stereo bars. See slider bar framework
sticky notes, storyboarding with, 43–44
stories/storylines
    checklist for, 174
    concise, 72–73
    engaging, 268

stories/storylines (continued)
   history lessons, 45–46
   key points via, 62, 104–106
   logical, 73, 272
   pyramid structures for, 50
   sentence titles for clear, 57–58
   slides omitted for, 273–274
   STAR/STARC to structure, 106
   SUCCESs method for, 106–109, 268
   telling a clear story, 4, 61, 284–286
   up-front answers in, 46–50, 105, 285
storyboarding, 43–45, 64, 65, 179
Storytelling with Data (Knaflic), 122
strategic pillar framework, 147
stress, 227–229, 242
studio, home, 245–252
style/formatting, 31–33, 174
subjects, 38
subject titles, 57, 58, 59
Success = Opportunity + Preparation, 24
SUCCESs method, 106–109, 268
summarization, 276
support/challenge matrix, fig. 7.34, 210
supporting ideas, 48, 49
surprise/unexpected stories, 107, 109
Swinford, Echo, 198

T

tables, 74–77, 190
taglines, 57
talkers, 272
talk track. *See* speech
target diagram, 142–143
tautologies/redundancy, 91
teaching vs. expertise, 133–134
technology
   add-ins/extensions, 171–172
   alignment tools, 206
   challenges of, 243, 251–252
   collaboration software, 31
   home studio setup, 245–252
   hybrid/virtual environments, 25
   presentation software, 13–14, 187–188
   Touch Up My Appearance tool, 257–258
   virtual engagement tools, 254
TED Talks, 25, 78, 197, 198, 207, 233, 272
telling a clear story, 4, 61, 284–286
templates, 198, 201, 203, 206–207, 214–216, 288
Terberg, Julie, 198, 200
text-dense slides, 192–193
"Thank you" slides, 277
"The Effect of Expert Power on Consensus Decision-Making" (Polk), 220
Think Fast Talk Smart: The Podcast, 271
3D charts, 113–114
3D formatting, 189
3F (facts, feelings, follow-up) framework, fig. 1.10, 21–22
3P (prepare, practice, pump up) framework, 229
timely endings, 276
Times New Roman, 197, 199, 200, 208
Titivillus, 181
titles
   design considerations, 201
   presentation, 38–39
   sentence titles, 56–68
   slide titles, 56–59, 64, 174
toasts, 271
tornado charts, 144
Torrance, Megan, 8, 188, 189, 190
Touch Up My Appearance tool, 257–258
town hall meetings, 278
transitions, 96
transparency, 129
Trapp, Kathryn, 30
trend displays, 74, 110, 128
Tufte, Edward, 188
Twain, Mark, 266
two-by-two matrixes, 141
typos, 161–162, 178, 181
Tyson, Mike, 235

U

"um," saying, 264–268
umbrella framework, 139–140
unaided recall, 226
The Under (or Over) Confidence Trap, 7, 219–238, 256

V

Value Proposition Design (Osterwalder), 52–53
value propositions, fig. 2.20, 52–54
Venn, John, 142
Venn diagrams, 142
vertical relationships, 48
videoconferencing. *See* virtual meetings
video setups, 247–248, 250, 252, 259
Vigen, Tyler, 114
The Virtual Fatigue Trap, 7, 230, 241–260
virtual meetings
    accessibility for, 214
    challenges of, 242
    engaging the audience in, 253–255
    fatigue minimization, 252
    home studio setup, 245–252
    hybrid environments, 259
    performance adjustments for, 256
    questions slide for, 278
    rules for, 253
    security for, 258
    setting considerations and, 24, 25
    virtual fatigue, 242–245, 252
vision deficiency, 213
visual cues, 272
visualization, 226, 227–228
visualizing data, 73–77, 98, 110–125, 126, 189
voice. *See* speech
voiceover. *See* speech
Voice over Internet Protocol (VoIP), 243
volume of speech, 231–233
vomit drafts, 179
vyopta, 244

W

walk-up song, 229
wall of text slides, 72, 136, 148
waterfall charts, 74, 112–113
webinars, 222
weighing decisions framework, 147
weight, shifting back and forth, 234
WHAT (why? how? anecdote, thanks!) framework, 271
whiteboards, virtual, 255
white space, 186, 194–195, 204, 205
Whittaker, James, 220
"Whose Shoes Are You Still Tying?" (Hunsaker), 30
Whyte, William H., 17
Wicked Bible, 182
WIIFM (what's in it for me?), 270
word art, 188
word diets, 73, 90–93, 100, 224, 273, 284, 290
wording
    concise, 22, 72–73, 272, 288
    consistent formatting for, 31–33
    design considerations, 201–202
    filler words, 264–268
    font size, 27
    images and, 81
    layout, 209
    legibility, 211–212, 213
    minimalist, 26
    noise and designing, 187–188
    parallel structure, 164–165
    sentence titles, 56–68
    text-dense slides, 192–193
    wall of text slides, 72, 136
    word diets, 90–93
    writing like you speak, 162–163
word play, 151
work, showcasing your, 3
writer's block, 16, 45, 179
writing like you speak, 162–163, 168, 172, 183

Y

"You've Visualized Your Data, Now Actualize Your Promotion" (Polk), 8

Z

Z (Gutenberg) pattern, 192, 196
Ziglar, Zig, 24

About the Authors

John Polk is the president of John Polk & Associates and a former professor of data visualization at the University of Richmond's Robins School of Business. John created a presentation design workshop at Capital One and, along with Justin and other experts, trained over 10,000 associates. John earned a master's in industrial engineering from Virginia Tech.

Justin Hunsaker is a lead consultant at John Polk & Associates. He won the Barlow Monarch Innovation Honorable Mention for KeyBank's Small Business Review. Throughout his career, Justin has launched new products and coached associates at all levels at multiple Fortune 500 banks and tech startups. Justin earned an executive master's of technology management from the University of Pennsylvania and the Wharton School.

John and Justin met at Capital One, leading strategy and analysis teams for a combined 30 years across operations and marketing. During that time, they wrote and influenced thousands of presentations and coached hundreds of associates, from new college hires to senior executives, on effective presentation design.

John and Justin now teach workshops and coach leaders to design and deliver presentations that engage, influence, and drive action, from startups to Fortune 500 companies. They are on a mission to rid the world of poor presentations and the poor decisions that come with them while giving leaders the tools to communicate their stories effectively.

Sources: Courtesy of Marty Polk and Todd Rafalovich

John Polk & Associates
Design and Deliver Presentations That Drive Action

Our mission is to rid the world of poor presentations ... and the poor decisions that come with them.

Workshops
Workshops leverage the science behind communication and influence to give participants practical ways to tell their stories, visualize their data, reduce noise, and deliver their presentations confidently.

Coaching & Consulting
Through one-on-one and group coaching, we help individuals improve their communication and influencing skills by raising their game on presentation design and delivery. We also collaboratively build critical presentations, like pitch decks and town hall meetings.

Presentation Toolkits
We partner with organizations to establish professional, branded presentation templates and customizable slide libraries that enable teamwork and dramatically reduce presentation development time.

For more information, a free consultation, or to sign up for our newsletter check out:

 johnpolkandassociates.com

✉ john.polk@johnpolkandassociates.com

justin.hunsaker@johnpolkandassociates.com

 linkedin.com/in/johnwpolk/

linkedin.com/in/justinhunsaker/